STUDY AND REVIEW GUIDE
TO ACCOMPANY

PSYCHOLOGY
IN ACTION

KAREN HUFFMAN ◆ 6TH EDITION

Study and Review Guide Prepared by:

Karen Huffman / Palomar College

Richard Hosey

John Wiley & Sons, Inc.

New York • Chichester • Weinheim • Brisbane • Singapore • Toronto

Cover Art: ©*Lightbulb IV*, 1992, by Paul Giovanopoulos.

To order books or for customer service call 1-800-CALL-WILEY (225-5945).

ISBN 0-471-41582-0

Printed in the United States of America

10 9 8 7 6 5 4 3 2 1

Printed and bound by Courier Kendallville, Inc.

TABLE OF CONTENTS

TIPS FOR USING THIS STUDY AND REVIEW GUIDE

Congratulations! Your decision to buy and use this study guide is an important step toward student success. It is carefully designed to help you learn the most important material in your textbook (in the shortest possible time), to improve your performance on quizzes and exams, and ultimately to help you achieve the highest grade possible in your first introduction to psychology course.

This study guide is coordinated with your text, <u>Psychology in Action</u> (6th ed.), and is divided into seven major sections: *Chapter Outlines, Learning Objectives, Key Terms, Active Learning Exercises, Chapter Overview, Self-Tests,* and *Answers.* These seven sections are explained and identified throughout each chapter with the following boxes and icons:

OUTLINE   (<u>S</u>urvey & <u>Q</u>uestion)

This outline is intended to help you *survey* the chapter. As you read through the various sections, write down any *questions* or comments that come to mind in the space provided. This is a valuable part of active learning and the SQ4R method. It not only makes your reading time more enjoyable and active, but it also increases your retention and understanding of the material.

Core and Expanded LEARNING OBJECTIVES   (<u>R</u>ead, <u>R</u>ecite & w<u>R</u>ite)

While *reading* the chapter, stop periodically and *recite* (or repeat in your own words) the answers to the following learning objectives. It will also help your retention if you *write* your answer in the space provided. (Page numbers refer to the text <u>Psychology in Action</u>, 6th Ed.)

KEY TERMS (Review)

The *review* step in the SQ4R method is very important to your performance on quizzes and exams. Upon completion of this chapter, you should be able to define the following terms.

ACTIVE LEARNING EXERCISES (Recite)

The *recite* step in the SQ4R method requires you to be an ACTIVE learner. By completing the following exercises, you will test and improve your mastery of the chapter material, which will also improve your performance on quizzes and exams. Answers to some exercises appear at the end of this study guide chapter.

CHAPTER OVERVIEW (Review)

The following CHAPTER OVERVIEW provides a narrative overview of the main topics covered in the chapter. Like the Visual Summary found at the end of each chapter in the text, this narrative summary provides a final opportunity to *review* chapter material.

SELF-TESTS (Review & wRite)

Completing the following SELF-TESTS will provide immediate feedback on how well you have mastered the material. In the *crossword puzzle* and *fill-in exercises*, write the appropriate word or words in the blank spaces. The *matching exercise* requires you to match the terms in one column to their correct definitions in the other. For the *multiple-choice questions* in Practice Tests I and II, circle or underline the correct answer. If you are unsure of any answer, highlight or specially mark the item, and then go back to the text for further review. Correct answers are provided at the end of this study guide chapter.

ANSWERS
The following answers to active learning exercises, the crossword puzzle, fill-ins, matching exercises, and practice tests 1 and 2 provide immediate feedback on your mastery of the material. Try not to simply memorize the answers. When you are unsure of your "guess" or make an error, be sure to go back to the textbook and carefully review. This will greatly improve your scores on classroom exams and quizzes.

Did you notice that most of these sections have terms in parentheses, such as (Survey & Question), (Read, Recite & wRite), and (Review & wRite)? This is because both your study guide and text, Psychology in Action, are designed around the best-known studying technique—the SQ4R method. The symbols "S,Q, R, R, R, R" stand for:

Survey

Before you begin reading each chapter of the text, you should skim it. Note the title, major headings and subheadings, and figure captions. Then read the interim summaries that come before each set of review questions sprinkled throughout the chapter. Finally, carefully examine the visual summary at the end of the chapter. This survey helps organize the material into a larger unit that will help focus your attention during later careful reading and studying.

The "Survey" step also provides a "map" or "big picture" of the chapter contents. If you were new to the United States and planning a car trip from California to New York, you wouldn't jump in your car and simply start driving. However, most students do jump into their texts and start reading the first page with no idea of what road signs to look for or what lies ahead. To make the most of your car trip to New York, you would begin with a large map of the entire United States and try to plan the most efficient route. Similarly, since you are "new" to the country of psychology, you need to begin with a large overall road map--the SURVEY step of the SQ4R method.

Question

As you are surveying the material, ask yourself questions about what you are going to read. (What did your instructor say about this topic when it was assigned? What questions do the headings and subheadings suggest?

What will I learn in this chapter? How can I use this information in my everyday life?) Questions aid retention because they require active participation on your part and increase personal relevance of the material.

Read

The survey and question procedure provides a natural lead-in to careful reading. While reading the chapter, attempt to answer the questions you generated, as well as paying close attention to all figures, tables, and **boldfaced** terms. Read in small units from one major heading to the next. In Chapter 6 of your textbook, you will note that cramming or massed learning is not a good method for studying, retention, or retrieval of information. Space your studying throughout the time period allocated by your instructor for the assigned chapters. This method of "distributed versus massed practice" has been scientifically proven to be more effective than cramming because you retain more information and will remember it longer.

Recite

"Recite" means to go over what you just read by orally summarizing, making notes, and/or completing the review questions in the text (and the active learning exercises in this study guide). Have you ever found yourself having to reread sections of a text because your mind wandered off as you were studying? Do you find that you can spend hours studying and yet remember little of what you've read? This is because you are not "reciting." A well-known principle of education states that learning is much more effective when people are *actively* responding to the material than when they are *passive* recipients. By orally summarizing, taking notes, completing the review questions and active learning exercises, you will be taking an active role in your studying—and your grades will improve!

Review

Reviewing is a combination of the total SQ4R formula. Briefly repeat the survey and questioning you did before you began the chapter, reread all your notes (from the text, your class lecture notes, and notes in this study guide). Check your memory by completing the review questions in the text and the self-tests in this study and reviewguide.

w<u>R</u>ite

Writing is a very important element in learning. By writing a response and taking notes while reading or listening to lectures, you will retain more than simply listening to a lecture or silently reading a text. This study guide is purposely designed in a workbook format to allow space for writing responses to the learning objectives, your definitions for the key terms, your responses to the activities, and your answers to the sample self-tests. Taking this study and review guide with you to class is also an important aid in organizing your lecture notes.

The SQ4R method can be used with any textbook. However, your <u>Psychology in Action</u> (6th Ed.) textbook and this study and review guide have been carefully designed to maximize this technique. We hope you will try this method and actively use this study and review guide. Research finds those students who purchase and USE study guides generally do better on exams and overall course performance. Your text has numerous " tools for student success," your instructor is available to assist and inspire you, and this study and review guide is here to guide and support your studying efforts. The next step is yours. Best wishes for an exciting journey in the new country called "Psychology."

Karen Huffman/Palomar College
Richard Hosey

1 Introduction and Research Methods

OUTLINE (<u>S</u>urvey & <u>Q</u>uestion)

This outline is intended to help you *survey* the chapter. As you read through the various sections, write down any *questions* or comments that come to mind in the space provided. This is a valuable part of active learning and the SQ4R method. It not only makes your reading time more enjoyable and active, but it also increases retention and understanding of the material.

TOPIC	NOTES

I. UNDERSTANDING PSYCHOLOGY

    A. What is Psychology?

    B. Goals of Psychology

    C. Careers in Psychology

II. DOING RESEARCH IN PSYCHOLOGY

    A. The Scientific Method

B. Experiments

C. Nonexperimental Studies

Critical Thinking/Active Learning: Becoming a Better Consumer of Scientific Research

Research Highlight: An Elegant Study of Therapeutic Touch

D. Ethical Problems

III. PERSPECTIVES IN PSYCHOLOGY

A. Psychology's Past

B. Psychology's Present

Gender and Cultural Diversity: Are There Cultural Universals?

Core and Expanded LEARNING OBJECTIVES (Read, Recite & wRite)

While *reading* the chapter, stop periodically and *recite* (or repeat in your own words) the answers to the following learning objectives. It will also help your retention if you *write* your answer in the space provided. (Page numbers refer to the text Psychology in Action, 6th Ed.)

Core Learning Objectives
These objectives are found at the beginning of each chapter of Psychology in Action (6th ed.).

1. What is psychology? What are its goals and main career specialties?

2. What is the scientific method?

3. How do psychologists conduct experiments?

4. What are the advantages and disadvantages of nonexperimental studies?

5. What are the major research and ethical issues and biases?

6. Who are the important contributors to psychology's past, and what are the primary perspectives that guide modern psychology?

Sigman Freud - discovered psychology
Pethwen - behaviorism
Skinner - behaviorism
rogers/maslow - humanistic

Expanded Learning Objectives

These objectives offer more detail and a more intensive way to study the chapter.

Upon completion of CHAPTER 1, the student should be able to:

1. Define psychology, and describe the difference between psychology and pseudopsychology (pp. 4-6).

2. Define critical thinking and describe its three components (p. 4).

3. List and describe the four goals of psychology, and explain the difference between basic and applied research (p. 6).

4. Describe the difference between a psychiatrist and psychologist, and describe the ten major career options in psychology (pp. 8-9).

5. List and describe the six basic steps involved in scientific research; define theory, hypothesis, and operational definitions (pp. 10-13).

6. Define statistics, and describe the relevance of publication, replication, and citations in determining the legitimacy of research results (pp. 12-13).

7. Define experiment, independent and dependent variables, experimental and control groups, and extraneous variables (pp. 13-15, 17).

8. Describe the following possible sources of, and solutions to, bias in research: experimenter bias, the double-blind study, placebo; ethnocentrism; and sample bias, including the difference between populations and samples (pp. 15-17).

9. Discuss the merits and limitations of the following nonexperimental research techniques: naturalistic observation, survey, and case study (pp. 18-20).

10. Describe a correlational study and the three kinds of correlations; determine the strength of a correlation from the correlation coefficient (pp. 20-22).

11. Discuss the issue of ethics in animal research, and describe the following ethical considerations for human research: informed consent, debriefing, deception, and participant confidentiality; state the role of Human Research Committees. State the rules regarding confidentiality in clinical or counseling psychology (pp. 23-26).

12. Describe the similarities and differences between the following six major schools of psychology: experimental, structuralism, functionalism, psychoanalytic, gestalt, and behaviorism (pp. 26-30).

13. Name four women or minorities who have contributed to the field of psychology (pp. 30-31).

14. Briefly describe the seven perspectives in psychology today, and explain the eclectic approach, which is prevalent in modern psychology (pp. 31-32).

15. Describe the importance of cultural psychology in today's world, then describe and provide an example of a culturally universal behavior (pp. 33-34).

KEY TERMS (<u>R</u>eview)

The *review* step in the SQ4R method is very important to your performance on quizzes and exams. Upon completion of this chapter, you should be able to define the following terms.

Applied Research: *When known psychology is used in a real life application*

Basic Research: *research done to study theortical questions*

Case Study: *a detailed study of a singal participant*

Control Group: *in a study they are the group that is manipulated to test the hypothisis*

Correlational Study: *Study wefre things are compared to each other and show how strongly related they are to each other*

Critical Thinking: *Objectivly evaluctating comparing analyzing and synthesizing information*

Debriefing: *a necessary aspect of deception research where researches explain th purpose of the experiment*

Dependent Variable (DV): *it is what is measured due to the changing independent variable*

Double-Blind Study: _is when the participant and the researcher don't know the treatment_

Ethnocentrism: _belief that your culture is the same as everyone elses_

Experiment: _a controled scientific procedure_

Experimental Group: _the group of participants in an experiment_

Experimenter Bias: _tendence of of experimeters to influence results_

Extraneous Variables: _____

Hypothesis: _an estimated guess_

Independent Variable (IV) _what is being changed in the group_

Informed Consent: _____

Interaction: _____

Meta-Analysis: _____

Naturalistic Observation: _____

_____

Nature-Nurture Controversy: _____

_____

Operational Definition: _____

_____

Placebo: _____

_____

Psychology: _____

_____

Random Assignment: _____

_____

Sample Bias: _____

_____

Survey: _____

_____

Theory: _____

_____

ACTIVE LEARNING EXERCISES   (Recite)

The *recite* step in the SQ4R method requires you to be an ACTIVE learner. By completing the following exercises, you will test and improve your mastery of the chapter material, which will also improve your performance on quizzes and exams. Answers to some exercises appear at the end of this study guide chapter.

ACTIVE LEARNING EXERCISE I

For each of the three studies:
- Decide whether the study is correlational or experimental.
- If the study is correlational, briefly describe how the variables are related and whether the correlation is positive, negative, or zero.
- If the study is experimental, identify the independent variable (IV) and dependent variable (DV).

Study I
A Dartmouth study found that lifetime earnings for women who graduate from college is approximately the same as that of men who graduate from high school.

Study II
An Australian study found that MSG does not cause people to be sick, as previously reported. The researcher informed participants he was studying ingredients in a new soft drink and fed them either MSG or a placebo in the drink. The same number and type of symptoms were found in both the MSG and the placebo groups.

Study III
USA Today reported a major University study that found couples who live together before marriage are more likely to divorce than couples who don't.

ACTIVE LEARNING EXERCISE II

To help you understand and appreciate the complexity of the experimental method, think of a specific problem or topic that you are interested in studying. For example, "Does caffeine increase studying effectiveness?" Now answer the following:

1. What would be your hypothesis?

2. What would be the independent and dependent variable(s)?

3. List possible experimental controls for the experiment.

4. Could your hypothesis also be tested with nonexperimental methods? If so, describe them.

ACTIVE LEARNING EXERCISE III

<u>Applying</u> <u>Abstract</u> <u>Thinking</u>   (A Cognitive Skill)

In Chapter 1 of your textbook, you learned useful research terminology that can be used to also evaluate reports from politicians, advertisers, teachers, the news media, and even close friends. The following exercise will allow you to actively evaluate these sources of information. Read each "research" report and decide what is the <u>primary</u> problem or research limitation. In the space provided, make one of the following marks:

CC = The report is misleading because correlational data are used to suggest causation.

CG = The report is inconclusive because there was no control group.

EB = The results of the research were unfairly influenced by experimenter bias.

SB = The results of the research are questionable because of sample bias.

_____ 1. William owns a company in New York City that makes shoes for women. He is concerned with slumping sales and decides to conduct a survey in one of his factories to determine how female employees feel about shoes produced in Italy.

_____ 2. At a major league baseball park, researchers found that beer and soft-drink sales are highest when color advertising is used on all billboards.

_EB_ 3. After failing an important exam in his psychology class, Alex decides to personally interview fellow classmates regarding their opinion of the professor's teaching techniques.

IV color - no color
DV amount of sales

CHAPTER OVERVIEW (Review)

The following CHAPTER OVERVIEW provides a narrative overview of the main topics covered in the chapter. Like the Visual Summary found at the end of each chapter in the text, this narrative summary provides a final opportunity to *review* chapter material.

I. Understanding Psychology

Psychology is the scientific study of behavior and mental processes. It emphasizes the empirical approach and the value of **critical thinking**. Psychology is not the same as common sense, "pop psychology," or pseudopsychology. The goals of psychology are to *describe, explain, predict,* and *change* behavior and mental processes. To meet these goals, psychologists conduct either **basic research**, which studies theoretical issues, or **applied research**, which seeks to solve specific, real-world problems. There are many opportunities for a career in psychology. Some professional areas are grouped under the heading of basic research, including experimental, biopsychology or neuroscience, cognitive, gender and cultural, developmental, and social psychology. Applied areas include clinical, counseling, industrial/organizational, educational, and school psychology.

II. Doing Research in Psychology

The scientific method consists of six carefully planned steps: (1) reviewing the literature for existing **theories**, (2) formulating a testable hypothesis, (3) designing the study and collecting the data, (4) analyzing the data and accepting or rejecting the **hypothesis**, (5) publishing followed by replication and scientific review, and (6) building further theory. The steps are arranged in a circle to show the circular, cumulative nature of science.

The experimental method is the only research method that can be used to identify cause-and-effect relationships. **Independent variables** are the factors the experimenter manipulates and **dependent variables** are measurable behaviors of the participants. Experimental controls include having one control group and one or more experimental groups, and holding **extraneous variables** constant.

To safeguard against the researcher problem of **experimenter bias**, researchers employ blind observers, single-blind and **double-blind studies,** and **placebos**. To control for **ethnocentrism**, they use cross-cultural sampling. In addition, to offset participant problems with **sample bias**, researchers use random/representative sampling and **random assignment.** To control for participant bias, they rely on many of the same controls in place to prevent experimenter bias, such as double-blind studies. They also attempt to assure anonymity, confidentiality, and sometimes use deception.

Unlike experiments, nonexperimental methods cannot determine the causes of behavior, but they can describe specifics, determine relationships, and help with prediction. **Naturalistic observation** is used to study and describe behavior in its natural habitat. **Surveys** use interviews or questionnaires to obtain information on a sample of participants. Individual **case studies** are in-depth studies of a participant.

Correlational studies examine how strongly two variables are related (+1.00 to –1.00) and whether the relationship is positively, negatively, or not at all (zero) correlated. Correlational studies and the correlation coefficient provide important research findings and valuable predictions. However, it is important to remember that *correlation does not imply causation.*

Psychologists are expected to maintain high ethical standards in their relations with human and animal research participants, as well as with clients in therapy. The APA has published guidelines detailing these ethical standards.

III. Perspectives in Psychology

Among the early schools of psychology, the experimentalists focused on the study of experience and the use of introspection, whereas the structuralists sought to identify elements of consciousness and how those elements formed the structure of the mind. Functionalists studied how mental processes help the individual adapt to the environment.

A later pioneer in psychology, Sigmund Freud, developed psychoanalytic theory to explain psychological problems developed from unconscious conflicts. Behaviorism emphasizes observable behaviors and stimulus-response relationships. The Gestalt school studied organizing principles of perceptual processes.

Seven major perspectives guide modern psychology: biopsychology or neuroscience, cognitive, behavioral, sociocultural, evolutionary, humanistic, and psychodynamic. These seven perspectives permeate the field of psychology and will be discussed in great detail in later chapters.

SELF-TESTS (Review & wRite)

Completing the following SELF-TESTS will provide immediate feedback on how well you have mastered the material. In the *crossword puzzle* and *fill-in exercises*, write the appropriate word or words in the blank spaces. The *matching exercise* requires you to match the terms in one column to their correct definitions in the other. For the *multiple-choice questions* in Practice Tests I and II, circle or underline the correct answer. If you are unsure of any answer, highlight or specially mark the item, and then go back to the text for further review. Correct answers are provided at the end of this study guide chapter.

CROSSWORD PUZZLE FOR CHAPTER 1

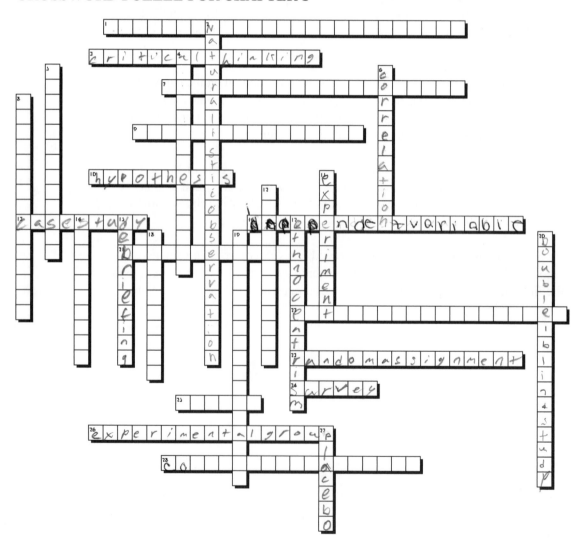

ACROSS

1 The longstanding dispute over the relative contributions of nature (heredity) and nurture (environment) to the development of behavior and mental processes.

3 The process of objectively evaluating, comparing, analyzing, and synthesizing information.

7 A precise description of how the variables in a study will be observed and measured.

9 The tendency of experimenters to influence the results of a research study in the expected direction.

10 A statement of a predicted relationship between two or more variables.

13 An in-depth study of a single research participant. case study

16 In an experiment, a variable that is manipulated by the experimenter to determine its causal effect on the dependent variable.

21 Research conducted to study theoretical questions without trying to solve a specific problem.

22 Variables that are not directly related to the hypothesis under study and that the experimenter does not actively attempt to control (e.g., time of day and heating of room).

23 Occurs when participant's chances of being assigned to each group in an experiment are equal; thereby assuring any later differences between people in the experimental and control conditions must be the result of the treatment. random assignment

24 Nonexperimental research technique that assesses behaviors and attitudes of a sample or population. survey

25 A system of interrelated, accumulated research findings used to explain a set of observations and generate testable hypotheses.

26 In a controlled experiment, the group of participants that receives the independent variable. experimental group

28 A form of research that studies relationships between variables without the ability to infer causal relationships.

DOWN

2 The systematic recording of observable behavior in the participant's natural state or habitat with little or no experimenter intervention.

4 Research that uses the principles and discoveries of psychology for practical purposes, to solve real-world problems.

5 A statistical procedure for combining and analyzing data from many studies.

6 A process where multiple factors mutually influence the outcome-as in the interaction between heredity and environment.

8 A participant's agreement to take part in a study after being told what to expect. informed consent

11 A carefully controlled scientific procedure conducted to determine whether certain variables manipulated by the experimenter have a causal effect on other variables. experiment

12 In a controlled experiment, the group of participants that receive a zero level of the independent variable and that is used to assess the effects of the independent variable or treatment.

14 The tendency for the sample of participants in a research study to be atypical of a larger population.

15 A necessary and important aspect of deception research in which the participants are informed after the research about the purpose of the study, the nature of the anticipated results, and any deceptions used. debriefing

17 The belief that behavior in your culture is typical of all cultures. Also, viewing one's own ethnic group (or culture) as central and "correct" and then judging the rest of the world according to this standard. *ethnocentrism*

18 The scientific study of behavior and mental processes. *behaviorism*

19 The variable that is observed and measured for change in an experiment; thought to be affected by (or dependent on) the manipulation of the independent variable.

20 A study in which neither the participant nor the experimenter knows which treatment is being given to the participant or to which group the participant has been assigned. *Double-blind*

21 An inactive substance or fake treatment used as a control technique, usually in drug research, or given by a medical practitioner to a patient. *placebo*

FILL-IN EXERCISES

1. Your text defines psychology as the _____ (p. 4).

2. The goals of psychology are to _____ (p. 5). *D.E. P.C.*

3. Basic research studies _____, whereas applied research is conducted to _____ (pp. 5-6).

4. The causes of behavior can be determined by using the _____ method of research (p. 11).

5. A(n) _____ is a factor that is selected and manipulated by the experimenter and is totally independent of anything the research participant does (p. 12).

6. _____ studies describe how strongly two variables are related (p.   ).

7. When researchers _____ their research participants, they explain the reasons for conducting the research and clear up any misconceptions or concerns (p. 24).

8. Explaining behavior in terms of unconscious drives and conflicts is key to the _____ perspective (p. 29).

9. _____ emphasizes the importance of the inner, subjective self and stresses the positive side of human nature (p. 30).

10. The six steps in the SQ4R method for active reading are _____, _____, _____, _____, _____, and _____ (p. 38).

MATCHING EXERCISES

Column A   Column B

a. Behaviorism   1.____ Studies how mental processes help adaptation.
b. Cognitive Psychology   2._i__ Emphasizes influence of the unconscious mind.
c. Cultural Psychology   3._a__ Focuses on mental processing of information.
d. Evolutionary Perspective 4.____ Focuses on sensations and feelings and perception.
e. Functionalism   5._h__ Studies the biology of behavior.
f. Gestalt Psychology   6._f__ Believes the whole is greater than the sum of the parts.
g. Humanistic Psychology   7._d__ Derived from theory of evolution and natural selection.
h. Psychobiology   8._c__ Studies influence of culture and ethnicity on behavior.
i. Psychoanalytic Theory   9._a__ Focuses on objective or observable behaviors.
j. Structuralism.   10.____ Emphasizes inner, subjective self and positive nature.

PRACTICE TEST I

D. E. P. C

$\frac{11}{20}$ | u 6 $\frac{13}{14}$ $\frac{13}{20}$

1. Which of the following are the goals of psychology?
    a. describe, manipulate, control, and examine behavior
    (b) describe, explain, predict, and change behavior
    c. predict, control, examine, and change behavior
    d. manipulate, control, explain, and change behavior

2. Basic research is conducted to study _____.
    a. basic psychological needs such as hunger, socialization, and the need for praise
    b. theoretical questions that may or may not have real-world applications
    c. the goals of psychology
    d. a specific real-world problem

3. Applied research is conducted to study _____.
    a. how people apply knowledge in an educational setting
    b. theoretical questions that may or may not have real-world applications
    c. the goals of psychology
    d. a specific real-world problem

4. Amanda studies changes in human behavior from conception to death. She is a(n) _____
    psychologist.
    a. comparative
    b. evolutionary
    c. developmental
    d. interspecies

5. The belief that behavior in your culture is typical of behavior in all other cultures is one definition of
   _____.
   a. ideology
   b. ethnocentrism
   c. prejudice
   d. ethnic typing

6. Only the experiment allows one to investigate _____.
   a. relationships
   b. correlations
   c. causation
   d. the goals of psychology

7. An educated guess or a possible explanation for a behavior being studied, that is expressed as a
   prediction or a statement of cause and effect is a(n) _____.
   a. correlation
   b. experiment
   c. hypothesis
   d. theory

8. An experimenter wishes to see if there is a difference between two types of memory techniques.
   She teaches one group of participants Technique A and another group Technique B. Then she gives
   each group a list of words to memorize. Two weeks later she tests the participants to see how many
   of the words they have remembered. What is the dependent variable in this experiment?
   a. number of words in the list
   b. memory techniques
   c. sex of the experimenter
   d. number of words remembered

9. What is the independent variable in the experiment described in the previous question?
   a. number of words in the list
   b. memory techniques
   c. sex of the experimenter
   d. number of words remembered

10. When participants are not exposed to any amount or level of the independent variable, they are
    members of the _____.
    a. control condition
    b. experimental condition
    c. observation group
    d. out-of-control group

11. The tendency of experimenters to influence the results of their experiment in an expected direction is called _____.
    a. experimenter bias
    b. control bias
    c. observational bias
    d. experimental bias

12. When neither the researcher nor the participants in an experiment know whether the treatment or independent variable has been given to any participant, the research design can be called _____.
    a. reliable
    b. double-blind
    c. valid
    d. deceptive

13. When researchers systematically observe the behavior of animals or humans in their natural state or habitat, they are conducting a(n) _____.
    a. experiment
    b. naturalistic observation
    c. case study
    d. survey

14. _____ is generally credited with being the founder of experimental psychology.
    a. Sigmund Freud
    b. Wilhelm Wundt
    c. William James
    d. G. Stanley Hall

15. The school of psychology that sought to study the elements of conscious experience was _____.
    a. functionalism
    b. Gestalt whole
    c. behaviorism behavior
    d. structuralism

16. Wilhelm Wundt is credited as the founder of _____ psychology.
    a. behaviorist
    b. functionalist
    c. experimental
    d. humanistic

17. Who developed psychoanalytic theory?
    a. Freud
    b. James
    c. Wundt
    d. Watson

18. _____ emphasized objective, observable behaviors.
    a. Functionalism
    b. Gestalt psychology
    c. Freud
    d. Behaviorism

19. Gestalt psychology studied the _____.
    a. psyche
    b. perception of wholes
    c. elements of perception
    d. patterns of stimulus and response

20. The _____ approach recognizes the value of using several perspectives to explain human behavior and mental processes.
    a. Gestalt
    b. humanistic
    c. eclectic
    d. Freudian

PRACTICE TEST II

1. The process of objectively evaluating, comparing, analyzing, and synthesizing information is known as _____.
    a. psychology
    b. critical thinking
    c. behaviorism
    d. the scientific method

2. You dread going to the grocery store because you got lost there when you were a child. This illustrates psychology's goal of _____ behavior.
    a. describing
    b. explaining
    c. predicting
    d. changing

3. The goal of _____ is to tell "what" occurred, whereas the goal of _____ is to tell "why."
    a. health psychologists; biological psychologists
    b. description; explanation
    c. psychologists; psychiatrists
    d. pseudopsychologists; clinical psychologists

4. _____ rely on nonscientific or deliberately fraudulent methods to explain personality.
    a. Pseudopsychologies
    b. Sociologists
    c. Astronomers
    d. Counselors

5. _____ research explores new theories and advances general scientific understanding; whereas _____ research attempts to solve real-world problems.
    a. Experimental; nonexperimental
    b. Correlational; survey
    c. Basic; applied
    d. Theoretical; hypothetical

6. In an experiment, the researcher _____.
    a. isolates one or more variables and examines their effects on a behavior
    b. controls the dependent variable and measures the independent variable
    c. deceives subjects, manipulates variables, and makes correlations
    d. observes one behavior to the exclusion of all other variables

7. In the statement, "This causes that," *this* is the _____.
    a. constant
    b. independent variable
    c. dependent variable
    d. hypothesis

    IV   male Female
    dV   level of math skill

8. Experimenter bias occurs when the researcher _____.
    a. studies only what is interesting to him or her
    b. changes the results to fit the hypothesis
    c. unintentionally provides subtle cues about the purpose of the study, which affects the results
    d. takes credit for the work done by his or her research assistants

9. Participants in the _____ are treated exactly the same as participants in the _____ , except they are not exposed to the independent variable.
    a. experiment; nonexperiment
    b. survey; case study
    c. selection group; placebo group
    d. control group; experimental group

10. Someone who systematically records behavior in a participant's normal habitat is engaged in _____.
    a. naturalistic observation
    b. voyeurism
    c. a case study
    d. random observation

11. The only research method that allows you to make cause-and-effect statements is the _____.
    a. representative survey
    b. controlled case study
    c. laboratory observation
    d. experiment

12. The relationship between the color of your shoes and your teacher's mood today can be called a _____.
    a. spurious correlation
    b. zero correlation
    c. random sampling
    d. negative correlation

13. Sometimes _____ is used in order to create a realistic situation with genuine reactions from participants.
    a. trickery
    b. deception
    c. a nonmonetary incentive
    d. case observation

14. The explanation a research provides to participants about the research process when it is over is called a(n) _____.
    a. case conference
    b. study's footnote
    c. debriefing
    d. exit interview

15. With regard to animal studies in psychology, the use of aversive treatment such as electrical shock is _____.
    a. extremely rare
    b. common for species that do not feel pain
    c. banned by animal care committees
    d. acceptable only if pain medication is provided

16. Which of the following terms are properly matched?
    a.   psychoanalysis and uniqueness
    b.   Gestalt and wholeness
    c.   functionalism and unconscious conflict
    d.   psychobiology and introspection

17. Observable behaviors are the primary focus in which of the following approaches to psychology?
    a.   humanistic
    b.   psychodynamic
    c.   behaviorism
    d.   cognitive

18. Someone who believes that behavior is the result of complex chemical and biological events within the brain is called a(n) _____.
    a.   information processor
    b.   ecological psychologist
    c.   evolutionary psychologist
    d.   psychobiologist

19. A _____ emphasizes the common evolutionary history of all people and studies the biological bases of social behavior.
    a.   ethologist
    b.   ethnologist
    c.   sociobiologist
    d.   psychobiologist

20. The expression and recognition of basic emotions may be a _____.
    a.   cultural universal
    b.   practice found only in Western cultures
    c.   universal practice amongst adolescents, but not adults
    d.   relatively new practice in the history of mankind

ANSWERS
The following answers to active learning exercises, the crossword puzzle, fill-ins, matching exercises, and practice tests 1 and 2 provide immediate feedback on your mastery of the material. Try not to simply memorize the answers. When you are unsure of your "guess" or make an error, be sure to go back to the textbook and carefully review. This will greatly improve your scores on classroom exams and quizzes.

CROSSWORD PUZZLE FOR CHAPTER 1

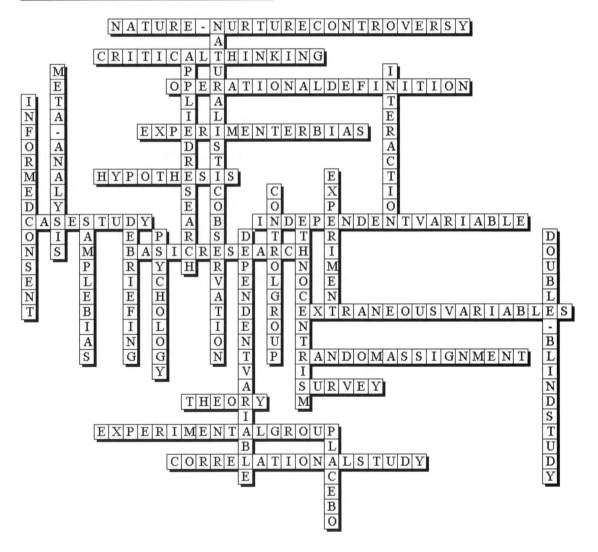

ACTIVE LEARNING EXERCISE I

Study I correlational, positive correlation; **Study II** experimental, IV = MSG or placebo, DV = symptoms of sickness; **Study III** correlational, positive

ACTIVE LEARNING EXERCISE III

1. SB   2. CG   3. EB

FILL-IN EXERCISES

1. scientific study of behavior and mental processes; 2. describe, explain, predict, and change; 3. theoretical questions, answer real-world questions; 4. experimental; 5. Independent variable; 6. correlational; 7. debrief; 8. psychoanalytic; 9. Humanistic psychology; 10. survey, question, read, recite, review, and wRite.

MATCHING EXERCISES

a. 9, b. 3, c. 8, d. 7, e. 1, f. 6, g. 10, h. 5, i. 2, j. 4

PRACTICE TEST I		PRACTICE TEST II	
1. b (p. 5)	11. a (p. 15)	1. b (p. 4)	11. d (p. 19)
2. b (p. 5)	12. b (p. 15)	2. b (p. 5)	12. b (p. 20)
3. d (p. 6)	13. b (p. 17)	3. b (pp. 6-8)	13. b (p. 24)
4. c (p. 7)	14. b (p. 28)	4. a (p. 8)	14. c (p. 24)
5. b (p. 15)	15. d (p. 28)	5. c (p. 11)	15. a (p. 24)
6. c (pp. 11, 21)	16. c (p. 28)	6. a (p. 11)	16. b (p. 27)
7. c (p. 11)	17. a (p. 29)	7. b (p. 12)	17. c (p. 30)
8. d (p. 13)	18. d (p. 29)	8. c (p. 15)	18. d (p. 31)
9. b (p. 12)	19. b (p. 30)	9. d (p. 15)	19. c (p. 32)
10. a (p. 13)	20. c (p. 31)	10. a (p. 17)	20. a (p. 34)

2 Neuroscience and Biological Foundations

TOPIC	NOTES

I. BIOLOGICAL FOUNDATIONS

   A. An Overview of the Nervous System

   B. Neurons as the Basic Building Blocks

   C. How Neurons Communicate

   D. Chemical Messengers in the Nervous System

II. A TOUR THROUGH THE BRAIN

A. Tools for Exploration

B. Lower-Level Brain Structures

C. The Cerebral Cortex

D. Two Brains in One?

Critical Thinking/Active Learning: Understanding Central Nervous System Anatomy and Function

Research Highlight: Rewiring, Repairing, and Transplanting Brains and Spinal Cords

III. GENETICS AND EVOLUTION

A. Behavioral Genetics

Research Highlight: Breakthrough—The Human Genome is Mapped!

B. Evolutionary Psychology

Gender and Cultural Diversity: The Evolution of Sex Differences

Core and Expanded LEARNING OBJECTIVES (Read, Recite & wRite)

While *reading* the chapter, stop periodically and *recite* (or repeat in your own words) the answers to the following learning objectives. It will also help your retention if you *write* your answer in the space provided. (Page numbers refer to the text Psychology in Action, 6th Ed.)

Core Learning Objectives
These objectives are found at the beginning of each chapter of Psychology in Action (6th ed.).

1.   How is the nervous system organized?

2.   What are neurons, and how do they communicate information throughout the body?
       Neurons are a bunch of nerves

3.   What are the best tools for studying the brain?

4.   What are the lower-level structures of the brain, and what are their roles in behavior and

      mental processes?

5.   How does the cortex control behavior and mental processes?

6.   How do the left and right hemispheres of the brain affect behavior and mental processes?

7.   How are heredity and evolution linked to human behavior?

Expanded Learning Objectives
These objectives offer more detail and a more intensive way to study the chapter.

Upon completion of CHAPTER 2, the student should be able to:

1. Define neuroscience. Define the major divisions of the nervous system, list the subdivisions of the central nervous system, and describe the functions of the spinal cord (pp. 46-48).

2. Describe the functions of the major subdivisions of the peripheral nervous system, and describe the functions of the parasympathetic and sympathetic nervous systems (pp. 48-50).

3. Draw a neuron, label its parts, and describe the function of each part (p. 51).

4. Describe the electrochemical process involved in an action potential (pp. 52-53).

5. Define neurotransmitter and explain how neurotransmitters act to excite or inhibit action potentials. Describe the effects of the major neurotransmitters: serotonin, acetylcholine, dopamine, norepinephrine, epinephrine, and GABA (pp. 53-55).

6. Explain how neurotransmitters are related to some diseases, poisons, and mind-altering drugs; define agonistic and antagonistic effects, and describe the role of endorphins (pp. 55-57).

7. Describe the function of the endocrine system and list its major glands (pp. 57-58).

8. Describe major tools for studying the brain (pp. 59-61).

9. Identify the location of the cerebellum and the three parts of the brain stem; describe the functions of each of these brain structures (pp. 62-63).

10. Identify the location and functions of each part of the subcortical brain; identify the parts of the limbic system involved with memory, aggression, and fear (pp. 63-65).

11. Describe the cerebral cortex; identify the location and describe the function of the four cortical lobes, and identify the location and function of important areas in each lobe (pp. 65-70).

12. Define lateralization and describe the specialized and interdependent functions of the brain's left and right hemispheres; describe what has been learned from split-brain research (pp. 70-73).

13. Describe recent research regarding neuroplasticity and neurogenesis, and the role of stem cells in the treatment of various brain dysfunctions (pp. 73, 76).

14. Describe how behavioral genetics has combined the fields of genetics and psychology in furthering our understanding of human behavior (pp. 76-79).

15. Describe recent research regarding mapping the human genome (p. 79).

16. Describe how evolutionary psychologists use Darwin's principles of natural selection and genetic mutations to explain human behavior (pp. 80-81).

17. Describe recent research regarding gender differences related to the brain and behavior (pp. 79; 81-82).

 **KEY TERMS** (Review)

The *review* step in the SQ4R method is very important to your performance on quizzes and exams. Upon completion of this chapter, you should be able to define the following terms.

Action Potential: *electro chemical impulse that carries information along the axon of a neuron*

Amygdala: *lower level brain structure b, Part of the limbic system, involved w/ emotion*

Association Areas: _____

_____

Autonomic Nervous System (ANS): _Subdivision of peripheral nervous system_

Axon: _Structure of nerve cell that carries impulses from cell body to terminal buttons_

Behavioral Genetics: _____

Brainstem: _responsible for automatic survival function_

Cell Body: _____

Central Nervous System (CNS): _____

Cerebellum: _located behind the brain stem controls smooth movement, balance._

Cerebral Cortex: _outside surfce of the 2 cerebral hemisphere and regulates complex behavior, reciving sensations motor control (higher mental process_

Chromosome: _____

Corpus Callosum: _bridge between the two hemispheres of the brain_

Dendrites: _nerve parts that recives neural impulses and brings them to the soma or cell body_

Endocrine System: *System of glands that secret hormons into the blood stream*

Endorphins: *involved in pain control pleasure & memory*

Evolutionary Psychology: _____

Frontal Lobes: *Cortical lobes in the front of the brain which control speech production thinking personality emotion & memory*

Gene: _____

Glial Cells: *give nerves nutritional support*

Heritability: _____

Hormones: *chemicals that react to specific enzymes*

Hypothalamus: *controls endocrine system and regulates hunger thirst sex and aggression*

Lateralization: _____

Limbic System: *group of brain structures involved w/ emotion motivation memory & learning*

Localization of Function: _____

_____

Medulla: _Part of ~~the~~ brainstem that is responsible for automatic
functions, heart rate breathing rate_

Myelin Sheath: _____

_____

Natural Selection: _____

_____

Neurogenesis: _____

_____

Neuron: _____

_____

Neuroplasticity: _____

_____

Neuroscience: _____

_____

Neurotransmitter: _____

_____

Occipital Lobes: _back of the brain, vision/perseption_

_____

Parasympathetic Nervous System: _____

_____

Parietal Lobes: *part of the brain where bodily sensations are interpreted*

Peripheral Nervous System (PNS): _____

_____

Pons: *Top of the brain stem involved w/ ~~responsible~~ for respiration movement walking sleep and dreaming*

Reticular Formation (RF): *Screens incoming info and arouses the cortex*

_____

Somatic Nervous System (SNS): *Controls skeletal movement*

_____

Split-Brain: _____

_____

Stem Cell: _____

_____

Sympathetic Nervous System: _____

_____

Synapse: *Gap between the terminal buttons of one nerve and the dendrites of another*

Temporal Lobes: *Controls hearing and language comprehension memory and some emotional*

Thalamus: *part of brain stem that relays sensory messages to the cerebral cortex*

ACTIVE LEARNING EXERCISES (Recite)

The *recite* step in the SQ4R method requires you to be an ACTIVE learner. By completing the following exercises, you will test and improve your mastery of the chapter material, which will also improve your performance on quizzes and exams. Answers to some exercises appear at the end of this study guide chapter.

ACTIVE LEARNING EXERCISE I

For each of the following behaviors, identify which of the sensory projection areas would receive incoming neural impulses. Write down the cerebral lobes receiving the input (frontal, parietal, occipital, or temporal).

1. Looking at a picture _____.

2. Feeling a rough texture with your right hand _____.

3. Listening to music on headphones _____.

4. Catching a baseball with your left hand _____.

5. Reading silently _____.

ACTIVE LEARNING EXERCISE II

Using information from Chapter 2, fill in the appropriate label or term in the space next to the corresponding number or letter.

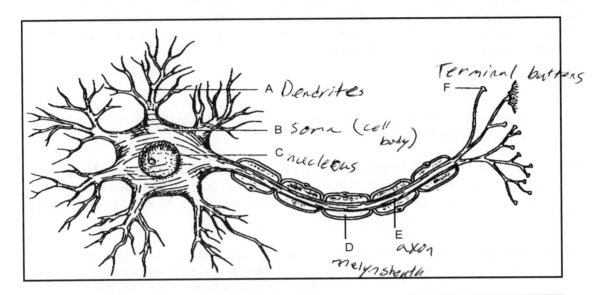

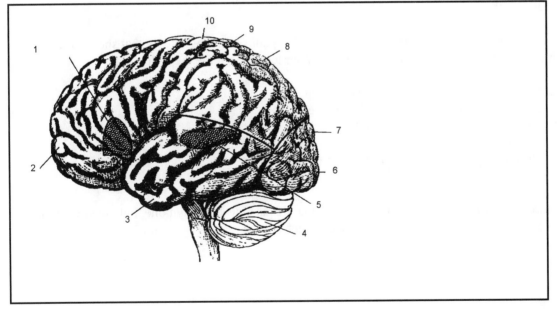

ACTIVE LEARNING EXERCISE III

<u>Clarifying</u> <u>Terms</u> <u>and</u> <u>Concepts</u>   (A Cognitive Skill)

An important element of active learning and critical thinking is clarity of thought. A clear thinker understands that simply defining a term is not evidence of true understanding. One must be able to extend basic definitions to higher, more complex applications. The following exercise will help clarify your understanding of brain terminology and function.

<u>The</u> <u>Setting</u>

You are a famous neurosurgeon who specializes in brain damage. In each of the following cases, make a "diagnosis" (using information from Chapter 2).

Case 1: A 56-year-old man has suffered a recent stroke. He speaks in a curious manner resembling fluent English but the phrases make no sense. You find that he comprehends your verbal or written instructions perfectly and can even write them down, but cannot repeat them verbally. You diagnose the problem as a lesion in the _____ .

Case 2: A 7-year-old boy is having serious difficulties learning to read. At age 5, his corpus callosum was sectioned to prevent epileptic seizures. His mother points out that he is very intelligent and she cannot understand why reading is so difficult for him. You explain that his reading difficulties are probably related to the fact that _____ .

Case 3: An intelligent businesswoman comes to you and explains rather agitatedly that she awoke yesterday morning to find she could no longer read. Your tests determine the following:

1. She is totally blind in the right visual field.
2. She speaks fluently and comprehends speech.
3. She can write with her right hand but cannot read what she has written.
4. She can copy written words but only with her left hand.

You turn to your puzzled assistant and remark that this is indeed a tough one, but you are willing to bet you will find brain damage in at least two areas, which are the _____ and _____ .

CHAPTER OVERVIEW (<u>R</u>eview)

The following CHAPTER OVERVIEW provides a narrative overview of the main topics covered in the chapter. Like the Visual Summary found at the end of each chapter in the text, this narrative summary provides a final opportunity to *review* chapter material.

I. Biological Foundations

Neuroscience is an interdisciplinary field that studies how biological processes, especially activity in the brain and nervous system, relate to behavior. The **central nervous system** is composed of the brain and the spinal cord. The spinal cord is the communications link between the brain and the rest of the body below the neck. It is involved in all voluntary and reflex responses of the body below the neck.

The **peripheral nervous system** includes all nerves going to and from the brain and spinal cord. Its two major subdivisions are the **somatic nervous system** and the **autonomic nervous system.** The somatic nervous system includes all nerves carrying incoming sensory information and outgoing motor information to and from the sense organs and skeletal muscles. The autonomic nervous system includes the nerves outside the brain and spinal cord that maintain normal functioning of glands, heart muscle, and the smooth muscle of blood vessels and internal organs.

The autonomic nervous system is further divided into two branches, the **parasympathetic** and the **sympathetic**, which tend to work in opposition to one another. The parasympathetic nervous system normally dominates when a person is relaxed. The sympathetic nervous system dominates when a person is under physical or mental stress. It mobilizes the body for fight or flight by increasing heart rate and blood pressure and slowing digestive processes.

Neurons are cells that transmit information throughout the body. They have three main parts: **dendrites**, which receive information from other neurons; the **cell body**, which provides nourishment and "decides" whether the axon should fire; and the **axon**, which sends along the neural information. **Glial cells** support and provide nutrients for neurons in the CNS.

The axon is specialized for transmitting neural impulses, or **action potentials**. During times when no action potential is moving down the axon, the axon is at rest. The neuron is activated, and an action potential occurs, when the charge within the neuron becomes more positive than the charge outside the cell's membrane. Action potentials travel more quickly down myelinated axons because the **myelin sheath** serves as insulation.

Information is transferred from one neuron to another at synapses by chemicals called **neurotransmitters.** Neurotransmitters bind to receptor sites much as a key fits into a lock, and their effects can be *excitatory* or *inhibitory*. Most psychoactive drugs affect the nervous system by acting directly on receptor sites for specific neurotransmitters or by increasing or decreasing the amount of neurotransmitter that crosses the **synapse**.

In addition to neurotransmitters, there are two other important chemical messengers—endorphins and hormones. Neuromodulators (such as **endorphins**) increase or decrease the effects of neurotransmitters. **Hormones** are released from glands in the **endocrine system** directly into the bloodstream. They regulate levels of critical chemicals in the body.

II. A Tour Through the Brain

Researchers study the brain through dissection of brains of cadavers, lesion techniques, which involve destroying part of an animal's brain to study resultant changes in behavior, and direct observation or case studies. Electrical recording techniques involve implanting electrodes into the brain or on its surface to study the brain's electrical activity. CT, PET, MRI, and fMRI scans are sophisticated techniques for studying intact, living brains.

The most important lower-level brain structures are the brain stem, cerebellum, thalamus, hypothalamus, and limbic system. The **brain stem** controls automatic functions such as heartbeat and breathing, the cerebellum contributes to balance, muscle coordination, and some higher mental operations. Parts of the brain stem (the **pons** and **medulla**) are involved in sleeping, waking, dreaming, and control of automatic bodily functions, whereas the **reticular formation** screens incoming information and arouses the cortex. The **cerebellum** maintains smooth movement, balance, and some aspects of perception and cognition. The **thalamus** is the major incoming sensory relay area of the brain. The **hypothalamus** is involved in emotion and in drives associated with survival, such as regulation of body temperature, thirst, hunger, sex, and aggression. The **limbic system** is a group of brain structures (including the **amygdala**) involved with emotional behavior and memory.

The left and right cerebral hemispheres of the brain take up most of the room inside the skull. The outer covering of the hemispheres, the **cerebral cortex,** is divided into four lobes. The **frontal lobes** control movement and speech and are involved with self-awareness and planning ahead. The **parietal lobes** are the receiving area for sensory information. The **temporal lobes** are concerned with hearing and language. The occipital lobes are dedicated to vision and visual information processing.

The two hemispheres of the brain are linked by the **corpus callosum**, through which they communicate and coordinate. However, **split-brain** research shows that each hemisphere does perform somewhat separate functions. In most people, the left hemisphere is dominant in verbal skills, such as speaking and writing, and also for analytical tasks. The right hemisphere appears to excel at nonverbal tasks, such as spatio-manipulative skills, art and music, and visual recognition. Recent research shows the brain can reorganize and change its structure and function throughout the lifespan (**neuroplasticity**), and create new nerve cells (**neurogenesis**) from **stem cells.**

III. Genetics and Evolution

Genes are strings of chemicals that hold the code for certain traits that are passed on from parent to child, and they can be dominant or recessive. Genes are found on long strands of DNA molecules called **chromosomes**. **Behavioral geneticists** use twin studies, adoption studies, family studies, and genetic abnormalities to explore genetic contributions to behavior and make estimates of heritability.

Evolutionary psychology is the branch of psychology that looks at evolutionary changes related to behavior. Several different processes, including **natural selection**, mutations, and social and cultural factors can affect evolution.

SELF-TESTS (Review & wRite)

Completing the following SELF-TESTS will provide immediate feedback on how well you have mastered the material. In the *crossword puzzle* and *fill-in exercises*, write the appropriate word or words in the blank spaces. The *matching exercise* requires you to match the terms in one column to their correct definitions in the other. For the *multiple-choice questions* in Practice Tests I and II, circle or underline the correct answer. If you are unsure of any answer, highlight or specially mark the item, and then go back to the text for further review. Correct answers are provided at the end of this study guide chapter.

CROSSWORD PUZZLE FOR CHAPTER 2

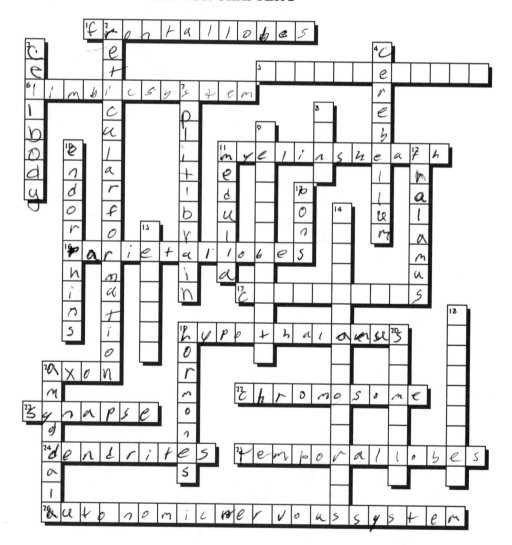

ACROSS

1 Cortical lobes in the front of the brain, which govern motor control, speech production, and higher functions, such as thinking, personality, emotion, and memory. '

5 The division of nonneuronal cells to produce neurons.

6 An interconnected group of lower-level brain structures involved with the arousal and regulation of emotion, motivation, memory, and many other aspects of behavior and mental processes.

11 A layer of fatty insulation wrapped around the axon of some neurons, which increases the rate at which nerve impulses travel along the axon. *myelin sheath* *myelin sheath*

16 Cortical lobes at the top of the brain where bodily sensations are interpreted.

17 Nervous system cells that provide structural, nutritional, and other support for the neuron; also called glia or neuroglia.

19 A tiny structure in the brain that lies under the thalamus and regulates emotions and drives, such as hunger, thirst, sex, and aggression. *hypothalamus*

21 A long, tube-like structure that conveys impulses away from the neuron's cell body toward other neurons or to muscles or glands. *axon*

22 Threadlike strands of DNA (deoxyribonucleic acid) molecules that carry genetic information.

23 The junction between the axon tip of the sending neuron and the dendrite or cell body of the receiving neuron.. *Synaptic gap*

24 Branching neuron structures that receive neural impulses from other neurons and convey impulses toward the cell body. *Dendrites*

25 Cortical lobes above the ears involved in auditory (hearing), language comprehension, memory, and some emotional control. *Temporal lobes*

26 Subdivision of the peripheral nervous system (PNS) that controls involuntary functions, such as heart rate and digestion. It is further subdivided into the sympathetic nervous system, which arouses, and the parasympathetic nervous system, which calms. *autonomic*

DOWN

2 A diffuse set of neurons found in the core of the brain stem that are responsible for screening incoming information and arousing the cortex.

3 The part of the neuron that contains the cell nucleus, as well as other structures that help the neuron carry out its functions.

4 The brain area responsible for maintaining smooth movement, balance, and some aspects of perception and cognition. *Cerebellum*

7 A surgical separation of the brain's two hemispheres used medically to treat severe epilepsy. Split-brain patients provide data on the functions of the two hemispheres.

8 A segment of DNA that occupies a specific place on a particular chromosome and carries the code for hereditary transmission.

9 The proportion of observed variance in a particular trait (such as intelligence) that can be attributed to inherited genetic factors in contrast to environmental ones.

10 Chemical substances in the nervous system that are similar in structure and action to opiates; involved in pain control, pleasure, and memory. *endorphins*

11 A structure in the brain stem responsible for automatic body functions such as breathing and heart rate. *Medulla*

12 A brain structure located on top of the brain stem that relays sensory messages to the cerebral cortex. *Thalamus*

13 A structure located at the top of the brain stem that is involved with functions such as respiration, movement, waking, sleep, and dreaming. *Pons*

14 So-called "quiet areas" in the cerebral cortex involved in interpreting, integrating and acting on information processed by other parts of the brain.

15 Individual nerve cells responsible for processing, storing, and transmitting information throughout the body.

18 The part of the brain that begins as a continuation of the spinal cord and ends deep within the cortex; it is responsible for automatic, survival functions.

19 Chemicals manufactured by endocrine glands and circulated in the bloodstream to produce bodily changes or maintain normal bodily functions. *hormones*

20 Precursor (immature) cells that give birth to new specialized cells. A stem cell holds all the information it needs to make bone, blood, brain--any part of a human body-and can also copy itself to maintain a stock of stem cells.

21 An almond-shaped lower-level brain structure that is part of the limbic system and involved in emotion. *amygdala*

FILL-IN EXERCISES

1. The two major divisions of the nervous system are the *CNS*, which consists of the brain and spinal cord, and the *PNS* which consists of all nerves outside the CNS (p. 46).

2. The *Somatic* is involved in reflexes and relaying neural information to and from the brain (p. 47).

3. The *Parasympathetic* part of the autonomic nervous system is dominant during normal, relaxed times, whereas the _____ is dominant during times of mental or physical stress (p. 48).
    Sympathetic

4. Individual nerve cells responsible for processing, storing, and transmitting information throughout the body are known as _____ (p.50).

5. The fatty insulation on some axons that helps insulate and speed neural messages is known as the _____ (p. 51).
    Myelin Sheath

6. Most poisons and drugs have their effect at the _____ (p. 55).

7. The _____ is responsible for maintaining smooth movement, balance, and some aspects of perception and cognition (p. 63).

8. The *cerebellum* maintains homeostasis and regulates emotions and drives, such as hunger, thirst, sex, and aggression (p. 64).

9. The *occipital* lobes are responsible for vision and visual perception (p. 69).

10. Specialization of the hemispheres of the brain was first discovered as a result of _____ (p. 70).

MATCHING EXERCISE

$\frac{10}{10}$

Column A   Column B

a. Neuron 7   ✓1. __J__ Receive information from other neurons.
b. Temporal Lobes 10   ✓2. __e__ Integrates incoming information from dendrites.
c. Myelin Sheath 9   ✓3. __i__ Transmits messages from one hemisphere to the other.
d. Parietal Lobes 5   ✓4. __h__ Electrochemical impulse that travels down the axon.
e. Cell Body 2   ✓5. __d__ Interprets bodily sensations.
f. Amygdala 6   ✓6. __f__ Part of the limbic system particularly involved in emotion.
g. Brain Stem 8   ✓7. __a__ Cells that transmit information throughout the body.
h. Action Potential 4   ✓8. __g__ Controls automatic functions like the heartbeat.
i. Corpus Callosum 3   ✓9. __c__ Fatty insulation that speeds up action potential.
j. Dendrites 1   ✓10. __b__ Involved in audition and language comprehension.

PRACTICE TEST I

$\frac{16}{20}$ $?\frac{4}{20}$

1. Cells within your body specialized for conducting information are called _____.
    a. dendrites
    b. neurons
    c. axons
    d. nucleotides

2. The three major parts of a neuron are the _____.
    a. glia, dendrites, and myelin
    b. myelin, dendrites, and axon
    c. dendrites, axon, and cell body
    d. axon, glia, and myelin

3. The _____ consists of all the nerves that connect to sensory receptors and control skeletal muscles.
    a. parasympathetic nervous system
    b. spinal cord
    c. somatic nervous system
    d. action potential

4. _____ provide structural, nutritional, and other support for the neuron.
    a. Dendrites
    b. Axons
    c. Nurturing bodies
    d. Glial cells

b 5.   The neurotransmitter _____ is a suspected factor in Parkinson's disease (PD) and schizophrenia.
   a.   acetycholine
   b.   dopamine
   c.   serotonin
   d.   all of these options

c 6.   The synapse is the point where _____.
   a.   the soma attaches to the dendrite
   b.   neurotransmitters are manufactured
   c.   information transfers from neuron to neuron
   d.   the action potential begins

b 7.   Chemical messengers that are secreted into the synapse are called _____.
   a.   ions
   b.   neurotransmitters
   c.   nucleotides
   d.   neurocommunicators

d 8.   The principle whereby an axon either fires or does not fire an action potential is called the _____
   a.   sodium-potassium
   b.   axon terminal
   c.   shotgun
   d.   all-or-none

d 9.   _____ are manufactured by endocrine glands and circulated in the bloodstream to produce bodily changes or maintain normal bodily functions.
   a.   Endorphins
   b.   Neurotransmitters
   c.   Endoseals
   d.   Hormones

d 10. The parasympathetic and sympathetic are the major divisions of the _____ nervous system.
   a.   automatic
   b.   somatic
   c.   central
   d.   autonomic

b 11. The parasympathetic nervous system is dominant when a person is _____.
   a.   stressed
   b.   relaxed
   c.   frightened
   d.   angry

C 12. The system of glands that secrete hormones into the bloodstream is called the _____ system.
- a. lympathic
- b. hormonal
- © endocrine
- d. reticular activating

d 13. The major divisions of the central nervous system are _____.
- a. sympathetic and parasympathetic
- b. somatic and autonomic
- c. gray matter and white matter
- d. brain and spinal cord

b 14. The frontal, parietal, occipital, and temporal lobes make up the _____.
- a. brain
- b. cerebral cortex
- c. subcortex
- d. brain stem

C 15. If you are accidentally hit on the head and you see flashes of light, most likely the blow activated cells in the _____.
- a. frontal lobes
- b. temporal lobes
- © occipital lobes
- d. parietal lobes

a 16. The limbic system, the thalamus, and the hypothalamus are all _____.
- ⓐ lower-level brain structures
- b. cortical areas
- c. brain stem areas
- d. spinal cord areas

b 17. Damage to the medulla can lead to loss of _____.
- a. vision
- b. respiration
- c. hearing
- d. smell

d 18. Split-brain research has indicated that, in most people, the left hemisphere is responsible for _____ abilities.
- a. musical
- b. spatial
- c. artistic
- d. language

19. The brain's ability to reorganize and change its structure and function throughout the life span is known as _____.
    a.   rejuvenation
    b.   neurogenesis
    c.   semipermeable processes
    d.   neuroplasticity

20. Three types of brain scans are the _____.
    a.   CAT, DOG, RAN
    b.   PET, CAT, MRI
    c.   BW, LEF, SS
    d.   KSU, HSU, CSU

PRACTICE TEST II

1. Neurons are the basic units in the _____.
    a.   nervous system
    b.   synapses
    c.   dendrites
    d.   body

2. The _____ integrates incoming information, absorbs nutrients, and produces proteins necessary for the functioning of the neuron.
    a.   axon hillock
    b.   myelin sheath
    c.   synaptic gap
    d.   cell body

3. An action potential is a(n) _____ impulse that travels through a neuron.
    a.   ganglial
    b.   muscular
    c.   electrochemical
    d.   neuroelectrical

4. The proportion of observed variance in a particular trait (such as intelligence) that can be attributed to inherited genetic factors in contrast to environmental ones is known as _____.
    a.   behavioral genetics
    b.   genetic determinism
    c.   heritability
    d.   Mendelian factors

5. Neurotransmitters are _____.
   a. charged ions that carry action potentials down the axon
   b. hormones that pass electrical energy from the dendrite into the soma
   c. chemical messengers that are released from an axon and stimulate dendrites on another neuron
   d. lubricants and nutrients needed by the soma to keep the neuron alive

6. Some drugs, called agonists, work by _____ the action of neurotransmitters.
   a. speeding up
   b. blocking
   c. slowing down
   d. mimicking

7. Precursor (or immature) cells that produce new specialized cells are called _____ cells.
   a. maternal
   b. primoridial
   c. stem
   d. embryonic

8. An interconnected group of lower-level brain structures particularly responsible for emotions is known as the _____.
   a. subcortical center
   b. homeostatic controller
   c. limbic system
   d. master endocrine gland

9. The _____ lobes govern motor control, speech production, and higher functions, such as thinking, personality, emotion, and memory.
   a. parietal
   b. master
   c. frontal
   d. temporal

10. The sensory and motor nerves that go to and from the central nervous system, body organs, and skeletal muscles make up the _____ nervous system.
    a. somatic
    b. fight or flight
    c. autonomic
    d. peripheral

11. The _____ system prepares your body to respond to stress.
    a. central nervous
    b. sympathetic
    c. peripheral
    d. somatic

12. A reflex arc occurs in the _____.
    a.   skeletal muscles
    b.   brain
    c.   spinal cord
    d.   reticular activating system

13. A stroke that damages Broca's area would affect a person's ability to _____.
    a.   make speech sounds
    b.   read and write
    c.   understand language
    d.   read, write, and understand language

14. Specialization of the left and right hemispheres of the brain for particular operations is known as _____.
    a.   centralization
    b.   asymmetrical processing
    c.   localization of function
    d.   lateralization

15. The occipital lobes contain the sensory projection areas for _____.
    a.   vision
    b.   hearing
    c.   smell and taste
    d.   touch and pain

16. The corpus callosum _____.
    a.   maintains your balance
    b.   keeps you breathing
    c.   connects your right and left cerebral hemispheres
    d.   is the center of your personality

17. The brainstem is involved with your _____.
    a.   ability to move and maintain posture
    b.   sense of touch and pain
    c.   basic survival functions
    d.   emotional behavior

18. If Hannibal Lecter removed and ate the _____ of your brain, you would no longer understand language.
    a.   corpus callosum
    b.   association areas
    c.   Wernicke's area
    d.   parietal lobes

19. In the lesion technique for studying the brain, brain tissue is _____.
    a.   replaced
    b.   destroyed
    c.   destroyed, then replaced
    d.   injected with chemicals

20. Split-brain patients _____.
    a.   do not exist
    b.   have split personalities
    c.   cannot name an object if they hold it in their left hand without looking at it
    d.   deteriorate gradually at first and usually die within a year

ANSWERS
The following answers to active learning exercises, the crossword puzzle, fill-ins, matching exercises, and practice tests 1 and 2 provide immediate feedback on your mastery of the material. Try not to simply memorize the answers. When you are unsure of your "guess" or make an error, be sure to go back to the textbook and carefully review. This will greatly improve your scores on classroom exams and quizzes.

ACTIVE LEARNING EXERCISE I

1. right and left occipital lobes; 2. left parietal lobe; 3. left and right temporal lobes; 4. right frontal lobe; 5. vision = left and right occipital lobes, language processing = left parietal lobe.

ACTIVE LEARNING EXERCISE II

Neuron Drawing a. dendrite, b. cell body (soma), c. nucleus, d. myelin sheath, e. axon, f. terminal branches of axon.

Brain Drawing 1. Broca's area, 2. frontal lobe, 3. temporal lobe, 4. cerebellum, 5. Wernicke's area, 6. occipital lobe, 7. visual cortex, 8. parietal lobe, 9. somatosensory cortex, 10. motor cortex.

ACTIVE LEARNING EXERCISE III

Case 1: Left hemisphere, in the frontal and temporal lobes, probably Broca's area.

Case 2: He had his corpus callosum severed, and his frontal, temporal, and occipital lobes are not integrating information.

Case 3: Left occipital lobe, corpus callosum.

CROSSWORD PUZZLE FOR CHAPTER 2

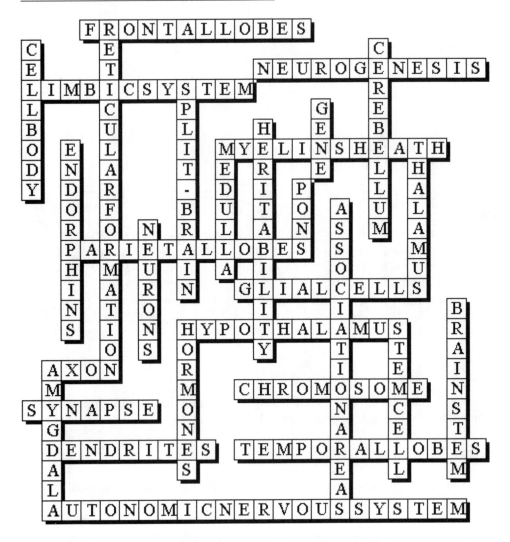

FILL-IN EXERCISES

1. central nervous system, peripheral nervous system; 2. spinal cord; 3. parasympathetic, sympathetic; 4. neurons; 5. myelin sheath; 6. synapse; 7. cerebellum; 8. hypothalamus; 9. occipital; 10. split-brain research.

MATCHING EXERCISES

a. 7, b. 10, c. 9, d. 5, e. 2, f. 6, g. 8, h. 4, i. 3, j. 1

PRACTICE TEST I		PRACTICE TEST II	
1. b (p. 50)	11. b (pp. 48-49)	1. a (p. 50)	11. b (p. 48)
2. c (p. 51)	12. c (p. 57)	2. d (p. 51)	12. c (p. 47)
3. c (p. 48)	13. d (p. 46)	3. c (p. 52)	13. a (p. 67)
4. d (p. 51)	14. b (p. 66)	4. c (p. 78)	14. d (p. 70)
5. b (p. 54)	15. c (p. 69)	5. c (p. 53)	15. a (p. 69)
6. c (p. 53)	16. a (p. 59-65)	6. d (p. 56)	16. c (p. 70)
7. b (p. 53)	17. b (p. 63)	7. c (p. 76)	17. d (p. 63)
8. d (p. 53)	18. d (p. 72)	8. c (p. 64)	18. c (p. 69)
9. d (p. 57)	19. d (p. 74)	9. c (p. 66)	19. b (p. 59)
10.d (p. 48)	20. a (p. 59)	10. d (p. 48)	20. c (p. 70)

3 Stress and Health Psychology

TOPIC	NOTES

I. HEALTH PSYCHOLOGY IN ACTION

A. What Health Psychologists Do

B. Smoking

C. Binge Drinking

      Gender and Cultural Diversity: Binge Drinking Around the World

D. Chronic Pain

II. STRESS AND ITS ROLE IN HEALTH

A. Sources of Stress

B. Results of Stress

    Research Highlight: Procrastination, Performance, and Health

III. STRESS AND SERIOUS ILLNESS

A. Cancer

B. Cardiovascular Disorders

IV. COPING WITH STRESS

A. Emotion-Focused Forms of Coping

B. Problem-Focused Forms of Coping

    Critical Thinking/Active Learning: Is Your Job Stressful?

C. Resources for Effective Coping

D. Active Coping Strategies

Core and Expanded LEARNING OBJECTIVES (Read, Recite & wRite)

While *reading* the chapter, stop periodically and *recite* (or repeat in your own words) the answers to the following learning objectives. It will also help your retention if you *write* your answer in the space provided. (Page numbers refer to the text Psychology in Action, 6th Ed.)

Core Learning Objectives
These objectives are found at the beginning of each chapter of Psychology in Action (6th ed.).

1. What is health psychology? Can health psychologists help with problems related to smoking, binge drinking, and chronic pain?

2. What is stress and what are its major sources and results?

3. How is stress related to serious illnesses like cancer and coronary heart disease?

4. What techniques and resources are available to help people cope with stress?

Expanded Learning Objectives
These objectives offer more detail and a more intensive way to study the chapter.

Upon completion of CHAPTER 3, the student should be able to:

1. Define health psychology and state how it is related to life expectancy; identify major occupational options for health psychologists (pp. 88-89).

2. Describe the consequences of cigarette smoking; explain psychological, social, and biological factors that lead to smoking; and describe methods for prevention and quitting (pp. 89-91).

3. Discuss binge drinking on college campuses and around the world; describe how to reduce the social rewards that contribute to this problem (pp. 92-94).

4. Describe the role of psychologists in helping people deal with chronic pain (pp. 94-45).

5. Differentiate between stress and stressors, eustress and distress (p. 96).

6. Describe research findings related to Holmes and Rahe's Social Readjustment Rating Scale, chronic stressors, daily hassles, frustrations, burnout, and conflict; differentiate between the three basic conflicts (pp. 96-99).

7. Describe the physiological effects of stress, including the general adaptation syndrome, the suppression of the immune system, and the development of physical disorders (pp. 101-103).

8. Describe how stress is related to cancer (pp. 104-105).

9. Explain the relationship between stress and heart disease, focusing on the autonomic nervous system, fatty deposits in the arteries, and cholesterol ratios (pp. 105-106).

10. Differentiate between Type A and Type B personalities; describe the research related to Type A personalities and heart disease; compare the shotgun and target behavior approaches to behavior modification (p. 106).

11. Describe the three attitudes common in people with the hardiness trait, and how these can affect stress (p. 107).

12. Contrast emotion-focused and problem-focused forms of coping with stress, and provide an example of each (pp. 108-110).

13. List coping resources and describe how each improves coping (pp. 110-111).

14. Explain how exercise, biofeedback, and relaxation can reduce stress (pp. 111-112).

KEY TERMS (Review)

The *review* step in the SQ4R method is very important to your performance on quizzes and exams. Upon completion of this chapter, you should be able to define the following terms.

Approach-Approach Conflict: _____

_____

Approach-Avoidance Conflict: _____

_____

Avoidance-Avoidance Conflict: _____

_____

Burnout: _____

_____

Chronic Pain: _____

_____

Conflict: _____

_____

Defense Mechanisms: _____

_____

Distress: _____

_____

Emotion-Focused Forms of Coping: _____

_____

Eustress: _____

_____

Frustration: _____

_____

General Adaptation Syndrome (GAS): _____

_____

Hardiness: _____

_____

Hassles: _____

_____

Health Psychology: _____

_____

Locus of Control: _____

_____

Problem-Focused Forms of Coping: _____

_____

Psychoneuroimmunology: _____

_____

Stress: _____

_____

Type-A Personality: _____

_____

Type-B Personality: _____

_____

ACTIVE LEARNING EXERCISES (Recite)

The *recite* step in the SQ4R method requires you to be an ACTIVE learner. By completing the following exercises, you will test and improve your mastery of the chapter material, which will also improve your performance on quizzes and exams. Answers to some exercises appear at the end of this study guide chapter.

ACTIVE LEARNING EXERCISE I

After reading pages 108-110 of the text, try identifying both an emotion-focused and a problem-focused coping strategy for each of the following situations:

1. It is the first day of classes for a new semester and about five minutes into your first class you realize you are in classroom 242 not room 424. This is a physics class not a psychology class.

2. Your significant other has just told you that he/she is in love with someone else and is getting married next August.

3. Your car has stalled on a deserted country road. As you start to get out to check the problem, two large dogs run up to your door and start barking and growling at you.

4. Your car insurance has just been cancelled because of a mistake in your driving record.

5. You come to your history class expecting a normal lecture class, but you discover this is the day of the first major examination.

ACTIVE LEARNING EXERCISE II

<u>Making</u> <u>Sound</u> <u>Decisions</u> (A Cognitive Skill)

Good decision-makers take full responsibility for their own future. They realize they are the only ones who can truly evaluate the merits and potential costs of each alternative. A critical thinker also recognizes that decisions are often stressful, but cannot be avoided. Avoiding a decision is, in fact, making one without the benefit of a careful analysis of the problem. To improve your decision-making skills, we offer the following exercise (adapted from Seech, 1987):

1. At the top of the chart, identify an ongoing personal conflict as approach-approach, avoidance-avoidance, or approach-avoidance.

2. On the lines in the left-hand column, list all possible alternatives or possible courses of action. Although the wording of the "approach-approach" discussion may imply only two choices, most conflicts involve several options or alternatives. Identifying all your options will require a good deal of homework. Read up on your problem. Talk to as many people as you can.

3. Now list the logical outcome or consequence of each alternative, regardless of whether the consequence is significant or insignificant and regardless of whether it is a certain or a possible outcome.

4. Next assess both the probability and significance of each outcome. Using a 0 to 5 rating scale (0 = won't occur and 5 = certain to occur), assign a numerical rating for the likelihood that each consequence will actually occur. Using a similar 0 to 5 rating scale (0 = no significance and 5 = high significance), assess the importance you place on each consequence.

5. Now review the chart. In some cases, you may find it helpful to multiply your probability and significance ratings and then compare your results for the various alternatives. In other cases, you will find it difficult to assign numerical values to complex issues and feelings. Even in the most difficult decisions, however, the thinking and evaluation elicited by this chart may provide useful insights to your conflict. Also note the feelings you associate with each alternative. Careful decision making tries to integrate feelings and cognitions.

6. After you've reviewed each alternative, ask yourself which choice is most in line with your overall goals and values. Some alternatives may look more-or less appealing when weighed against long-term relationship plans, career goals, and personal belief systems. You may want to discuss your chart with a trusted friend before you make a final decision.

7. Once you make your decision, commit yourself and give it all you've got. Throw away your expectations. Many decisions don't turn out the way we imagine, and if we focus on the way it is supposed to be we miss enjoying the way it is. On the other hand, if the decision is wrong, don't be afraid to change or correct your course. ("When you're in a hole, stop digging!")

TYPE OF CONFLICT: _____

    Alternatives   Logical Outcome   Probability   Significance

1.

2.

3.

CHAPTER OVERVIEW (Review)

The following CHAPTER OVERVIEW provides a narrative overview of the main topics covered in the chapter. Like the Visual Summary found at the end of each chapter in the text, this narrative summary provides a final opportunity to *review* chapter material.

I. Health Psychology in Action

Health psychology is the study of the relationship between psychological behavior and physical health and illness, with an emphasis on wellness and the prevention of illness. As researchers, health psychologists study psychological issues that affect physical health and find ways to help patients cope with medical procedures and health problems. As practitioners, health psychologists work with patients alongside health care professionals to help reduce psychological distress and unhealthy behaviors and educate the general public about health risks and health maintenance.

Because smoking is the single most preventable cause of death and disease in the United States, prevention and cessation of smoking are of primary importance to all health practitioners, including health psychologists. Smoking prevention programs involve educating the public about short- and long-term consequences of smoking, trying to make smoking less socially acceptable and helping nonsmokers resist social pressures to smoke. Most approaches to help people quit smoking include cognitive and behavioral techniques to aid smokers in their withdrawal from nicotine, and nicotine replacement therapy (using patches, gum, and pills).

Binge drinking is a serious problem, which can lead to rape or assault, and even to death from alcohol poisoning or automobile and other accidents. It occurs when a man has five or more drinks in a row and a woman has four or more. To reduce binge drinking, we must overcome the myths about drinking and teach the facts. We must also reduce or remove the social rewards.

Chronic pain is continuous or recurrent pain that persists over a period of six months or more. Although psychological factors rarely are the source of chronic pain, they can encourage and intensify it. Increased activity, exercise, and dietary changes help to reduce chronic pain. Health psychologists also use behavior modification, biofeedback, and relaxation techniques to treat chronic pain.

II. Stress and Its Role in Health

Stress is the body's arousal, both physical and mental, to situations or events that we perceive as threatening or challenging. A situation or event, either pleasant or unpleasant, that triggers arousal and causes stress is known as a stressor.

The major sources of stress are life changes, chronic stressors, hassles, burnout, frustration, and conflicts. Chronic stressors are ongoing events such as poor working conditions. **Hassles** are little everyday life problems that pile up to cause major stress. Persistent hassles and a loss of idealism in your work situation can lead to a form of physical, mental, and emotional exhaustion known as **burnout.** **Frustration** has to do with blocked goals, whereas **conflict** involves two or more competing goals. Conflicts can be classified as **approach--approach, avoidance--avoidance,** or **approach--avoidance.**

When stressed, the body undergoes physiological changes. The sympathetic branch of the autonomic nervous system is activated, increasing heart rate and blood pressure. This sympathetic activation is beneficial if people need to fight or flee, but in today's world, it generally has negative consequences.

Hans Selye described a generalized physiological reaction to severe stressors, which he called the **general adaptation syndrome (GAS)**. It has three phases: the alarm reaction, the resistance phase, and the exhaustion phase. Prolonged stress can suppress the immune system, which can render the body susceptible to a number of diseases.

III. Stress and Serious Illness

Cancer appears to result from an interaction of heredity, environment (for example, smoking), and immune system deficiency. Stress may be an important cause of decreased immunity. The leading cause of death in the United States is heart disease. Risk factors in heart disease include smoking, stress, obesity, a high-fat diet, lack of exercise, and **Type A personality** (if it includes cynical hostility). The two main approaches to modifying Type A behavior are the shotgun approach and the target behavior approach. People with psychological **hardiness** are less vulnerable to stress because of three distinctive personality characteristics—commitment, control, and challenge.

IV. Coping with Stress

The two major forms of coping with stress are **emotion-focused** and **problem-focused**. Emotion-focused forms change how we view stressful situations. Problem-focused forms deal directly with the situation or the factor causing the stress so as to decrease or eliminate it.

The ability to cope with a stressor also depends on the resources available to a person. Resources include health and energy, positive beliefs, an internal **locus of control**, social skills, social support, and material resources. Exercise and progressive relaxation are active methods people can use to cope with stress.

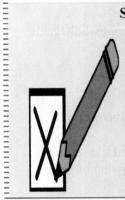

SELF-TESTS (Review & wRite)

Completing the following SELF-TESTS will provide immediate feedback on how well you have mastered the material. In the *crossword puzzle* and *fill-in exercises*, write the appropriate word or words in the blank spaces. The *matching exercise* requires you to match the terms in one column to their correct definitions in the other. For the *multiple-choice questions* in Practice Tests I and II, circle or underline the correct answer. When you are unsure of any answer, be sure to highlight or specially mark the item and then go back to the text for further review. Correct answers are provided at the end of this study guide chapter.

CROSSWORD PUZZLE FOR CHAPTER 3

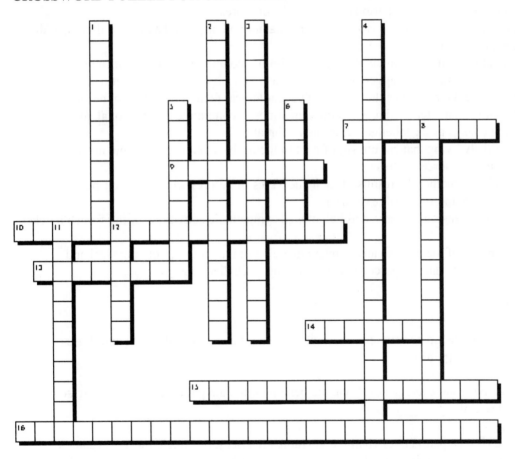

ACROSS

7 A negative emotional state caused by an inability to choose between two or more incompatible goals or impulses.

9 Unpleasant, objectionable stress.

10 Unconscious strategies used to distort reality and relieve anxiety and guilt

13 Pleasant, desirable stress.

14 A state of physical, emotional, and mental exhaustion attributable to long-term involvement in emotionally demanding situations.

15 Set of behavior characteristics consistent with a calm, patient, relaxed attitude toward life.

16 As described by Selye, a generalized physiological reaction to severe stressors consisting of three phases: the alarm reaction, the resistance phase, and the exhaustion phase.

DOWN

1 Continuous or recurrent pain over a period of six months or more.

2 The study of the relationship between psychological behavior and physical health and illness, with an emphasis on wellness and the prevention of illness.

3 Set of behavior characteristics that includes intense ambition, competition, drive, constant preoccupation with responsibilities, exaggerated time urgency, and a cynical, hostile outlook.

4 An interdisciplinary field that studies the effects of psychological factors on the immune system.

5 A resilient personality characteristic based on three qualities: a commitment to personal goals, control over life, and viewing change as a challenge rather than a threat.

6 Little problems of daily living that are not significant in themselves, but they accumulate and sometimes become a major source of stress.

8 A person's belief about whether the results of their successes or failures are under their personal control (internal) or outside their control (external).

11 An unpleasant state of tension, anxiety, and heightened sympathetic activity resulting from a blocked goal.

12 A nonspecific response of the body to any demand made on it; the arousal, both physical and mental, to situations or events that we perceive as threatening or challenging.

FILL-IN EXERCISES

1. The study of the relationship between psychological behavior and physical health and illness is known as _____ (p. 88)

2. An increase in activity and exercise levels can be beneficial to pain patients because exercise increases the release of _____ (p. 94).

3. According to the U.S. Department of Health and Human Services, the single most preventable cause of death and disease in the United States is _____ (p. 89).

4. _____ occurs when a man consumes 5 or more drinks in a row or a woman consumes 4 or more (p. 92)

5. The text defines stress as " a _____ response of the body to any _____ made on it (p. 96).

6. Selye called _____ beneficial, pleasant, or desirable stress (p. 96).

7. Having to choose between two alternatives that will both lead to undesirable results is known as a(n) _____ conflict (p. 99).

8. The three-phase bodily response to chronic stress (Selye's general adaptation syndrome), includes the _____, the _____, and the _____ (p. 102).

9. Being hard driving, competitive, ambitious, impatient, and hostile is characteristic of the _____ personality; whereas having a laid-back, calm, relaxed attitude toward life is typical of the _____ personality (p. 106).

10. If you decide to confront a coworker to tell him/her that they are not doing their share of the work, you are using a _____ coping strategy (p. 108).

MATCHING EXERCISES

Column A

Column B

a. Problem-Focused Strategy
b. Defense Mechanisms
c. Hassles
d. Frustration
e. Burnout
f. Type A personality
g. Psychoneuroimmunology
h. Approach-Avoidance
i. Hans Selye
j. Conflict

1._____ Small everyday problems.
2._____ Studies effect of psychological function on immune system.
3._____ Exhaustion from emotionally demanding situations.
4._____ Unpleasant state from two or more competing goals.
5._____ Conflict with both desirable and undesirable goals.
6._____ Unconscious strategies that protect the ego.
7._____ Deals directly with the stress with problem-solving.
8._____ Alarm reaction, resistance, and exhaustion phase.
9._____ Unpleasant state resulting from blocked goal.
10._____ Ambitious, competitive, hard driving.

PRACTICE TEST I

1. The study of the relationship between psychological behavior and physical health/illness, with a large emphasis on "wellness" and the prevention of illness, is the definition of _____.
    a.   environmental psychology
    b.   Gestalt psychology
    c.   humanistic psychology
    d.   health psychology

2. Which of the following statements about chronic pain is true?
    a.   Chronic pain should never last longer than a few days.
    b.   It has been estimated that as many as one-third of all Americans have, at one time or another, suffered from chronic pain.
    c.   Chronic pain is the leading cause of drug addiction in the 45- to 60-year-old age group.
    d.   Chronic pain is necessary for survival.

3. Which of the following has been used in an attempt to alleviate chronic pain?
    a.   monosodium glutamate therapy
    b.   biofeedback
    c.   epinephrine injections
    d.   complaint-catharsis therapy

4. Naturally produced brain chemicals that reduce pain perception are called _____.
    a.   opiates
    b.   adrenaline
    c.   endorphins
    d.   epinephrine

5. According to the U.S. Department of Health and Human Services, what is the single most preventable cause of death and disease in the United States?
    a.   cigarette smoking
    b.   lack of exercise
    c.   overeating
    d.   heart disease

6. Why do young people start smoking?
    a.   peer pressure
    b.   imitation of role models
    c.   want to look mature
    d.   all of these options

7. Hans Selye defines stress as the _____.
    a. reaction of the autonomic nervous system to a specific challenge imposed from outside the body
    b. nonspecific response of the body to any demand made on it
    c. activation of the sympathetic nervous system
    d. intellectual response made to any stressor

8. Distress _____.
    a. a stimulus that causes stress
    b. relative to each culture and everyone within a culture will experience the same stressors
    c. roughly equivalent to punishment
    d. unpleasant, objectionable stress

9. The three phases of the general adaptation syndrome are _____.
    a. preparation, alarm reaction, incubation
    b. alarm reaction, incubation, resistance
    c. alarm reaction, resistance, exhaustion
    d. incubation, resistance, exhaustion

10. Trying to decide which of two equally good concerts to attend on a Friday night is a(n) _____.
    a. approach-avoidance conflict
    b. avoidance-avoidance conflict
    c. approach-approach conflict
    d. transitory positive conflict

11. The _____ controls the physiological changes associated with stress.
    a. spinal cord
    b. autonomic nervous system
    c. thalamus
    d. brain and spinal cord

12. This is **NOT** a factor known to contribute to the onset of cancer.
    a. heredity
    b. essential hypertension
    c. environment
    d. immune system changes

13. A heart attack is _____.
    a. a disorder of the lining of the heart
    b. death of heart muscle tissue
    c. elevated blood pressure that leads to death
    d. elevated blood pressure because of kidney failure

14. The Type-A behavior pattern is associated with _____.
    a.   chronic pain
    b.   cancer
    c.   smoking cigarettes
    d.   heart disease

15. _____ is **NOT** a type of heart disease.
    a.   atherosclerosis
    b.   stroke
    c.   angina
    d.   heart attack

16. Slow normal speech, relaxed and comfortable posture, and a good sense of humor are characteristics of _____.
    a.   brain disease
    b.   Type-A behavior
    c.   Type-B behavior
    d.   Alzheimer's disease

17. Many psychological defense mechanisms are examples of _____.
    a.   emotion-focused forms of coping with stress
    b.   psychosis
    c.   problem-focused forms of coping with stress
    d.   hassles

18. Which of the following is a good resource for effective coping with stress?
    a.   positive beliefs
    b.   health and energy
    c.   social skills
    d.   all of these options

19. Hardiness is _____?
    a.   high levels of phenylalanine
    b.   a resilient personlaity characteristic
    c.   aerobic stamina
    d.   none of these options

20. Life changes may affect health because they _____.
    a.   increase the number of hassles
    b.   cause us to reassess our life style
    c.   are always the result of something bad happening
    d.   are known to increase the level of cortisol above normal

PRACTICE TEST II

1. _____ is an unpleasant state of tension resulting from a blocked goal.
   a. Conflict
   b. Burnout
   c. Heart disease
   d. Frustration

2. The sympathetic nervous system _____.
   a. is also known as the "fight or flight" system
   b. increases heart rate
   c. releases hormones such as epinephrine and cortisol
   d. all of these options

3. _____ is an interdisciplinary field that studies the effects of psychological factors on the immune system.
   a. Health psychology
   b. Psychiatry
   c. Psychneuroimmunology
   d. None of these options

4. _____ is the major risk factor for coronary heart disease and lung cancer.
   a. Stress
   b. Binge drinking
   c. Smoking
   d. Conflict

5. Chronic pain from tension headaches and lower back pain has been effectively treated by _____.
   a. EMG biofeedback
   b. EEG biofeedback
   c. psychopharmacology
   d. prayer

6. A(n) _____ locus of control is associated with better coping skills.
   a. extrinsic
   b. internal
   c. heightened
   d. relaxed

7. An increase in acetylcholine and norepinephrine is associated with _____.
    a.   nicotine
    b.   any alcohol consumption
    c.   binge drinking
    d.   stress

8. Once you begin smoking, you continue because _____.
    a.   nicotine is addictive
    b.   it increases alertness
    c.   it stimulates the release of dopamine
    d.   all of these options

9. In the 1800's the major causes of death were _____, but today the major causes are _____.
    a.   starvation; obesity
    b.   accidents; stress-related illnesses
    c.   contagious diseases; noncontagious diseases
    d.   physiological; psychological

10. A pleasant, nonspecific physiological response to any internal or external demand is called _____.
    a.   eustress
    b.   love
    c.   happiness
    d.   euphoria

11. Having to choose between two or more alternatives that both lead to undesirable results is known as
    _____.
    a.   frustration
    b.   burnout
    c.   distress
    d.   avoidance-avoidance conflict

12. If you have a job that is demanding and requires a lot of concentration, without opportunities for
    advancement or creativity, it is most likely that you will _____.
    a.   quit
    b.   demand more money
    c.   experience more distress
    d.   experience more eustress

13. A conflict is defined as a negative emotional state caused by _____.
    a.   other people
    b.   your own cognitive appraisals
    c.   having to choose between incompatible goals
    d.   a blocked goal

14. Compared to non-procrastinators, students who procrastinate on class assignments _____.
    a.   get higher grades because they work better under pressure
    b.   drop out of college in greater numbers
    c.   have fewer illnesses because they are less stressed
    d.   receive lower grades on term papers

15. Chest pain due to an insufficient blood supply to the heart is called _____.
    a.   angina
    b.   heart disease
    c.   atherosclerosis
    d.   a heart attack

16. Hardy people see challenges as _____.
    a.   obstacles to self-actualization
    b.   opportunities for growth and improvement
    c.   a chance for purposeful activity and problem solving
    d.   opportunities for enlisting social support

17. When you focus on decreasing or eliminating a stressor, you are using _____.
    a.   emotion-focused coping
    b.   problem-focused coping
    c.   a problem-solving set
    d.   a practical defense mechanism

18. Unconscious strategies used to distort reality and relieve anxiety and guilt are known as _____.
    a.   problem-focused forms of coping
    b.   emotional approaches
    c.   burnout
    d.   defense mechanisms

19. Taking this practice test is a(n) _____ form of coping.
    a.   emotion-focused
    b.   overachiever's
    c.   problem-focused
    d.   ineffective

20. This is **NOT** an effective coping resource.
    a.   an external locus of control
    b.   an internal locus of control
    c.   positive beliefs
    d.   social support

ANSWERS

The following answers to active learning exercises, crossword puzzles, fill-ins, matching exercises, and practice tests 1 and 2 provide immediate feedback on your mastery of the material. Try not to simply memorize the answers. When you are unsure of your "guess" or make an error, be sure to go back to the textbook and carefully review. This will greatly improve your scores on classroom exams and quizzes.

CROSSWORD PUZZLE FOR CHAPTER 3

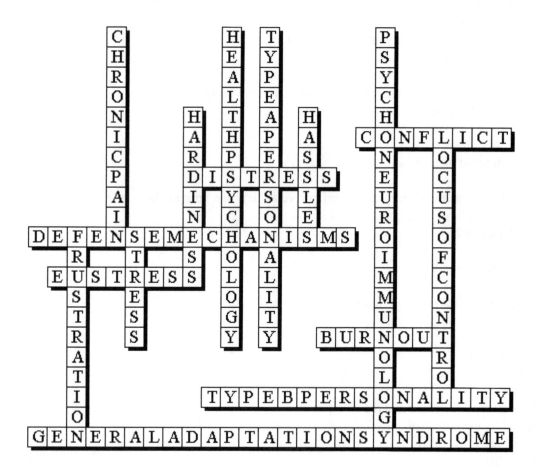

FILL-IN EXERCISES

a. health psychology; 2. endorphins; 3. cigarette smoking; 4. Binge drinking; 5. nonspecific, demand; 6. eustress; 7. avoidance-avoidance; 8. alarm reaction, phase of resistance, stage of exhaustion; 9. Type A, Type B; 10. Problem-focused.

MATCHING EXERCISES

a. 7, b. 6, c. 1, d. 9, e. 3, f. 10, g. 2, h. 5, i. 8, j. 4.

PRACTICE TEST I		PRACTICE TEST II	
1. d (p. 88)	11. b (p. 101)	1. d (p. 99)	11. d (p. 99)
2. d (p. 94)	12. b (p. 104)	2. d (p. 101)	12. c (p. 97)
3. b (p. 94)	13. b (p. 105)	3. c (p. 103)	13. c (p. 99)
4. c (p. 94)	14. d (p. 106)	4. c (p. 89)	14. d (p. 103)
5. a (p. 89)	15. b (p. 105)	5. a (p. 95)	15. a (p. 105)
6. d (p. 90)	16. b (p. 106)	6. b (p. 111)	16. b (p. 107)
7. b (p. 96)	17. a (p. 108)	7. a (p. 90)	17. b (p. 108)
8. d (p. 96)	18. d (p. 110)	8. d (p. 90)	18. d (p. 108)
9. c (p. 102)	19. b (p. 107)	9. c (p. 88)	19. c (p. 108)
10.c (p. 99)	20. a (p. 97)	10.a (p. 96)	20. a (p. 111)

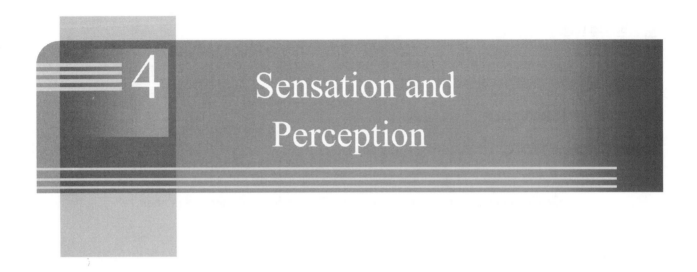

4 Sensation and Perception

OUTLINE (Survey & Question)

This outline is intended to help you *survey* the chapter. As you read through the various sections, write down any *questions* or comments that come to mind in the space provided. This is a valuable part of active learning and the SQ4R method. It not only makes your reading time more enjoyable and active, but it also increases retention and understanding of the material.

TOPIC	NOTES

I. EXPERIENCING SENSATIONS

A. Processing

B. Thresholds

C. Adaptation

II. HOW WE SEE AND HEAR

A. Vision

B. Hearing

   Research Highlight: Tracking Down the Genes for Deafness

III. OUR OTHER SENSES

A. Smell and Taste

   Gender and Cultural Diversity: Do Some People Smell Better Than Others?

B. The Body Senses

IV. PERCEPTION

A. Selection

B. Organization

   Gender and Cultural Diversity: Are the Gestalt Laws Universally True?

C. Interpretation

D. Subliminal Perception and ESP

   Critical Thinking/Active Learning: Problems with Believing in ESP

Core and Expanded LEARNING OBJECTIVES (<u>R</u>ead, <u>R</u>ecite & w<u>R</u>ite)

While *reading* the chapter, stop periodically and *recite* (or repeat in your own words) the answers to the following learning objectives. It will also help your retention if you *write* your answer in the space provided. (Page numbers refer to the text <u>Psychology in Action</u>, 6th Ed.)

Core Learning Objectives

These objectives are found at the beginning of each chapter of <u>Psychology in Action</u> (6th ed.).

1. How do our sensory organs gather sensory information and convert it into signals our brain can understand?

2. How do our eyes and ears enable us to see and hear?

3. How do our other sense enable us to experience the world?

4. How do we decide what to pay attention to in our environment?

5. How do we organize stimuli to perceive form, constancies, depth, and color?

6. What factors influence how we interpret sensations?

Expanded Learning Objectives
These objectives offer more detail and a more intensive way to study the chapter.

Upon completion of CHAPTER 4, the student should be able to:

1. Define and differentiate sensation and perception, and describe bottom-up and top-down processing (p. 118).

2. Explain transduction, sensory reduction, and coding in sensory processing (pp. 119-120).

3. Define psychophysics. Describe absolute and difference thresholds and the importance of sensory adaptation. Explain the gate-control theory of pain perception (pp. 120-122).

4. Describe the physical properties of light and light waves (pp. 123-124).

5. Diagram the eye, and explain how each structure contributes to the visual process (pp. 124-125).

6. Explain dark and light adaptation (p. 126).

7. Describe the physical properties of sound and sound waves (pp. 124, 126).

8. Diagram the ear, and explain how each structure contributes to the auditory process (p. 127).

9. Describe how place and frequency theories explain the detection of pitch and loudness (pp. 128-129).

10. Describe the causes of nerve deafness and current research into genetically caused deafness (pp. 129-130).

11. Describe olfaction, including basic anatomy, the lock-and-key theory, gender and cultural differences, and the role of pheromones in animals and humans (pp. 131-132).

12. Describe gustation, including basic anatomy, how it works, and causes of "picky" eating (p. 132).

13. Describe the skin senses and their functions (pp. 132-133).

14. Explain how the vestibular and kinesthetic senses provide information about the body (pp. 133-134).

15. Describe the differences between illusions, hallucinations, and delusions (p. 135).

16. Describe the role of selection in the process of perception. Describe the physiological and stimulus factors that influence selection (pp. 135-137).

17. List and discuss the Gestalt principles of perceptual organization. Describe cross-cultural research on the universality of these principles (pp. 138-140).

18. Explain the concept of perceptual constancy as it relates to size, shape, color, and brightness (pp. 140-142).

19. Explain how a person perceives depth, describing both binocular and monocular depth cues (pp. 143-146).

20. Discuss how both the trichromatic and opponent-process theories are needed to explain how humans perceive color (pp. 146-148).

21. Describe how perceptual adaptation, perceptual set, individual motivation, and frame of reference influence perceptual interpretation (pp. 148-149).

22. Discuss the research on subliminal perception (pp. 150-151).

23. Describe the different types of extrasensory perception; discuss criticisms regarding ESP research; and discuss how four types of faulty reasoning perpetuate ESP beliefs (pp. 151-153).

KEY TERMS (<u>R</u>eview)

The *review* step in the SQ4R method is very important to your performance on quizzes and exams. Upon completion of this chapter, you should be able to define the following terms.

Absolute Threshold: _____

_____

Accommodation: _____

_____

Amplitude: _____

_____

Audition: _____

_____

Binocular Cues: _____

_____

Bottom-Up Processing: _____

_____

Cochlea: _____

_____

Coding: _____

_____

Cones: _____

_____

Convergence: _____

_____

Dark Adaptation: _____

_____

Depth Perception: _____

_____

Difference Threshold: _____

_____

Extrasensory Perception (ESP): _____

_____

Farsightedness: _____

_____

Feature Detectors: _____

_____

Figure and Ground: _____

_____

Frequency: _____

_____

Frequency Theory: _____

_____

Gate-Control Theory of Pain: _____

_____

Gustation: _____

_____

Habituation: _____

_____

Hue: _____

_____

Illusion: _____

_____

Kinesthesis: _____

_____

Monocular Cues: _____

_____

Nearsightedness: _____

_____

Olfaction: _____

_____

Opponent-Process Theory: _____

_____

Perception: _____

_____

Perceptual Constancy: _____

_____

Perceptual Set: _____

_____

Pheromones: _____

_____

Pitch: _____

_____

Place Theory: _____

_____

Psychophysics: _____

_____

Retina: _____

_____

Retinal Disparity: _____

_____

Rods: _____

_____

Selective Attention: _____

_____

Semicircular Canals: _____

_____

Sensation: _____

_____

Sensory Reduction: _____

_____

Subliminal: _____

_____

Top-Down Processing: _____

_____

Transduction: _____

_____

Trichromatic Theory: _____

_____

Wavelength: _____

_____

 **ACTIVE LEARNING EXERCISES** (Recite)

The *recite* step in the SQ4R method requires you to be an ACTIVE learner. By completing the following exercises, you will test and improve your mastery of the chapter material, which will also improve your performance on quizzes and exams. Answers to some exercises appear at the end of this study guide chapter.

ACTIVE LEARNING EXERCISE I

In the blank space next to each letter, write the name of the eye structure that corresponds to the letter in the diagram.

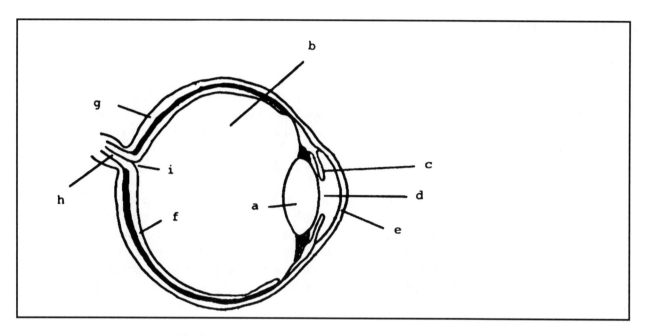

ACTIVE LEARNING EXERCISE II

Auditory Perception

Have you noticed that music often sounds better when it is played loudly, but not to the point that it hurts your ears? This is primarily because very high and very low frequencies are not perceived as well at a low volume. The music sounds "flat."

To try this yourself, find a stereo system with separate bass and treble controls and a "loudness" button. Set the bass and treble controls to their middle position, while making sure the "loudness" button is off.

Now choose your favorite music, turn on the stereo, and then increase the volume until the music sounds best to you. (Be careful not to overdo the volume. As you discovered in the text, loud noises can permanently damage your hearing.) Try decreasing the volume. The music should begin to seem "flat" or not as pleasing as before. Experiment with increasing only the low or high bass and treble. Turn on the "loudness" button and note how the music automatically sounds better. This button is specifically designed to amplify the highs and lows.

This exercise may help you enjoy your music more without excessive volume (and potential hearing loss). Just make sure that you can perceive all frequencies, not just those in the middle range.

ACTIVE LEARNING EXERCISE III

Empathizing (An Affective Skill)

In Chapter 4, you read about Helen Keller, an extraordinary woman who was blind from birth. The following exercise will improve your ability to empathize a bit with her and other visually handicapped people you might know. As you have read in the text, noncritical thinkers view everything and everyone else in relationship to themselves. They fail to understand or appreciate another's thoughts, feelings, or behaviors, as critical thinkers do.

Find a partner to take you on a "blind walk" for at least 20 to 30 minutes. Have the person first blindfold you, and then lead you on a walk filled with varied sensory experiences. Go up a hill, over a gravel driveway, across a dirt field full of potholes, past a bakery, through the school cafeteria, next to a rough wall, past an open freezer door, through a quiet library or the noisy student union, and so on. Try to identify each of these varied sensory experiences. Remind your partner not to give hints regarding your location. Now exchange roles and lead your partner on a similar "blind walk."

What happened when you or your partner were without your sense of sight? Did you adapt? Could you navigate better and more easily identify your location by the end of the "blind walk?" How did you compensate for your lack of sight? Did you substitute another sense for your sense of sight?

_____

_____

_____

_____

CHAPTER OVERVIEW (Review)

The following CHAPTER OVERVIEW provides a narrative overview of the main topics covered in the chapter. Like the Visual Summary found at the end of each chapter in the text, this narrative summary provides a final opportunity to *review* chapter material.

I. Experiencing Sensations

Sensation refers to the process of receiving, converting, and transmitting information from the outside world, whereas **perception** is the process of selecting, organizing, and interpreting raw sensory data into useful mental representations of the world.

Sensory processing includes transduction, reduction, and coding. **Transduction** converts stimuli into neural impulses that are sent to the brain, and we cope with the vast quantities of sensory stimuli through the process of **sensory reduction**. Each sensory system is specialized to **code** its stimuli into unique sets of neural impulses that the brain interprets as light, sound, touch, and so on.

The **absolute threshold** is the smallest magnitude of a stimulus we can detect. The **difference threshold** is the smallest change in a stimulus that we can detect. The process of **sensory adaptation** decreases our sensitivity to constant, unchanging stimuli.

II. How We See and Hear

Light is a form of energy that is part of the electromagnetic spectrum. The **wavelength** of a light determines its **hue**, or color; the **amplitude**, or the height of a light wave, determines its *intensity*. The range of light waves determines its *complexity*. The function of the eye is to capture light and focus it on visual receptors that convert light energy to neural impulses. Light enters through the pupil and lens to the retina, and then travels along the optic nerve to the brain. Cells in the **retina** called **rods** are specialized for night vision, whereas **cones** are specialized for color and fine detail.

The sense of hearing is known as **audition**. We hear sound via sound waves, which result from rapid changes in air pressure caused by vibrating objects. The wavelength of these sound waves is sensed as the **pitch** of the sound, whereas the amplitude of the waves is perceived as *loudness*. The range of sound waves is sensed as *timbre*, the purity or complexity of the tone. The outer ear conducts sound waves to the middle ear, which in turn conducts vibrations to the inner ear where hair cells in the **cochlea** transduce mechanical energy into neural impulses. The neural message is then carried along the auditory nerve to the brain.

III. Our Other Senses

The sense of smell (**olfaction**) and the sense of taste (**gustation**) are called the chemical senses and are closely interrelated. The receptors for olfaction are at the top of the nasal cavity. According to the lock-and-key-theory, we can smell different odors because each three-dimensional odor molecule fits into only one type of receptor. These receptors are sensitive to four basic tastes: salty, sweet, sour, and bitter.

The body senses are the skin senses, the vestibular sense, and the **kinesthetic** sense. The skin senses detect pressure, temperature, and pain. They protect the internal organs and provide basic survival information. The vestibular apparatus is located in the inner ear. The kinesthetic sense provides the brain with information about body posture and orientation, as well as body movement. The kinesthetic receptors are spread throughout the body in muscles, joints, and tendons.

IV. Perception

The selection process allows us to choose which of the billions of separate sensory messages will eventually be processed. **Selective attention** allows us to direct our attention to the most important aspect of the environment at any one time. **Feature detectors** are specialized cells in the brain that distinguish between different sensory inputs. The selection process is very sensitive to changes in the environment. We **habituate** to unchanging stimuli and pay attention when stimuli change in intensity, novelty, location, and so on.

The Gestalt psychologists set forth laws explaining how people perceive form. The most fundamental principle is the distinction between **figure and ground**. Other principles include proximity, continuity, closure, contiguity, and similarity. Through the **perceptual constancies** of size, shape, color, and brightness, we are able to perceive a stable environment, even though the actual sensory information we receive may be constantly changing. These constancies are based on our prior experiences and learning.

Depth perception allows us to accurately estimate the distance of perceived objects and thereby perceive the world in three dimensions. But how do we perceive a three-dimensional world with two-dimensional receptors called eyes? There are two major types of cues: **binocular cues**, which require two eyes, and monocular cues, which only require one eye. The binocular cues are **retinal disparity** and **convergence**. **Monocular cues** include linear perspective, aerial perspective, texture gradients, interposition, light and shadow, relative size, accommodation, and motion parallax.

Color perception is explained by a combination of two color theories. The **trichromatic theory** proposes three color systems maximally sensitive to blue, green, and red. The **opponent-process theory** also proposes three color systems but holds that each is sensitive to two opposing colors---blue and yellow, red and green, and black and white---and that they operate in an on-off fashion. The trichromatic system operates at the level of the retina, whereas the opponent-process system occurs at the level of the brain.

Interpretation, the final stage of perception, can be influenced by perceptual adaptation, perceptual set, and individual motivation and frame of reference. **Subliminal** (below the threshold) messages can be perceived without our knowing awareness. However, there is little or no evidence of subliminal persuasion. **Extrasensory perception (ESP)** is the supposed ability to perceive things that go beyond the normal senses. ESP research has produced "fragile" results, and critics condemn its lack of experimental control and replicability.

SELF-TESTS (Review & wRite)

Completing the following SELF-TESTS will provide immediate feedback on how well you have mastered the material. In the *crossword puzzle* and *fill-in exercises*, write the appropriate word or words in the blank spaces. The *matching exercise* requires you to match the terms in one column to their correct definitions in the other. For the *multiple-choice questions* in Practice Tests I and II, circle or underline the correct answer. When you are unsure of any answer, be sure to highlight or specially mark the item and then go back to the text for further review. Correct answers are provided at the end of this study guide chapter.

CROSSWORD PUZZLE FOR CHAPTER 4

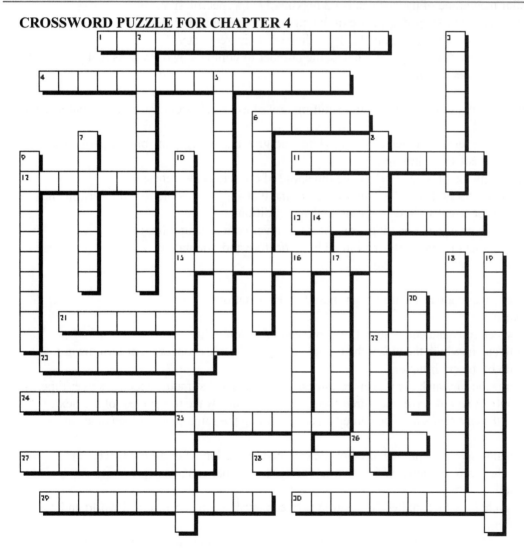

ACROSS

1 By organizing perception in three-dimensions-even though the images that strike the retina are two-dimensional-we can perceive distance.

4 The process of filtering and analyzing incoming sensations that occurs before a neural impulse is sent to the cortex.

6 The three-part process that converts a particular sensory input into a specific sensation.

11 The process of selecting, organizing, and interpreting sensory data into usable mental representations of the world.

12 The height of a light or sound wave; pertaining to light, it refers to brightness.

13 Airborne chemicals released from one individual that affect another individual's behavior, including recognition of family members, aggression, territorial marking, and sexual mating.

15 Theory that explains how we hear higher-pitched sounds; for each distinct higher pitch, hair cells located on the basilar membrane of the cochlea bend maximally at a specific spot.

21 The three-chambered, snail-shaped structure in the inner that contains the receptors for hearing.

22 The highness or lowness of tones or sounds, depending on their frequency.

23 How often a light or sound wave cycles. That is, the number of complete wavelengths that pass a point in a given time (e.g., per second).

24 The sense of taste.

25 The process of receiving, translating, and transmitting raw sensory data from the external and internal environments to the brain.

26 Visual receptors in the retina that detect black, white, and gray and are responsible for peripheral vision. They are most sensitive in dim light.

27 Pertaining to any stimulus presented below the threshold of conscious awareness.

28 Visual receptors concentrated near the center of the retina that are responsible for color vision and fine detail. They are most sensitive in daylight or well-lit conditions.

29 The process by which energy stimulating a receptor is converted into neural impulses.

30 The sensory system that provides information on body posture and orientation.

DOWN

2 A readiness to perceive in a particular manner, based on expectations.

3 The sense of hearing.

5 The process by which rods and cones adjust to allow vision in dim light.

6 A binocular depth cue in which the closer the object, the more the eyes converge, or turn inward.

7 A false impression of the environment.

8 A sensory phenomenon in which the perceived intensity of a repeated stimulus decreases over time.

9 The length of a light or sound wave, measured from the crest of one wave to the crest of the next.

10 The tendency for the environment to be perceived as remaining the same even with changes in sensory input.

14 The visual dimension seen as a particular color; determined by the length of a light wave.

16 The tendency of the brain to ignore environmental factors that remain constant.

17 The sense of smell.

18 The branch of psychology that studies the relation between attributes of the physical world and our psychological experience of them.

19 A visual acuity problem that results when the cornea and lens focus an image behind the retina.

20 The light-sensitive inner surface of the back of the eye, which contains the receptor rods and cones plus other neurons that help in processing visual information

FILL-IN EXERCISES

1. _____ involves receiving, translating, and transmitting raw sensory data from the external and internal environments to the brain (p. 118).

2. The process of selecting, organizing, and interpreting sensory data into usable mental representations of the world is known as _____ (p. 118).

3. The branch of psychology that studies the relation between attributes of the physical world and our psychological experience of them is known as _____ (p. 120).

4. In light waves, the wavelength determines _____ and amplitude _____ (p. 123).

5. Light waves enter the eye through a rough transparent shield called the _____, they then pass through a small opening called the _____; and are then focused by the elastic _____ on the _____ at the back of the eye (p. 124).

6. _____ results from the movement of air molecules in a particular wave pattern (p. 127).

7. The idea that each odor molecule fits into only one type of smell receptor cell according to its shape is known as the _____ theory of olfaction (p. 131).

8. False impressions of the physical world produced by physical distortions (such as desert mirages) are known as _____ (p. 135).

9. A decrease in response of a sensory system to continuous stimulation is known as_____ ; whereas _____ involves the tendency of the brain to ignore environmental factors that remain constant (pp. 120, 135)

10. _____ theory proposes that color perception results from mixing three distinct color systems—red, green, and blue (p. 147).

MATCHING EXERCISES

Column A

a. Depth Perception
b. Transduction
c. Sensory Adaptation
d. Cones

Column B

1. ____ "Psychic" abilities beyond the known senses.
2. ____ Band of radiant energy from the sun.
3. ____ Bulging and flattening of the lens to allow focusing.
4. ____ A part of the retina containing no visual receptors.

e. Audition   5. ____ Decrease in response due to continuous
                                           stimulation.
f. Olfaction   6. ____ Receptors that respond to color and fine detail.
g. Blind Spot   7. ____ The sense of hearing.
h. Accommodation   8. ____ The sense of smell.
i. Electromagnetic Spectrum   9. ____ Ability to perceive distance and three dimensions.
j. Extrasensory Perception   10. ____ Receptors converting stimulus into neural impulse.

PRACTICE TEST I

1. The process of receiving, transducing, and transmitting information from the outside world is called
    _____.
    a.   perception
    b.   detection
    c.   sensation
    d.   integration

2. The process of converting a physical stimulus into a nerve impulse is called _____.
    a.   reduction
    b.   conduction
    c.   transduction
    d.   neural stimulation

3. The lowest or quietest sound people can hear is their _____.
    a.   threshold of excitation
    b.   absolute threshold
    c.   difference threshold
    d.   low point

4. The _____ of light determines its hue, and the _____ determines its brightness.
    a.   wavelength, amplitude
    b.   pitch, wavelength
    c.   timbre, amplitude
    d.   wavelength, frequency

5. The receptors in the eye responsible for daylight and color vision are the _____; the receptors in the
    eye responsible for dim light vision are the _____.
    a.   rods, cones
    b.   hair cells, cilia
    c.   lens, cornea
    d.   cones, rods

6. The frequency of a sound wave is sensed as the _____ of a sound.
   a. pitch
   b. intensity
   c. loudness
   d. height

7. The chemical senses are _____.
   a. taste and touch
   b. taste and smell
   c. vision and audition
   d. touch and smell

8. Airborne chemicals released from one individual that affect another individual's behavior are known as _____.
   a. olfactory attractants
   b. sexual odorificants
   c. pheromones
   d. olfactory hormones

9. The skin senses include pressure, pain, and _____.
   a. posture
   b. movement
   c. balance
   d. warmth and cold

10. The sense of balance is called the _____ sense.
   a. auditory
   b. gustatory
   c. kinesthetic
   d. vestibular

11. The process of selecting, organizing, and interpreting sensory data into a usable mental representation of the world is the definition of _____.
   a. sensation
   b. perception
   c. transduction
   d. adaptation

12. Subliminal messages, those messages presented below threshold, can affect behavior in which of the following ways?
    a.   They can help you learn while asleep.
    b.   They can cause you to change your behavior to comply with the message.
    c.   They can improve your memory for things that you learn while awake.
    d.   None of these options.

13. Which of the following is one of the Gestalt principles of organization?
    a.   roundness
    b.   isolation
    c.   symmetry
    d.   figure and ground

14. Monocular and binocular are two categories of _____.
    a.   depth perception
    b.   size adaptations
    c.   perceptual constancies
    d.   visual corrections

15. When an observer moves, near objects seem to pass quickly, intermediate objects seem to pass rather slowly, and far objects seem to stand almost still. The name of this monocular cue is _____.
    a.   linear perspective
    b.   accommodation
    c.   relative size
    d.   motion parallax

16. The _____ theory of color vision states that there are three different color systems (red, green, and blue).
    a.   trichromatic
    b.   opponent-process
    c.   tri-receptor
    d.   lock-and-key

17. Which of the following is **NOT** correct?
    a.   brighter objects are usually seen as closer
    b.   larger objects are usually seen as farther away
    c.   the object that obscures another object is seen as closer
    d.   distant objects appear fuzzy because of dust and haze in the air

18. The muscular cue to distance caused by both eyes turning in or out to focus on an object is called _____.
    a.   binocular rivalry
    b.   retinal disparity
    c.   convergence
    d.   accommodation

19. According to the Gestalt principle of proximity, objects that _____.
    a.   continue a pattern will be grouped together
    b.   are close together will be grouped together
    c.   are similar in size or shape will be grouped together
    d.   all of these options

20. Concerning ESP (extrasensory perception), research suggests that people should be _____.
    a.   believers
    b.   doing more research to support ESP
    c.   very skeptical of ESP claims
    d.   developing their own ESP

PRACTICE TEST II

1. The conversion of stimulus energy into neural impulses is called _____.
    a.   coding
    b.   transduction
    c.   transference
    d.   reception

2. Sensory adaptation occurs when _____.
    a.   one sensory system takes over for another that has been damaged
    b.   information from several sensory systems are organized together in the brain
    c.   a sensory system becomes less responsive to continuous stimulation
    d.   a stroke or other brain damage prevents full sensory capability

3. Light travels through the cornea to the _____.
    a.   pupil, lens, and retina
    b.   lens, pupil, and retina
    c.   vitreous humor, aqueous humor, and retina
    d.   retina on the back of the lens

4. _____ is the process that occurs when your visual system shifts from cones to rods upon entering a dark room.
    a.   Light adaptation
    b.   Sensory adaptation
    c.   Dark adaptation
    d.   Accommodation

5. Which of the following is an example of pitch?
    a.   you switch the lever on your telephone from soft to loud
    b.   your mother raises her voice when you ignore her
    c.   you can barely hear your television because of the traffic noise outside
    d.   your neighbor's car alarm alternates between high and low tones

6. _____ results from stimulation of receptor cells in the nose.
    a.   Audition
    b.   Pheromones
    c.   Olfaction
    d.   Vestibular sense

7. Rock concerts, blaring radios, and raucous pep rallies are _____.
    a.   adolescent rites of passage
    b.   signs of a good time
    c.   damaging to auditory receptor cells
    d.   the reason parents lose their sanity by age 50

8. Smell and taste can be adversely affected by _____.
    a.   heart disease
    b.   the common cold
    c.   spicy food
    d.   all of these options

9. African men and women have a _____ androstenone (a component of sweat) than American men and women.
    a.   greater ability to detect
    b.   significantly lower ability to detect
    c.   milder sensitivity to
    d.   lower responsiveness to

10. Light stimulation of both pressure and pain receptors results in the sensation of _____.
    a.   itching
    b.   tickling
    c.   vibration
    d.   all of these options

11. The gate control theory is founded on the knowledge that pain signals travel slower than other sensory messages because the pain nerve fibers are _____.
    a. not myelinated
    b. myelinated
    c. smaller
    d. larger

12. The process of _____ explains why several people witnessing the same event give different accounts of what actually happened.
    a. sensation
    b. perception
    c. accommodation
    d. assimilation

13. _____ are false impressions of the environment; whereas _____ are sensory perceptions that occur without external stimulus.
    a. Hallucinations; delusions
    b. Delusions; Illusions
    c. Illusions; delusions
    d. Illusions; hallucinations

14. Habituation occurs when _____.
    a. a sensory system stops responding to a continuous stimulus
    b. the brain begins to ignore constant environmental factors
    c. you repeat the same behavior until it becomes automatic
    d. all of these options

15. The tendency for the environment to be perceived as remaining the same even with changes in sensory input is known as _____.
    a. habituation
    b. sensory adaptation
    c. perceptual constancy
    d. sensory sensitivity

16. A binocular cue to distance in which the separation of the eye causes different images to fall on each retina is known as _____.
    a. convergence
    b. retinal disparity
    c. perceptual constancy
    d. perceptual adaptation

17. Blue-yellow, red-green, and black-white are associated with the _____ theory of color perception.
    a.   trichromatic
    b.   opponent-process
    c.   nativist
    d.   empiricist

18. The trichromatic theory explains color vision at the level of the _____.
    a.   thalamus
    b.   hypothalamus
    c.   retina
    d.   lens

19. Stimuli presented below the threshold of conscious awareness are called _____.
    a.   telekinesis
    b.   hallucinations
    c.   illusions
    d.   subliminal

20. The fact that the same person will demonstrate extrasensory abilities in one laboratory study but not another suggests that _____.
    a.   replication of studies is a waste of time
    b.   the studies were probably not valid
    c.   the researcher or the participant was biased against ESP
    d.   ESP is not a reliable phenomenon

ANSWERS

The following answers to active learning exercises, crossword puzzles, fill-ins, matching exercises, and practice tests 1 and 2 provide immediate feedback on your mastery of the material. Try not to simply memorize the answers. When you are unsure of your "guess" or make an error, be sure to go back to the textbook and carefully review. This will greatly improve your scores on classroom exams and quizzes.

CROSSWORD PUZZLE FOR CHAPTER 4

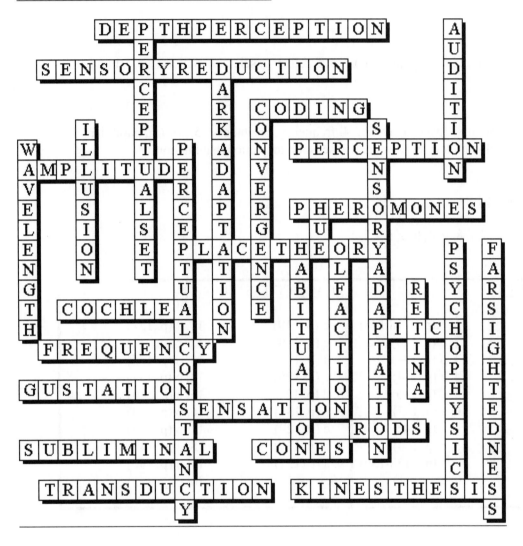

ACTIVE LEARNING EXERCISE I

Anatomy of the eye

a. lens, b. vitreous humor, c. iris, d. pupil, e. cornea, f. retina, g. sclera, h. optic nerve, i. blind spot.

FILL-IN EXERCISES

1. sensation; 2. perception; 3. psychophysics; 4. frequency, brightness; 5. cornea, pupil, lens, retina; 6. sound; 7. lock-and-key; 8. Illusions; 9. sensory adaptation, habituation; 10. Trichromatic.

MATCHING EXERCISES

a. 9, b. 10, c. 5, d. 6, e. 7, f. 8, g. 4, h. 3, i. 2, j. 1.

PRACTICE TEST I		PRACTICE TEST II	
1. c (p. 118)	11. b (pp. 118,135)	1. b (p. 119)	11. c (p. 121)
2. c (p. 118)	12. d (p. 150)	2. c (p. 120)	12. b (pp. 118,135)
3. b (p. 120)	13. d (p. 138)	3. a (p. 124)	13. d (p. 135)
4. a (p. 123)	14. a (p. 144)	4. c (p. 126)	14. b (p. 137)
5. d (p. 125)	15. d (p. 146)	5. d (p. 127)	15. c (p. 140)
6. a (p. 127)	16. a (p. 147)	6. c (p. 131)	16. b (p. 144)
7. b (p. 131)	17. b (p. 146)	7. c (p. 129)	17. b (p. 147)
8. c (p. 132)	18. c (p. 144)	8. b (p. 131)	18. c (p. 147)
9. d (p. 133)	19. b (pp. 138-139)	9. a (p. 131)	19. d (p. 150)
10.d (p. 133)	20. c (p. 151)	10. c (p. 133)	20. d (p. 151)

5 States of Consciousness

OUTLINE (Survey & Question)

This outline is intended to help you *survey* the chapter. As you read through the various sections, write down any *questions* or comments that come to mind in the space provided. This is a valuable part of active learning and the SQ4R method. It not only makes your reading time more enjoyable and active, but it also increases retention and understanding of the material.

TOPIC   **NOTES**

I. UNDERSTANDING CONSCIOUSNESS

    A. How Do We Define It?

    B. How Do We Describe It?

II. SLEEP AND DREAMS

    A. The Power of Circadian Rhythms

B. Stages of Sleep

C. Theories of Sleep and Dreaming

Gender and Cultural Diversity: Variations and Similarities in Dreams

Critical Thinking/Active Learning: Interpreting Your Dreams

D. Sleep Disorders

III. DRUGS THAT INFLUENCE CONSCIOUSNESS

A. Understanding Drugs

B. Depressants

C. Stimulants

D. Opiates

E. Hallucinogens

F. Explaining Drug Use

Research Highlight: Addictive Drugs as the Brain's "Evil Tutor"

IV. ADDITIONAL ROUTES TO ALTERNATE STATES

A. Daydreams and Fantasies

B. Hypnosis

C. Meditation

Gender and Cultural Diversity: Consciousness Across Cultures

Core and Expanded LEARNING OBJECTIVES   (<u>R</u>ead, <u>R</u>ecite & w<u>R</u>ite)

While *reading* the chapter, stop periodically and *recite* (or repeat in your own words) the answers to the following learning objectives. It will also help your retention if you *write* your answer in the space provided. (Page numbers refer to the text <u>Psychology in Action</u>, 6th Ed.)

Core Learning Objectives
These objectives are found at the beginning of each chapter of <u>Psychology in Action</u> (6th ed.).

1. How can we define and describe consciousness?

2. What happens to consciousness while we sleep and dream?

3. How do psychoactive drugs affect consciousness?

4. How do alternate states of consciousness, like hypnosis, affect consciousness?

Expanded Learning Objectives
These objectives offer more detail and a more intensive way to study the chapter.

Upon completion of CHAPTER 5, the student should be able to:

1. Define consciousness and alternate states of consciousness (ASCs); describe the various levels of awareness, including the difference between controlled and automatic processing (pp. 157-160).

2. Identify common myths about sleep (p. 161).

3. Define circadian rhythms; discuss the effects of disruptions in circadian rhythms (pp. 161-163).

4. Describe problems associated with sleep deprivation. Describe how EEGs, EMGs, and EOGs are used to study sleep (pp. 163-164).

5. Describe the various physical changes associated with each stage of sleep, including the REM stage and non-REM Stages 1, 2, 3, and 4 (pp. 164-167).

6. Discuss possible biological causes of sleep, and describe how the repair/restoration theory of sleep differs from the evolutionary/circadian theory (pp. 168-169).

7. State gender and cultural differences and similarities in dreaming (pp. 169-170).

8. Differentiate between the psychoanalytic, biological, and cognitive views of dreaming (pp. 1170-171).

9. Describe the five major sleep disorders: insomnia, sleep apnea, narcolepsy, nightmares, and night terrors (pp. 1172-1174).

10. Define psychoactive drugs, drug abuse, addiction, psychological and physical dependence, and tolerance (pp. 174-177).

11. Define depressants; describe the effects of alcohol on the nervous system and behavior, and discuss why alcohol is a growing social concern (pp. 177-179).

12. Define stimulants; and describe the effects of nicotine and cocaine (pp. 178, 179-181).

13. Define opiates; and describe their effects on the nervous system and behavior (pp. 178, 181).

14. Define hallucinogens; and describe the effects of LSD and marijuana on the nervous system and behavior (pp. 178, 1181-183).

15. Briefly explain how drugs act as agonists and antagonists in the brain, and describe how psychoactive drugs can affect each of the four steps in neurotransmission (pp. 183-185).

16. Explain the major reasons people use and abuse drugs, and describe recent research regarding the importance of dopamine and glutamate on drug addiction (pp. 185-187).

17. Describe the purpose of daydreams and sexual fantasies (pp. 188).

18. Define hypnosis, and discuss five myths and controversies regarding its use. State how hypnosis is used today in medical and psychotherapy settings (pp. 188-190).

19. Define meditation, and discuss its potential benefits (pp. 190-191).

20. Discuss why there has been such a strong interest in alternate states of consciousness throughout history and across cultures; and explain the three major functions of ASCs for all cultures (pp. 191-192).

KEY TERMS (Review)

The *review* step in the SQ4R method is very important to your performance on quizzes and exams. Upon completion of this chapter, you should be able to define the following terms.

Activation-Synthesis Hypothesis: _____

_____

Agonist: _____

_____

Alternate States of Consciousness (ASCs): _____

_____

Antagonist: _____

_____

Automatic Processes: _____

_____

Circadian Rhythms: _____

_____

Consciousness: _____

_____

Controlled Processes: _____

_____

Depressants: _____

_____

Designer Drugs: _____

_____

Drug Abuse: _____

_____

Evolutionary/Circadian Theory: _____

_____

Hallucinogens: _____

_____

Hypnosis: _____

_____

Insomnia: _____

_____

Latent Content: _____

_____

Manifest Content: _____

_____

Meditation: _____

_____

Narcolepsy: _____

_____

Nightmares: _____

_____

Night Terrors: _____

_____

Opiates: _____

_____

Physical Dependence: _____

_____

Psychoactive Drugs: _____

_____

Psychological Dependence: _____

_____

Rapid Eye Movement (REM) Sleep: _____

_____

Repair/Restoration Theory: _____

_____

Sleep Apnea: _____

_____

Stimulants: _____

_____

Tolerance: _____

_____

Withdrawal: _____

_____

ACTIVE LEARNING EXERCISES (Recite)

The *recite* step in the SQ4R method requires you to be an ACTIVE learner. By completing the following exercises, you will test and improve your mastery of the chapter material, which will also improve your performance on quizzes and exams. Answers to some exercises appear at the end of this study guide chapter.

Active Learning Exercise I

Using the following list of common dream themes, please place a check mark next to each one you have ever experienced.

_____ 1. Snakes
_____ 2. Seeing yourself as dead
_____ 3. Being nude in public
_____ 4. School, teachers, studying
_____ 5. Sexual experiences
_____ 6. Arriving too late
_____ 7. Eating
_____ 8. Being frozen with fright
_____ 9. Death of a loved person
_____ 10. Being locked up
_____ 11. Finding money
_____ 12. Swimming
_____ 13. Falling
_____ 14. Being dressed inappropriately
_____ 15. Being smothered
_____ 16. Trying repeatedly to do something
_____ 17. Fire
_____ 18. Failing an examination
_____ 19. Flying
_____ 20. Being attacked or pursued

Now compare your responses to those of 250 other college students:

1. 49% 2. 33% 3. 43% 4. 71% 5. 66% 6. 64% 7. 62% 8. 58% 9. 57% 10. 56% 11. 56% 12. 52 %
13. 83% 14. 46% 15. 44% 16. 71% 17. 41% 18. 39% 19. 34% 20. 77%

How did you compare? Do you think your responses might differ from others due to your age, gender, culture, or other variables? How? If you would like to read more about the "universality of dreams," check out the following reference:

Griffith, R. M., Miyago, O., & Tago, A. (1958). The universality of typical dreams: Japanese vs. Americans. <u>American Anthropologist, 60,</u> 1173-1179.

Active Learning Exercise II

<u>Distinguishing Fact from Opinion</u> (A Cognitive Skill)

The topic of drugs often generates heated debate between people with different perspectives. When discussing controversial issues, it is helpful to make a distinction between statements of fact and statements of opinion. (A fact is a statement that can be proven true. An opinion is a statement that expresses how a person feels about an issue or what someone thinks is true.) Although it is also important to determine whether the facts are true or false, in this exercise simply mark "O" for opinion and "F" for fact to test your ability to distinguish between the two:

_____1. Marijuana is now one of America's principal cash crops.

_____2. Friends don't let friends drive drunk.

_____3. People who use drugs aren't hurting anyone but themselves.

_____4. Legalizing drugs such as cocaine, marijuana, and heroin would make them as big a problem as alcohol and tobacco.

_____5. The number of cocaine addicts is small compared with the number of alcoholics.

_____6. The American Medical Association considers alcohol to be the most dangerous of all psychoactive drugs.

_____7. Random drug tests are justified for personnel involved with public safety (e.g., air traffic controllers, police officers, etc.).

_____8. If parents use drugs, their children are more likely to use drugs.

_____9. Mothers who deliver cocaine-addicted babies are guilty of child abuse.

_____10. Alcohol abuse by pregnant mothers is one of the most important factors in mental retardation.

ANSWERS: Because answers may vary, we recommend discussing your responses with classmates and friends. Listening to the reasons others give for their answers often provides valuable insights and help in distinguishing between fact and opinion. (Adapted from Bach, 1988.)

CHAPTER OVERVIEW (Review)

The following CHAPTER OVERVIEW provides a narrative overview of the main topics covered in the chapter. Like the Visual Summary found at the end of each chapter in the text, this narrative summary provides a final opportunity to *review* chapter material.

I. Understanding Consciousness

Most of our lives are spent in normal, waking **consciousness**, an organism's awareness of its own self and surroundings. However, we also spend considerable time in various **alternate states of consciousness (ASCs),** such as sleep and dreaming, daydreams, sexual fantasies, chemically induced changes from psychoactive drugs, hypnosis, and meditation. Consciousness has always been difficult to study and define. William James described it as a "flowing stream." Modern researchers emphasize that consciousness exists along a continuum. **Controlled processes**, which require focused attention, are at the highest level of awareness. **Automatic processes**, which require minimal attention, are found in the middle of the continuum. Unconsciousness and coma are at the lowest level of awareness.

II. Circadian Rhythms and Stages of Sleep

Circadian rhythms affect our sleep and waking cycle so that disruptions due to shift work, jet lag, and sleep deprivation can cause serious problems. A typical night's sleep consists of four to five 90-minute cycles. The cycle begins in Stage 1 and then moves through Stages 2, 3, and 4. After reaching the deepest level of sleep, the cycle reverses up to the **REM** (rapid eye movement) state where the person often is dreaming.

III. Theories of Sleep and Dreaming

The exact function of sleep is not known, but according to the **repair/restoration theory**, it is thought to be necessary for its restorative value, both physically and psychologically. According to **evolutionary/circadian theory** it also has adaptive value. Sleep seems to be controlled by several neurotransmitters and by various areas of the brain.

Three major theories attempt to explain why we dream: The psychoanalytic/psychodynamic view says dreams are disguised symbols of repressed anxieties and desires. The biological (**activation-synthesis hypothesis**) perspective argues that dreams are simple by-products of random stimulation of brain cells. The cognitive view suggests that dreams are an important part of *information processing* of everyday experiences.

IV. Sleep Disorders

Many people suffer from numerous sleep problems, which fall into two major diagnostic categories— *dyssomnias* (including insomnia, sleep apnea, and narcolepsy) and *parasomnias* (such as nightmares and night terrors). People who have repeated difficulty falling or staying asleep, or awakening too early experience **insomnia**. A person with **sleep apnea** temporarily stops breathing during sleep, causing loud snoring or poor quality sleep. **Narcolepsy** is excessive daytime sleepiness characterized by sudden sleep attacks. **Nightmares** are bad dreams that occur during REM sleep. **Night terrors** are abrupt awakenings with feelings of panic that occur during non-REM sleep.

V. Drugs and Consciousness

Psychoactive drugs change conscious awareness or perception. Drug abuse refers to drug taking that causes emotional or physical harm to the individual or others, whereas addiction is a broad term referring to a person's feeling of compulsion to use a specific drug. Psychoactive drug use can lead to psychological dependence or physical dependence or both. **Psychological dependence** is a desire or craving to achieve the effects produced by a drug. **Physical dependence** is a change in bodily processes due to continued drug use that results in **withdrawal** symptoms when the drug is withheld. **Tolerance** is a physiological process whereby the user needs larger and more frequent doses of a drug to produce the desired effect.

The major categories of psychoactive drugs are **depressants, stimulants, opiates,** and **hallucinogens**. Depressant drugs slow the central nervous system, whereas stimulants activate it. Opiates numb the senses and relieve pain, whereas hallucinogens produce sensory or perceptual distortions.

Drugs act primarily by changing the effect of neurotransmitters in the brain. Drugs that act as **agonists** mimic neurotransmitters, whereas **antagonists** oppose or block normal neurotransmitter functioning. There are many reasons for drug use and abuse, which fall into the two main categories of environment and biology.

VI. Additional Routes to Alternate States

Daydreaming and sexual fantasies are common forms of mild ASCs. They serve many functions— primarily positive. **Hypnosis** is an alternate state of heightened suggestibility characterized by relaxation and intense focus. Hypnosis has been used to reduce pain and increase concentration, and as an adjunct to psychotherapy. **Meditation** is a group of techniques designed to focus attention and produce heightened awareness. Meditation can produce dramatic changes in physiological processes, including heart rate and respiration.

Although the study of consciousness has waxed and waned among psychologists, the public has historically been very interested---particularly in ASCs. Among peoples of all cultures, ASCs (1) are part of sacred rituals, (2) serve social interaction needs, and (3) provide individual rewards.

SELF-TESTS (Review & wRite)

Completing the following SELF-TESTS will provide immediate feedback on how well you have mastered the material. In the *crossword puzzle* and *fill-in exercises*, write the appropriate word or words in the blank spaces. The *matching exercise* requires you to match the terms in one column to their correct definitions in the other. For the *multiple-choice questions* in Practice Tests I and II, circle or underline the correct answer. When you are unsure of any answer, be sure to highlight or specially mark the item and then go back to the text for further review. Correct answers are provided at the end of this study guide chapter.

Crossword Puzzle for Chapter 5

ACROSS

2 Biological changes that occur on a 24-hour cycle. (Circa = about and dies = day)

8 Discomfort and distress, including physical pain and intense cravings, experienced after stopping the use of addictive drugs.

12 A chemical (or drug) that mimics the action of a specific neurotransmitter.

13 Drug taking that causes emotional or physical harm to the drug user or others.

16 A sleep disorder in which a person has persistent problems in falling asleep or staying asleep or awakens too early.

18 An organism's awareness of its own self and surroundings (Damasio, 1999). Consciousness is always about something. It concerns perceptions (of objects and events), thoughts (including verbal thought and mental images, such as dreams and daydreams), feelings, and actions (Farthing, 1992).

21 The true, unconscious meaning of a dream, according to Freudian dream theory.

23 Psychoactive drugs that act on the central nervous system to suppress or slow bodily processes and reduce overall responsiveness.

24 Abrupt awakenings from non-REM sleep accompanied by intense physiological arousal and feelings of panic.

25 Mental activities found at one extreme of the continuum of awareness; they require focused attention and generally interfere with other ongoing activities.

DOWN

1 A decreased sensitivity to a drug brought about by its continuous use.

3 A chemical (or drug) that opposes or blocks the action of a neurotransmitter.

4 A group of techniques designed to focus attention and produce a heightened state of awareness.

5 A disease marked by sudden and irresistible onsets of sleep during normal waking hours. (Narco = numbness, lepsy = seizure)

6 Drugs that produce sensory distortions or perceptual distortions.

7 The surface content of a dream, containing dream symbols that distort and disguise the true meaning of the dream, according to Freudian dream theory.

9 Mental activities requiring minimal attention; other ongoing activities are generally not affected.

10 A temporary cessation of breathing during sleep; one of the suspected causes of

11 Chemicals that affect the nervous system and cause a change in behavior, mental processes, and conscious experience.

14 A stage of sleep marked by rapid eye movements, high-frequency brain waves, and dreaming.

15 An alternate state of heightened suggestibility characterized by relaxation and intense focus.

17 Illicitly manufactured variations on known recreational drugs.

19 Drugs that are derived from opium and function as an analgesic or pain reliever. The word opium derives from the Greek word meaning juice.

20 Drugs that act on the brain and nervous system, to increase their overall activity and general responsiveness.

22 Anxiety-arousing dreams that generally occur near the end of the sleep cycle, during REM sleep.

FILL-IN EXERCISES

1. _____ is generally defined as an organism's awareness of its own self and surroundings (p. 158).

2. A mental state other than ordinary waking consciousness, such as sleep, dreaming, or hypnosis, is known as _____ (p. 158).

3. Mental activities that require focused attention, while generally interfering with other ongoing activities are known as _____ (p. 160).

4. REM sleep is also called _____ sleep because the brain is aroused and active, yet the sleeper's muscles are deeply relaxed and unresponsive (p. 166).

5. According to the _____ theory, sleep serves an important recuperative function, whereas the _____ theory suggests sleep is a part of circadian rhythms and evolved as a means to conserve energy and protect individuals from predators (p. 168).

6. The major sleep disorders include _____ (difficulty falling and staying asleep or awakening too early), _____ (temporary cessation of breathing during sleep), _____ (sudden and irresistible onsets of sleep during normal waking hours, _____ (anxiety-arousing dreams that generally occur during REM sleep), and _____ (abrupt awakenings from non-REM sleep with feelings of panic) (pp. 172-174).

7. _____ drugs affect the nervous system and cause a change in behavior, mental processes, and conscious experience (p. 175).

8. _____ refers to the mental desire or craving to achieve the effects produced by a drug; whereas _____ involves modifications of bodily processes requiring use of the drug for minimal functioning (p. 176).

9. _____ drugs act on the brain and nervous system to increase overall activity and responsiveness; whereas _____ drugs suppress or slow down bodily processes (pp. 177, 179).

10. An alternate state of heightened suggestibility characterized by relaxation and intense focus is known as _____ (p. 188).

MATCHING EXERCISES

Column A   Column B

a. Circadian Rhythms   1.____ Mental activities requiring minimal attention.
b. Biological View   2.____ Stage of sleep marked by rapid eye movements.
c. Sleep Apnea   3.____ Surface content of a dream.
d. Drug Abuse   4.____ Temporary cessation of breathing during sleep.
e. Automatic Processes   5.____ Mental state other than ordinary waking consciousness.
f. Cognitive View   6.____ Causes emotional or physical harm to drug user or others.
g. REM sleep   7.____ Dangerous stimulant.
h. Cocaine   8.____ Information processing theory of dreams.
i. Manifest Content   9.____ Biological changes that occur on a 24-hour cycle.
j. ASCs   10.____ Activation-synthesis hypothesis of dreaming.

PRACTICE TEST I

1. _____ is an organism's awareness of its own self and surroundings.
    a. Awareness
    b. Consciousness
    c. Alertness
    d. Central processing

2. _____ processes are mental activities that require minimal attention, without affecting other activities
    a. Controlled
    b. Peripheral
    c. Conscious
    d. Automatic

3. This is **NOT** one of the major reasons many cultures support the use of alternate states of consciousness.
    a. to seek spiritual enlightenment
    b. to facilitate social interactions
    c. to escape from stress and anxiety
    d. to heal unconscious wounds inflicted by societal taboos

4. Biological rhythms that occur on a 24-hour cycle are called _____.
    a. circadian rhythms
    b. synchronisms
    c. diurnal circuits
    d. nocturnal transmissions

5. _____ waves are associated with drowsy relaxation.
   a. Alpha
   b. Beta
   c. Theta
   d. Delta

6. With regard to sleep, research suggests that _____ is nature's first need.
   a. REM sleep
   b. non-REM sleep
   c. dreaming
   d. hypnogogic sleep

7. The _____ theory says that sleep allows us to replenish what was depleted during daytime activities.
   a. repair/restoration
   b. evolutionary/circadian
   c. supply-demand
   d. conservation of energy

8. _____ developed the theory that dreams are a coherent synthesis of random, spontaneous neuron activity.
   a. Freud
   b. Hobson and McCarley
   c. Watson and Skinner
   d. Maslow

9. Insomnia occurs when you persistently _____.
   a. have difficulty staying awake
   b. go to sleep too early
   c. awake too early
   d. all of these options

10. _____ is a disease marked by sudden and irresistible onsets of sleep during normal waking hours.
    a. Dyssomnia
    b. Parasomnia
    c. Narcolepsy
    d. Sleep apnea

11. _____ are chemicals that affect the nervous system and cause a change in behavior, mental processes, and conscious experience.
    a. Endocrinologists
    b. Psychoactive drugs
    c. Alternators
    d. Bio-neural drugs

12. A chemical that blocks the action of a neurotransmitter is called a(n) _____.
    a.   synaptic inhibitor
    b.   antagonist
    c.   alternator
    d.   receptor-blocker

13. A mental desire or craving to achieve the effects produced by a drug is known as _____.
    a.   withdrawal effects
    b.   dependency
    c.   psychological dependence
    d.   physical dependence

14. Requiring larger and more frequent doses of a drug to produce a desired effect is characteristic of _____.
    a.   withdrawal
    b.   tolerance
    c.   psychoactive dependence
    d.   all of these options

15. According to the American Medical Association, the drug that is the most dangerous and physically damaging is _____.
    a.   cocaine
    b.   nicotine
    c.   alcohol
    d.   heroin

16. Which of the following drugs is a central nervous system stimulant?
    a.   amphetamine
    b.   alcohol
    c.   heroin
    d.   barbiturates

17. Which of the following is **NOT** classified as a hallucinogen?
    a.   mescaline
    b.   psilocybin
    c.   amphetamines
    d.   LSD

18. Marijuana is classified in your text as a _____.
    a.   narcotic
    b.   hallucinogen
    c.   barbiturate
    d.   LSD derivative

19. This is **NOT** associated with hypnosis.
    a.   the use of imagination
    b.   broad, unfocused attention
    c.   a passive, receptive attitude
    d.   decreased pain

20. Research on the effects of meditation has found a(n) _____.
    a.   increase in blood pressure
    b.   reduction in stress
    c.   lack of evidence for changes in any physiological functions
    d.   increase in appetite

PRACTICE TEST II

1.   _____ processing can help us concentrate on more important tasks but can also lead to health or relationship problems.
    a.   Controlled
    b.   Unconscious
    c.   Automatic
    d.   Autonomic

2.   Most people spend almost _____ hours daydreaming in a 24-hour day.
    a.   3
    b.   5
    c.   8
    d.   12

3.   Which of the following is a parasomnia?
    a.   narcolepsy
    b.   nightmares
    c.   sleep apnea
    d.   parental insomnia

4. EEG is the abbreviation for _____, which is used to record brain waves.
    a.   electrical emissions graph
    b.   electroencephalograph
    c.   electro-energy grams
    d.   even elephants get grumpy

5. Your breathing is regular, your heart rate and blood pressure are slowing, and you can be awakened easily. It is most likely that you are in _____.
    a.   a hypnogogic transition between wakefulness and sleep
    b.   a daydreaming state
    c.   Stage 1 sleep
    d.   Stage 2 sleep

6. Which of the following is **NOT** characteristic of REM sleep?
    a.   irregular breathing
    b.   eyes moving back and forth
    c.   dreaming
    d.   low-frequency brain waves

7. _____ drugs act on the brain and nervous system to increase overall activity and responsiveness.
    a.   Stimulants
    b.   Opiates
    c.   Depressants
    d.   Hallucinogens

8. _____ drugs produce sensory distortions or perceptual illusions.
    a.   Opiate
    b.   Narcotic
    c.   Expensive
    d.   Hallucinogens

9. Narcolepsy is characterized by sudden episodes of _____.
    a.   nightmares in Stage 1 sleep
    b.   REM sleep in the middle of wakeful periods
    c.   epileptic seizures during Stage 4 sleep
    d.   not being able to breathe during any stage of sleep

10. This is **NOT** a characteristic of night terrors.
    a.   occurrence during non-REM sleep
    b.   panicky feelings
    c.   imbedded within a pleasant dream
    d.   intense physiological arousal

11. Drugs that are derived from the Greek word meaning "juice" and function as an analgesic are called
    _____.
    a.   parsomnias
    b.   insulin
    c.   opiates
    d.   nicotine

12. Alcohol can cause a coma or death when it reaches a level equal to or greater than _____.
    a.   .1%
    b.   .5%
    c.   .75%
    d.   .90%

13. Physical damage, severe addiction, and psychological dependence are all associated with the use of
    _____.
    a.   cocaine
    b.   Prozac
    c.   antipsychotic medication
    d.   all of these options

14. Jake uses this drug to relax and achieve a state of euphoria. Jaime uses the same drug as an
    analgesic. Jeremiah uses the drug to feel more content, and to make his experience of reality more
    pleasant. All three may experience life-threatening side effects with this drug.
    a.   cocaine
    b.   opiates
    c.   a sedative
    d.   lithium

15. Marijuana is a hard drug to classify because it _____.
    a.   has properties of a depressant and an opiate
    b.   in low doses it produces mild euphoria
    c.   in hig does it may produce hallucinations, delusions, and distortions of body image
    d.   all of these options

16. Some drugs, called receptor _____, have a molecular structure very similar to that of the body's own
    neurotransmitters.
    a.   antagonists
    b.   parasomniacs
    c.   catalysts
    d.   agonists

17. Dopamine and glutamate are two neurotransmitters implicated in _____.
    a.   drug-induced amnesia
    b.   the arousing effects of most drugs
    c.   the lowering of inhibitions under the influence of drugs
    d.   drug addiction

18. According to this model, deeply relaxed people with heightened suggestibility will allow a hypnotist
    to direct their fantasies and behavior.
    a.   altered state theory
    b.   suggestibility hypothesis
    c.   relaxation/role-playing theory
    d.   guided visualization explanation

19. Meditation is designed to _____.
    a.   decrease attentional focus
    b.   decrease your state of awareness
    c.   decrease focus by increasing awareness
    d.   focus attention and heighten awareness

20. Ninety percent of 488 societies surveyed by Bourguignon reported that they _____.
    a.   ban the use of non-medicinal psychoactive drugs
    b.   practice institutionally-recognized methods of altering consciousness
    c.   have severe drug-addiction problems
    d.   regulate the use of hypnosis, meditation, and other non-medical methods of altering
          consciousness

ANSWERS

The following answers to active learning exercises, fill-ins, matching exercises,
and practice tests 1 and 2 provide immediate feedback on your mastery of the
material. Try not to simply memorize the answers. When you are unsure of your
"guess" or make an error, be sure to go back to the textbook and carefully
review. This will greatly improve your scores on classroom exams and quizzes.

FILL-IN EXERCISES

1. consciousness; 2. alternate states of consciousness (ASCs); 3. controlled processing;
4. paradoxical; 5. repair/restoration, evolutionary/circadian; 6. insomnia, sleep apnea,
narcolepsy, nightmares, night terrors; 7. Psychoactive; 8. psychological dependence, physical
dependence; 9. stimulants, depressants; 10. hypnosis.

MATCHING EXERCISES

a. 9, b. 10, c. 4, d. 6, e. 1, f. 8, g. 2, h. 7, i. 3, j. 5.

CROSSWORD PUZZLE FOR CHAPTER 5

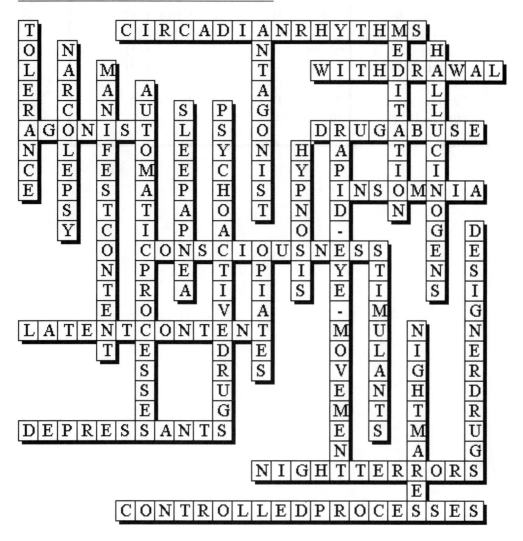

PRACTICE TEST I		PRACTICE TEST II	
1. b (p. 158)	11. b (p. 175)	1. c (p. 160)	11. c (p. 181)
2. d (p. 160)	12. b (p. 183)	2. c (p. 188)	12. b (p. 177)
3. d (pp. 192)	13. c (p. 176)	3. b (p. 174)	13. a (p. 181)
4. a (p. 162)	14. b (p. 176)	4. b (p. 164)	14. b (p. 181)
5. a (p. 165)	15. c (p. 179)	5. c (p. 165)	15. d (p. 182)
6. b (p. 167)	16. a (p. 179)	6. d (p. 166)	16. d (p. 185)
7. a (p. 168)	17. c (p. 181)	7. a (p. 179)	17. d (p. 186)
8. b (p. 170)	18. b (p. 182)	8. d (p. 181)	18. c (p. 189)
9. c (p. 172)	19. b (p. 188)	9. b (p. 174)	19. d (p. 190)
10.c (p. 174)	20. b (p.191)	10.c (p. 174)	20. b (p. 191)

OUTLINE (Survey & Question)

This outline is intended to help you *survey* the chapter. As you read through the various sections, write down any *questions* or comments that come to mind in the space provided. This is a valuable part of active learning and the SQ4R method. It not only makes your reading time more enjoyable and active, but it also increases retention and understanding of the material.

TOPIC	NOTES

I. CLASSICAL CONDITIONING

    A. Understanding Classical Conditioning

    B. Principles of Classical Conditioning

    C. Classical Conditioning in Real Life

II. OPERANT CONDITIONING

    A. Understanding Operant Conditioning

   B. Principles of Operant Conditioning

   C. Operant Conditioning in Real Life

        Critical Thinking/Active Learning: Using Learning Principles to Succeed in
        College

III. COGNITIVE-SOCIAL LEARNING

   A. Insight and Latent Learning

   B. Observational Learning

   C. Applications of Cognitive-Social Learning

        Gender and Cultural Diversity: Scaffolding as a Teaching Technique in Different
        Cultures

IV. NEUROSCIENCE AND EVOLUTION

   A. Neuroscience and Learning

        Research Highlight: Scanning the Brain for Learning

   B. Evolution and Learning

Core and Expanded LEARNING OBJECTIVES (Read, Recite & wRite)

While *reading* the chapter, stop periodically and *recite* (or repeat in your own words) the answers to the following learning objectives. It will also help your retention if you *write* your answer in the space provided. (Page numbers refer to the text Psychology in Action, 6th Ed.)

Core Learning Objectives
These objectives are found at the beginning of each chapter of Psychology in Action (6th ed.).

1. What is classical conditioning, and how can I apply it in everyday life?

2. What is operant conditioning, and how can I apply it in everyday life?

3. How and when do we learn according to cognitive-social theory?

4. What neurological changes take place during and after learning? What are the evolutionary advantages to learning?

Expanded Learning Objectives
These objectives offer more detail and a more intensive way to study the chapter.

Upon completion of CHAPTER 6, the student should be able to:

1. Define learning; explain how learned and innate behaviors are different; and define the most basic form of learning: conditioning (p. 198).

2. Explain the process of classical conditioning, describing the differences between an unconditioned, neutral, and conditioned stimulus, and an unconditioned, conditioned, and conditioned emotional response (pp. 198-203).

3. For classical conditioning: describe stimulus generalization, stimulus distinction, extinction, spontaneous recovery, and higher-order conditioning (pp. 203-205).

4. Describe how classical conditioning is related to prejudice, phobias, medical treatment, and politics (pp. 205-207).

5. Define operant conditioning and differentiate it from classical conditioning (pp. 199; 208).

6. Describe the contributions of Thorndike and Skinner related to operant conditioning (p. 209).

7. Define reinforcement, and punishment, and describe how a response is strengthened (pp. 210-212).

8. Describe the different schedules of reinforcement, and state the effect each schedule will have on response rate and extinction (pp. 212-213).

9. Describe how behaviors are shaped, and how they can be weakened; and describe the negative consequences of punishment (pp. 214-216; 218).

10. For operant conditioning, define stimulus generalization, stimulus discrimination, extinction, spontaneous recovery, and discriminative stimulus (pp. 216, 218).

11. Explain the importance of feedback, timing, consistency, and order of presentation on the effective use of both reinforcement and punishment (p. 217).

12. Describe how operant conditioning is related to prejudice, biofeedback, and superstitious behavior (pp. 219-221).

13. Define cognitive-social theory and describe insight and latent learning (pp. 222-223).

14. Describe the four processes involved in learning through observation; and describe how cognitive-social learning is related to prejudice, and the influence of various media (pp. 224-225).

15. Describe the cross-cultural use of scaffolding as a teaching technique, and explain how it combines the principles of shaping and modeling (pp. 225-227).

16. Describe the neurological changes that occur during and after learning (pp. 227-228).

17. Define biological preparedness and describe how it is related to learning (pp. 229-230).

KEY TERMS   (<u>R</u>eview)

The *review* step in the SQ4R method is very important to your performance on quizzes and exams. Upon completion of this chapter, you should be able to define the following terms.

Biofeedback: _____

_____

Biological Preparedness: _____

_____

Classical Conditioning: form of ^involuntary learning where UCS, is paired w/

NS to produce CR _____

Cognitive Map: _____

_____

Cognitive-Social Theory: _____

_____

Conditioned Emotional Response (CER): _____

_____

Conditioned Response (CR): _____

_____

Conditioned Stimulus (CS): *a learned stimulus that causes a conditial Response*

Continuous Reinforcement: *for every correct response*

_____

Discriminative Stimulus: _____

_____

Extinction: *Suppression of a behavior by showing* CS *stimulus w/o uCS*

Fixed Interval Schedule: *reinforcement only after a certian amount of time (Pay check)*

Fixed Ratio Schedule: *Partial reinforcement (buy 2 get 1 free)*

Higher Order Conditioning: _____

_____

Insight: _____

_____

Instinctive Drift: _____

_____

Learning: _____

_____

Negative Punishment: _____

_____

Negative Reinforcement: _____

_____

Operant Conditioning: *learning based on consequence.*

_____

Partial (Intermittent) Reinforcement: → *When only some of the correct answers are given*

Positive Punishment: *addition of something that decreases behavior ie more chores*

Positive Reinforcement: *addition of something that will increase behavior ie money*

Premack Principle: _____

_____

Primary Reinforcers: *food water other basic needs*

_____

Punishment: *↓ behavior*

_____

Reinforcement: *↑ behavior*

_____

Secondary Reinforcers: *learned reinforcers ; money, etc.*

_____

Shaping: _____

_____

Spontaneous Recovery: _reappourence ot extinct behaviors_

Stimulus Discrimination: _Only specific objects produce Response not generalized things_

Stimulus Generalization: _____

Unconditioned Response (UCR): _naturally occuring response to an UCS_

Unconditioned Stimulus (UCS): _a unlearned Stimules that naturally produces a UCR_

Variable Interval Schedule: _Job promotion_

Variable Ratio Schedule: _no set pattern gambling_

ACTIVE LEARNING EXERCISES (Recite)

The *recite* step in the SQ4R method requires you to be an ACTIVE learner. By completing the following exercises, you will test and improve your mastery of the chapter material, which will also improve your performance on quizzes and exams. Answers to some exercises appear at the end of this study guide chapter.

ACTIVE LEARNING EXERCISE I

Read each of the following examples.

I. If the situation is an example of classical conditioning, label the NS, UCS, UCR, CS, and CR.

II. If the situation is an example of operant conditioning, label whether it is positive or negative reinforcement, or positive or negative punishment.

SITUATION 1

A very bright (mildly painful) light is turned on a rat. The rat has learned that he can turn off the light by pressing a lever on the other side of his cage. As soon as the light comes on, the rat runs across the room and presses the lever.

A. The behavior of pressing the lever is an example of _____ conditioning.

B. If you chose classical, follow part I of the instructions; if you chose operant, follow part II.

SITUATION 2

When a mother strokes her infant's skin, the stroking creates pleasure responses in the baby. After this goes on for many days, the baby begins to show pleasure responses simply at the sight of the mother (before even being touched).

A. The baby's pleasure response is an example of _____ conditioning.

B. If you chose classical, follow part I of the instructions; if you chose operant, follow part II.

SITUATION 3

A patient in a mental hospital is very disruptive at mealtimes. She grabs food from the plates of those sitting near her and tries to cram the food into her mouth. Because this behavior of stealing food is very undesirable, a plan is developed whereby every time the patient steals food from other plates, she is immediately taken to a room without food.

A. The mental health staff is attempting to change the behavior of stealing through _____ conditioning.

B. If you chose classical, follow part I of the instructions; if you chose operant, follow part II.

SITUATION 4

Imagine you have a friend who keeps the temperature in her home so high that each occasion on which you visit her you find yourself perspiring. The last time you visited her, you noticed that you began to perspire and became uncomfortable as soon as you saw her house (before you even were inside).

A. Your perspiring behavior can be explained as _____ conditioning.

B. If you chose classical, follow part I of the instructions; if you chose operant, follow part II.

ACTIVE LEARNING EXERCISE II

Applying Knowledge to New Situations (A Cognitive Skill)

In Chapter 6, you learned about classical conditioning and that such learning can be applied to various situations in your own life. A critical thinker will be able to decipher the situations that are present during a learning experience. Such a thinker will also notice how often one stimulus situation is paired with another and that the two become associated with each other. However, identifying the neutral stimulus, the unconditioned stimulus (UCS), the unconditioned response (UCR), the conditioned stimulus (CS), and the conditioned response (CR) can be difficult unless you have had some practice. The following paragraphs describe classical conditioning situations. Your task is to identify the neutral stimulus, the UCS, the UCR, the CS, and the CR.

1. A researcher sounds a tone, then places a piece of meat into a dog's mouth, causing it to salivate. Eventually the sound of the tone alone causes the dog to salivate.

NS: _____

UCS: _____

UCR: _____

CS: _____

CR: _____

2. As your teenage son leaves the house and tells you "goodbye," he always slams the door. Recently, you've noticed that you flinch as soon as he says "goodbye."

NS: _____

UCS: _____

UCR: _____

CS: _____

CR: _____

3. A researcher flashes a light and then blows a puff of air into the research participant's eye. The participant automatically blinks. After a few trials, just the flash of light will cause the participant to blink.

NS: _____

UCS: _____

UCR: _____

CS: _____

CR: _____

CHAPTER OVERVIEW (Review)

The following CHAPTER OVERVIEW provides a narrative overview of the main topics covered in the chapter. Like the Visual Summary found at the end of each chapter in the text, this narrative summary provides a final opportunity to *review* chapter material.

I. Understanding Classical Conditioning

In **classical conditioning**, the type of learning investigated by Pavlov and Watson, an originally neutral stimulus (NS) is paired with an **unconditioned stimulus (UCS)** that causes a particular reflex or **unconditioned response (UCR).**   After several pairings, the neutral stimulus becomes a **conditioned stimulus (CS)** that alone will produce a **conditioned response (CR)** or **conditioned emotional response (CER)** that is the same as the original reflex response.

There are four conditioning sequences: delayed conditioning, simultaneous conditioning, trace conditioning, and backward conditioning. Delayed conditioning is the most effective and backward conditioning is the least effective.

Pavlov's work laid a foundation for Watson's insistence that psychology must be an objective science, studying only overt behavior, without considering internal, mental activity. He called this position *behaviorism*. As Watson discovered in his famous "Little Albert" study, emotional responses can be classically conditioned.

II. Principles and Applications of Classical Conditioning

In classical conditioning, **stimulus generalization** occurs when stimuli similar to the original CS elicit the CR. **Stimulus discrimination** takes place when only the CS elicits the CR. **Extinction** occurs when the UCS is repeatedly withheld, and the association between the CS and the UCS is broken. **Spontaneous recovery** happens when a CR that had been extinguished reappears with no prompting. In **higher order conditioning**, the NS is paired with a CS to which the participant has already been conditioned, rather than with a UCS.

Classical conditioning has many applications in everyday life. Through classical conditioning we can learn negative attitudes toward groups of people—and unlearn those attitudes. It is also used in behavior modification programs, some medical treatments, and to help patients change associations and reduce undesirable conditioned behavior. In addition, classical conditioning is the basis for a great deal of advertising.

III. Operant Conditioning

In **operant conditioning**, people or animals learn by the *consequences* of their responses. Whether behavior is reinforced or punished (consequences) determines whether the response will occur again. Thorndike and Skinner are the two major contributors to operant conditioning. Thorndike's *law of effect* states rewarded behavior is likely to reoccur. Skinner extended Thorndike's work to more complex behaviors, but emphasized only external, observable behaviors.

Operant conditioning involves several important terms and principles. **Reinforcement** is any procedure that results in an increase in a response, whereas **punishment** is any procedure that results in a decrease. To strengthen a response, we use **primary reinforcers**, *which* satisfy an unlearned biological need (e.g., sex, thirst), and **secondary reinforcers**, which have learned value (e.g. money). **Positive reinforcement** (adding something) and **negative reinforcement** (taking something away) increase the likelihood the response will occur again. *Escape learning* and *avoidance learning* are two of the learning procedures used to study negative reinforcement. According to the **Premack principle,** activities or behaviors that are more common or probable in one's life will act as reinforcers for activities that are less probable.

Continuous reinforcement rewards each correct response, whereas a **partial (intermittent) schedule** reinforces for some, not all, designated responses. The four partial reinforcement schedules are **variable ratio**, **variable interval, fixed ratio,** and **fixed interval.** Partial reinforcement schedules reinforce for some, but not all, responses. Complex behaviors can be trained through **shaping**, which refers to reinforcing successive approximations to the desired behavior.

To weaken a response, we use punishment**,** which decreases the likelihood of responding. **Positive punishment** (adding something) and **negative punishment** (taking something away) decrease the likelihood the response will occur again. Although some punishment is essential in social relations, it has serious side effects, including passive aggressiveness, increased aggression, and avoidance behavior. To be effective, punishment must be immediate, consistent, and moderate.

Operant conditioning has several applications in real life. It helps explain prejudice, which is sometimes learned through positive reinforcement and stimulus generalization. **Biofeedback**, another application, is the feeding back of biological information, such as heart rate or blood pressure, which a person uses to control normally automatic functions of the body. The third major application, superstitions, involves behaviors that are continually repeated because they are believed to cause desired effects, although in reality the behaviors are only accidentally related.

IV. Cognitive-Social Learning
Cognitive-social theory incorporates concepts of conditioning, but emphasizes thought processes, or cognitions, and social learning. According to this perspective, people learn through insight, latent learning, observation, and modeling.

Kohler, in working with chimpanzees, demonstrated that learning could occur with a sudden flash of **insight**. Tolman demonstrated that **latent learning** takes place in the absence of reward and remains hidden until some future time when it can be retrieved as needed. A **cognitive map** is a mental image of an area that a person or animal has navigated.

According to Bandura, observational learning is the process of learning how to do something by watching others and performing the same behavior in the future. To imitate the behavior of others, we must pay attention, remember, be able to reproduce the behavior, and be motivated by some reinforcement.

Cognitive-social theory helps explain prejudice and media influences. People often learn their prejudices by imitating and modeling the behavior they see in friends, family, and the media. The media affect our purchasing behaviors as well as our aggressive tendencies. Video games may have a particularly strong influence.

V. Neuroscience and Evolution
Learning and conditioning produce relatively permanent changes in biochemistry and various parts of the brain. But not all behaviors are learned. At least some behavior is *innate*, or inborn, in the form of either reflexes or instincts. It appears that all animals are programmed to engage in certain innate behaviors that have evolutionary survival benefits.

Through **biological preparedness** an organism is innately predisposed to form associations between certain stimuli and responses. Taste aversions are classically conditioned associations of food to illness that are rapidly learned, often in a single pairing, and reflect a protective survival mechanism for a species. Findings on **instinctive drift** show there are biological constraints on operant conditioning.

SELF-TESTS (Review & wRite)

Completing the following SELF-TESTS will provide immediate feedback on how well you have mastered the material. In the *crossword puzzle* and *fill-in exercises*, write the appropriate word or words in the blank spaces. The *matching exercise* requires you to match the terms in one column to their correct definitions in the other. For the *multiple-choice questions* in Practice Tests I and II, circle or underline the correct answer. When you are unsure of any answer, be sure to highlight or specially mark the item and then go back to the text for further review. Correct answers are provided at the end of this study guide chapter.

CROSSWORD PUZZLE FOR CHAPTER 6

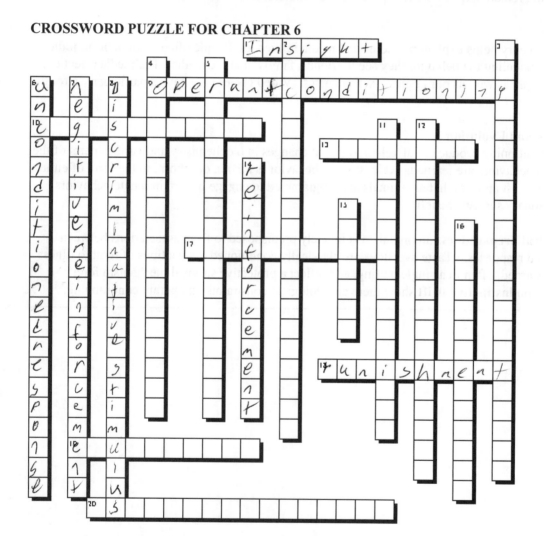

ACROSS

1 A sudden flash of understanding that occurs during problem solving.

9 Learning based on consequences. Behavior is strengthened if followed by reinforcement and diminished if followed by punishment

10 A mental image of a three-dimensional space that a person or animal has navigated.

13 A relatively permanent change in behavior or behavioral potential as a result of practice or

17 A procedure for electronically recording, amplifying, and feeding back information about internal bodily changes that would normally be imperceptible (such as blood pressure); aids voluntary regulation of these changes.

18 Any action or event that decreases the likelihood that a response will be repeated.

19 The gradual suppression of a behavior or a response that occurs when a CS is repeatedly

20 A biological constraint that occurs when an animal's learned responses shifts (or drifts) toward innate response patterns.

DOWN

2 Stimuli that increase the probability of a response because of their learned value, such as money and material possessions.

3 A theory of learning that emphasizes the role of thought and social learning in behavior.

4 The process of adding or presenting a stimulus that decreases the likelihood of that response occurring again.

5 Stimuli that increase the probability of a response because they satisfy a biological need, such as food, water, and sex.

6 The reflex response evoked by a stimulus without any learning required.

7 The process of taking away or removing a stimulus that increases the likelihood of that response occurring again.

8 The occurrence of a learned response to a specific stimulus but not to other, similar stimuli.

11 Using a response that has a high probability of occurrence to reinforce a response that has a lower probability of occurrence.

12 A partial schedule of reinforcement in which a participant must make a certain number of responses before being reinforced.

14 Any action or event that increases the probability that a response will be repeated.

15 A procedure in which reinforcement is delivered for successive approximations of the desired response.

16 Learning that occurs in the absence of a reward and remains hidden until some future time when it can be retrieved.

FILL-IN EXERCISES

1. *Pavlov* is credited with the discovery of classical conditioning (p. 198).

2. In classical conditioning, individuals learn _____ responses to stimuli through repeated pairings (p. 200).

3. The reflex response evoked by a stimulus without any required learning is known as _____ (p. 200).

4. _____ occurs when a previously extinguished response suddenly reappears (p. 204).

5. Learning based on consequences is called _____ (p. 208).

6. _____ involves any procedure resulting in an increase in a response; whereas _____ results in a decrease in a response (p. 209).

7. A response that is _____ reinforced will be learned more rapidly; whereas a response that is _____ reinforced will be more resistant to extinction (p. 212).

8. _____ involves reinforcing successive approximations to the desired behavior (p. 214).

9. A baseball player touching his right ear three times before batting may be an example of _____ (p. 220).

10. A teaching technique where the teacher reinforces successes of the student and models more difficult parts of the task is known as _____ (p. 226).

MATCHING EXERCISES

Column A

3 a. Spontaneous Recovery
9 b. Cognitive-Social Theory
8 c. Positive Punishment
7 d. Cognitive Map
6 e. Reinforcement
10 f. Classical Conditioning
1 g. Latent learning
4 h. Shaping
2 i. Extinction
5 j. Conditioned Stimulus (CS)

Column B

1. _g_ Occurs in the absence of a reward.
2. _i_ Gradual unlearning by presenting CS without the UCS.
3. _a_ Reappearance of a previously extinguished CR.
4. _h_ Reinforcing successive approximations.
5. _j_ Previously NS that now causes CR.
6. _e_ Anything likely to cause an increase in response.
7. _d_ Mental image of a three-dimensional space.
8. _c_ Something added that causes a decrease in response.
9. _b_ Focuses on thinking and social learning processes.
10. _f_ Involuntary response to a stimulus.

PRACTICE TEST I

1. A relatively permanent change in behavior, or behavior potential, as a result of practice or experience is the definition of _____.
    a.   learning
    b.   conditioning
    c.   behavior modification
    d.   modeling

2. When your mouth waters at the sight of a chocolate cake, it is an example of _____.
    a.   operant conditioning
    b.   social learning
    c.   vicarious conditioning
    d.   classical conditioning

3. Suppose a boy learns to fear bees by being stung when he touches a bee. In this situation the unconditioned STIMULUS is the _____.
    a.   bee
    b.   sting
    c.   fear
    d.   crying

4. Suppose a boy learns to fear bees by being stung when he touches a bee. In this situation the unconditioned RESPONSE is the _____.
    a.   bee
    b.   sting
    c.   fear
    d.   crying

5. Which of the following is the proper sequence of events in classical conditioning?
    a.   UCS-CS-UCR
    b.   CS-UCS-UCR
    c.   UCR-UCS-CS
    d.   UCR-CS-UCS

6. Once classical conditioning has occurred, the CR may be elicited by stimuli that are similar to the CS. This is called _____.
    a.   stimulus generalization
    b.   stimulus discrimination
    c.   spontaneous conditioning
    d.   replication of the effect

7. Higher order conditioning occurs when a(n) _____.
    a. previously neutral stimulus elicits a conditioned response
    b. neutral stimulus is paired with a conditioned stimulus
    c. neutral stimulus is paired with an unconditioned stimulus
    d. unconditioned response is paired with a conditioned stimulus

8. In classical conditioning, extinction occurs when the _____.
    a. conditioned stimulus is no longer paired with the unconditioned response
    b. conditioned stimulus is no longer paired with the unconditioned stimulus
    c. conditioned response is no longer paired with the unconditioned stimulus
    d. unconditioned stimulus is ambiguous

9. Anything that causes an increase in a response is a(n) _____.
    a. conditioned stimulus
    b. reinforcement
    c. punishment
    d. unconditioned stimulus

10. Anything that causes a decrease in a response is a(n) _____.
    a. conditioned stimulus
    b. reinforcement
    c. punishment
    d. unconditioned stimulus

11. Negative reinforcement and punishment are _____.
    a. the same
    b. the best ways to learn a new behavior
    c. not the same because negative reinforcement increases behavior and punishment
        decreases behavior
    d. not the same, even though they both decrease behavior

12. Making yourself study before you go to the movies is a good application of _____.
    a. negative reinforcement
    b. positive punishment
    c. fixed ratio schedule of reinforcement
    d. the Premack principle

13. Gamblers become addicted to their "sport" as a result of _____.
    a. previously generalized response discrimination
    b. previously extinguished response recovery
    c. partial (intermittent) reinforcement
    d. behavior being learned and not conditioned

14. If you reinforce your dog for sitting by giving him a treat every third time he sits, you are using a
   _____.
   a. continuous schedule of reinforcement
   b. random ratio reinforcement schedule
   c. fixed interval reinforcement schedule
   d. fixed ratio reinforcement schedule

15. In order for reinforcement or punishment to be effective, it must come _____.
   a. before the behavior
   b. after the behavior
   c. after the unconditioned stimulus
   d. before the unconditioned stimulus

16. A cue that signals when a particular response is likely to be followed by a certain type of
   consequence is known as a _____.
   a. primary reinforcer
   b. negative reinforcer
   c. discriminative stimulus
   d. variable ratio stimulus

17. Superstitious behavior occurs because _____.
   a. it has been reinforced on a fixed ratio schedule
   b. a person or an animal thinks the behavior causes a reinforcer when in reality the behavior and
      the reinforcement are not connected
   c. it is reinforced on a random ratio schedule
   d. the behavior and the reinforcement come in close proximity to one another, causing the
      superstitious behavior to increase in magnitude

18. Learning that occurs in the absence of a reward and remains hidden until some future time when it
   can be retrieved is called _____.
   a. latent learning
   b. insight
   c. spontaneous recovery
   d. trial-and-error learning

19. Albert Bandura's social learning theory emphasized _____.
   a. classical conditioning
   b. operant conditioning
   c. extinction
   d. modeling

20. Being innately predisposed to form associations between certain stimuli and responses is called
    _____.
    a. prejudice
    b. superstitious priming
    c. vicarious learning
    d. biological preparedness

PRACTICE TEST II

1. In Pavlov's classical conditioning experiments with dogs, salivation was the _____.
    a. unconditioned stimulus (UCS)
    b. conditioned response (CR)
    c. unconditioned response (UCR)
    d. both b and c

2. An emotional response that is evoked by a previously neutral event is called a(n) _____.
    a. conditioned emotional response (CER)
    b. gut automatic reaction (GAR)
    c. spontaneous emotional reaction (SES)
    d. elicited emotional response (EER)

3. John B. Watson and Rosalie Rayner demonstrated how the emotion of _____ could be classically
    conditioned.
    a. love
    b. anger
    c. joy
    d. fear

4. In Watson and Rayner's experiment, what was the neutral stimulus (NS)?
    a. The sight of the experimental room.
    b. A loud noise.
    c. A rabbit.
    d. A rat.

5. In Watson and Rayner's experiment, what was the conditioned emotional response(CER)?
    a. Avoidance behavior.
    b. Superstitious behavior
    c. Fear.
    d. None of these options

6. In Watson and Rayner's experiment, what was the conditioned stimulus (NS)?
    a.   The sight of the experimental room.
    b.   A loud noise.
    c.   A rabbit.
    d.   A rat.

7. In higher order conditioning, a neutral stimulus is paired with _____.
    a.   another neutral stimulus
    b.   a previously conditioned stimulus
    c.   two or more unconditioned stimuli
    d.   two or more unconditioned responses

8. Spontaneous recovery occurs when _____ suddenly reappears.
    a.   your lost wallet
    b.   a previously extinguished response
    c.   an extinct instinct
    d.   a forgotten stimulus-response sequence

9. Children may learn to salivate to McDonald's golden arches as a result of _____.
    a.   advertising
    b.   classical conditioning
    c.   higher-order conditioning
    d.   all of these options

10. Operant conditioning is an example of _____ in action.
    a.   Thorndike's law of effect
    b.   Skinner's law of reinforcement
    c.   Watson's rule of punishment
    d.   Pavlov's theory of stimulus-response

11. _____ are unlearned, usually satisfy a biological need, and increase the probability of a response.
    a.   Primary instincts
    b.   Secondary instincts
    c.   Primary reinforcers
    d.   Secondary reinforcers

12. Gamblers continue to put their money into slot machines because they pay off _____.
    a.   on a variable ratio
    b.   at variable intervals
    c.   at fixed intervals
    d.   on a fixed ratio

13. This is an example of passive aggressiveness that can be a side effect of punishment.
    a.   Janeel is late to dinner every night and never does her chores on time.
    b.   Erique refuses to do anything his father asks him to do, unless strictly supervised.
    c.   Gabe intentionally leaves food on dishes he puts in the dishwasher, knowing they will not get clean.
    d.   all of these options

14. When you use biofeedback equipment to lower your blood pressure, this provides you with a sense of accomplishment and a more relaxed physiological state. In this case, biofeedback is a(n) _____.
    a.   operant conditioning agent
    b.   fixed interval reinforcer
    c.   secondary reinforcer
    d.   conditioned stimulus

15. Insight is _____.
    a.   based on unconscious classical conditioning
    b.   divinely inspired
    c.   a sudden flash of understanding
    d.   an artifact of operant conditioning

16. Latent learning occurs without being rewarded and _____.
    a.   remains hidden until a future time when it is needed
    b.   is spontaneously recovered
    c.   serves no useful purpose
    d.   has been found only in nonhuman species

17. Observational learning theory suggests that we learn many behaviors by _____
    a.   imitating others
    b.   observing our inner processes
    c.   teaching others
    d.   shaping our own and others behaviors

18. "Follow my lead" could be a motto for _____.
    a.   classical conditioning
    b.   operant conditioning
    c.   latent learning
    d.   observational learning learning

19. In Albert Bandura's classic Bobo doll study, children acted aggressively because _____.
    a.   they were rewarded for their behavior
    b.   of observational learning
    c.   they were positively punished
    d.   all of these options

20. Scaffolding is a teaching technique that combines _____ to help a person learn complicated tasks.
    a. programmed instruction and classical conditioning
    b. vicarious conditioning and insight
    c. shaping and modeling
    d. reinforcement and rewards

ANSWERS

The following answers to active learning exercises, fill-ins, matching exercises, and practice tests 1 and 2 provide immediate feedback on your mastery of the material. Try not to simply memorize the answers. When you are unsure of your "guess" or make an error, be sure to go back to the textbook and carefully review. This will greatly improve your scores on classroom exams and quizzes.

ACTIVE LEARNING EXERCISE I

1. A. Operant, B. Negative Reinforcement; 2. A. Classical, B. NS = sight of mother, UCS = stroking, UCR = feelings of pleasure, CS = sight of mother, CR = feelings of pleasure; 3. A. Operant, B. Negative Punishment; 4. A. Classical, B. NS = sight of house, UCS = high temperature, UCR = perspiring, CS = sight of the house, CR = perspiring.

ACTIVE LEARNING EXERCISE II

1. NS: sound of the tone
    UCS: piece of meat
    UCR: salivating
    CS: sound of the tone
    CR: salivating

2. NS: saying "goodbye"
    UCS: loud noise from door slamming
    UCR: flinching
    CS: saying "goodbye"
    CR: flinching

3. NS: flash of light
    UCS: puff of air to the eye
    UCR: blinking
    CS: flash of light
    CR: blinking

CROSSWORD PUZZLE FOR CHAPTER 6

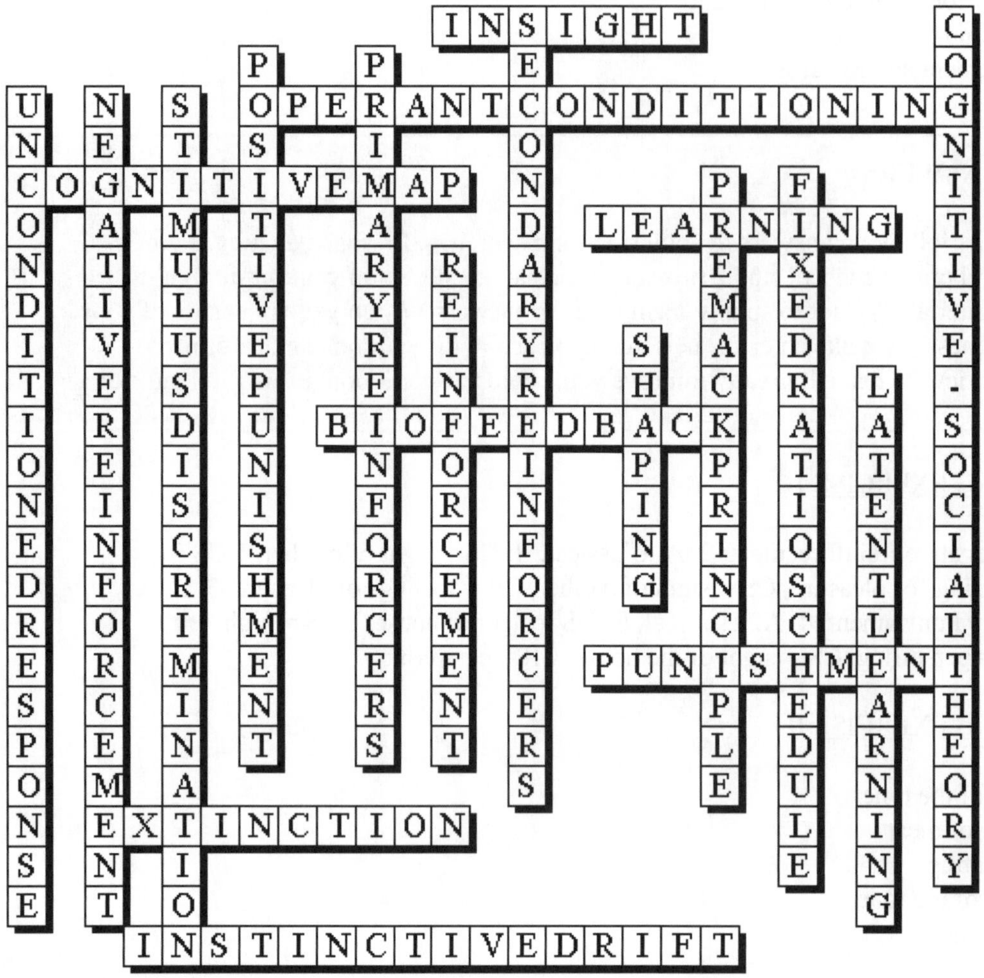
INSIGHT
COGNITIVE-SOCIALTHEORY
OPERANTCONDITIONING
UNCONDITIONEDRESPONSE
NEGATIVEREINFORCEMENT
STIMULUSDISCRIMINATION
POSITIVEPUNISHMENT
PRIMARYREINFORCERS
SECONDARYREINFORCERS
COGNITIVEMAP
LEARNING
PREMACKPRINCIPLE
FIXEDRATIOSCHEDULE
REINFORCEMENT
SHAPING
BIOFEEDBACK
LATENTLEARNING
PUNISHMENT
EXTINCTION
INSTINCTIVEDRIFT

FILL-IN EXERCISES

1. Ivan Pavlov; 2. involuntary; 3. an unconditioned response (UCR); 4. spontaneous recovery; 5. operant conditioning; 6. reinforcement, punishment; 7. continuously, partially; 8. shaping; 9. superstitious behavior; 10 scaffolding.

MATCHING EXERCISES

a. 3, b. 9, c. 8, d. 7, e. 6, f. 10, g. 1, h. 4, i. 2, j. 5.

PRACTICE TEST I		PRACTICE TEST II	
1. b (p. 198)	11. c (p. 211)	1. d (p. 200)	11. c (p. 210)
2. d (p. 198)	12. d (p. 211)	2. a (p. 202)	12. a (p. 213)
3. a (p. 200)	13. c (p. 212)	3. d (p. 202)	13. d (p. 218)
4. c (p. 200)	14. a (p. 212)	4. d (p. 202)	14. c (pp. 219,210)
5. b (p. 201)	15. b (p. 217)	5. c (p. 202)	15. c (p. 223)
6. a (p. 203)	16. c (p. 218)	6. d (p. 202)	16. a (p. 223)
7. d (p. 204)	17. b (p. 220)	7. b (p. 204)	17. a (p. 224)
8. b (p. 204)	18. a (p. 223)	8. b (p. 204)	18. d (p. 224)
9. b (p. 209)	19. d (p. 224)	9. d (p. 204)	19. b (p. 226)
10.c (p. 209)	20. d (p.229)	10.a (p.209)	20. c (p. 226)

7 Memory

OUTLINE (<u>S</u>urvey & <u>Q</u>uestion)

This outline is intended to help you *survey* the chapter. As you read through the various sections, write down any *questions* or comments that come to mind in the space provided. This is a valuable part of active learning and the SQ4R method. It not only makes your reading time more enjoyable and active, but it also increases retention and understanding of the material.

TOPIC	NOTES

I. WHAT IS MEMORY?

    A. Traditional Three-Stage Memory Model

    B. Encoding, Storage, and Retrieval

    C. Integrating the Two Major Approaches

    D. Biological Perspective

Research Highlight: Looking for Memory in All the Right Places

II. WHY DO WE FORGET?

A. Research Findings

Gender and Cultural Diversity: Cultural Differences in Memory

B. Theories of Forgetting

III. PROBLEMS WITH MEMORY

A. Organic Causes

B. Constructive Processes

C. Eyewitness Testimony and Repressed Memories

Critical Thinking/Active Learning: Exploring Your Memories

IV. IMPROVING MEMORY

A. Specific Tips

B. Seven Sins

Core and Expanded LEARNING OBJECTIVES (Read, Recite & wRite)

While *reading* the chapter, stop periodically and *recite* (or repeat in your own words) the answers to the following learning objectives. It will also help your retention if you *write* your answer in the space provided. (Page numbers refer to the text Psychology in Action, 6th Ed.)

Core Learning Objectives

These objectives are found at the beginning of each chapter of Psychology in Action (6th ed.).

1. What are the three major approaches that help explain memory?

2. What causes forgetting? How do we prevent forgetting of important information?

3. What are the key memory problems?

4. How can we improve our memory?

Expanded Learning Objectives

These objectives offer more detail and a more intensive way to study the chapter.

Upon completion of CHAPTER 7, the student should be able to:

1. List and describe the sequence of the three distinct storage systems in the traditional view of memory (pp. 236-238).

2. Describe the purpose, duration, and capacity of sensory memory (p. 238).

3. Describe the purpose, duration, and capacity of short-term memory; discuss the effects of chunking and maintenance rehearsal at this stage (pp. 238-239).

4. Describe the three parts of working-memory (p. 240).

5. Describe the purpose, duration, and capacity of long-term memory (pp. 240-241).

6. Describe the memory processing approach to memory, from encoding to storage to retrieval, and compare this to the parallel distributed processing approach (pp. 241-243).

7. Integrate the encoding process with short-term and long-term memory by describing the principles of organization and rehearsal as they apply to each of these stages of memory (pp. 244-246).

8. Integrate the storage process with long-term memory by describing the hierarchical systems and subsystems of long-term memory storage (pp. 246-248).

9. Integrate the retrieval process with long-term memory by describing retrieval cues, recognition, recall, and the encoding specificity principle (pp. 248-250).

10. Explain memory in terms of neuronal and synaptic changes, hormonal influences, and specific brain areas (pp. 250-253).

11. Discuss forgetting and describe how each of the following factors affects remembering: serial position, distributed versus massed practice, and cultural differences (pp. 254-257).

12. Describe theories of forgetting: interference, decay, retrieval failure, and motivated forgetting. Differentiate between proactive and retroactive interference (pp. 258-260).

13. Define amnesia, and differentiate between retrograde and anterograde amnesia; define Alzheimer's disease (pp. 260-262).

14. Describe how memory can be constructed and distorted (pp. 262-267).

15. Describe specific methods of improving your memory and provide examples of the various mnemonic devices (pp. 267-272).

KEY TERMS (Review)

The *review* step in the SQ4R method is very important to your performance on quizzes and exams. Upon completion of this chapter, you should be able to define the following terms.

Alzheimer's Disease (AD): _____

_____

Anterograde Amnesia: *inability to form new memories*

_____

Chunking: *grouping objects into units to store more info in short term memory*

Consolidation: _____

_____

Constructive Processes: _____

_____

Distributed Practice: _____

_____

Elaborative Rehearsal: *encoding technique that pairs old info w/ new info*

Encoding: *translating info into neural codes*

_____

Encoding Specificity Principle: _____

_____

Episodic Memory: *mental diary of a persons life*

_____

Explicit/Declarative Memory: *Subsystem of LTM that stores facts & info about personal life*

Implicit/Nondeclarative/Procedural Memory: *Subsystem of ~~LM~~ LTM that consist of skills learned and responses*

Long-Term Memory (LTM): *3rd stage storage of into for long periods of time infinite capacity and time*

Long-Term Potentiation (LTP): _____

_____

Maintenance Rehearsal: *repetion to hold contents of short term memory*

Massed Practice: _____

_____

Memory: *internal record process of receiving encoding store and organising into*

Misinformation Effect: _____

_____

Mnemonic: _____

_____

Parallel Distributed Processing Approach (PDP): _____

_____

Priming: _____

_____

Proactive Interference: *old info interfes w/new info* _____

_____

Procedural Memory: _____

_____

Recall: *general retrevial cue to search LTm* _____

_____

Recognition: *Process of mating cue to item in LTM* _____

_____

Relearning: _____

_____

Retrieval: *Process of retrieing info from memory* _____

_____

Retrieval Cue: _____

_____

Retroactive Interference: *new info interfers w/ old* _____

_____

Retrograde Amnesia: *Difficulty in remembering previously learned info*

_____

Semantic Memory: _____

_____

Sensory Memory: *1ˢᵗ stage of memory exact image is held for a few seconds*

Serial Position Effect: _____

_____

Short-Term Memory (STM): *2ⁿᵈ stage what is currently being worked w/ limit is 5-9 items for 30 sec*

Sleeper Effect: _____

_____

Source Amnesia: _____

_____

Storage: *Process of retaining neural codes over time*

_____

Tip-of-the-Tongue Phenomenon (TOT): _____

_____

Zeigarnik Effect: _____

_____

ACTIVE LEARNING EXERCISES (<u>R</u>ecite)

The *recite* step in the SQ4R method requires you to be an ACTIVE learner. By completing the following exercises, you will test and improve your mastery of the chapter material, which will also improve your performance on quizzes and exams. Answers to some exercises appear at the end of this study guide chapter.

ACTIVE LEARNING EXERCISE I

Using the Substitute Word System for Remembering Names

Now that you have learned the substitute word system, it can help improve your memory for names. Try converting a person's name into a visual image that will act as a memory retrieval cue.

Some names, like Sandy Storm, are easily visualized. However, you can also use this system with more common names, like "Brewster." Ask yourself, "Are there any words I can visualize that sound like the name?" If not, break the name into parts and imagine substitutes for them. For example, for the name "Brewster," substitute the word "rooster" or divide it into "brew" and "stir." With "rooster," imagine a big rooster with the facial features of the person named "Brewster." For "brew" and "stir," you might visualize a large mug of beer being stirred by an oar. Each of the images you choose should be absurd, exaggerated, or as distinctive as possible. The idea is to form a *lasting* image.

For practice, use the substitute word system and create corresponding vivid images for the following names: George Washington, Plato, Pearl Bailey, Heather Locklear, and Ricky Martin.

_____

_____

_____

_____

ACTIVE LEARNING EXERCISE II

<u>Gathering Data</u> (A Behavioral Skill)

Collecting up-to-date, relevant information is an important component of critical thinking. To help build this skill, as well as to gain important insights into memory strategies, try the following:

a.   Interview three classmates who do well on exams and that you believe have good memories. Ask about their study techniques and test taking strategies. Using the examples found in Appendix B of this study guide, ask which technique they find most useful? Now interview three classmates or friends who complain about their college grades and poor memories. Compare their study techniques and test taking strategies to those who remember well. What are the differences?

_____

_____

_____

_____

b.   Interview three people who have taken a reading improvement or speed-reading course. What methods were taught that increased reading speed and comprehension? What changes have they noticed in their college grades or exam performances after taking the course? Did they use any of the techniques or mnemonics discussed in the text?

_____

_____

CHAPTER OVERVIEW (Review)

The following CHAPTER OVERVIEW provides a narrative overview of the main topics covered in the chapter. Like the Visual Summary found at the end of each chapter in the text, this narrative summary provides a final opportunity to *review* chapter material.

I. Three-Stage Memory Model and Encoding, Storage, and Retrieval

The traditional three-stage memory model proposes that information must pass through each of three stages before being stored: *sensory memory*, *short-term memory*, and *long-term memory* to be retained in our memory system. **Sensory memory** preserves a brief replica of sensory information. It has a large capacity and information lasts from 2-3 seconds up to four seconds. Selected information is sent to short-term memory. **Short-term memory (STM),** also called *working memory*, involves memory for current thoughts. Short-term memory can hold 5 to 9 items for about 30 seconds before it is forgotten. Information can be stored longer than 30 seconds through **maintenance rehearsal** and the capacity of STM can be increased with **chunking**. **Long-term memory (LTM)** is relatively permanent memory storage with an unlimited capacity.

The encoding, storage, and retrieval approach sees memory as a *process*. It uses similarities between human memory and a computer's information processing system. Like typing on a keyboard, **encoding** translates information into neural codes that match the brain's language. **Storage** retains neural coded information over time, like saving material on the computer's hard drive or a disk. **Retrieval** gets information out of long-term memory storage and sends it to short-term memory to be used, whereas the computer retrieves information and displays in on the monitor.

The **Parallel Distributed Processing (PDP),** or *connectionist*, model explains that contents of our memory are represented as a vast number of interconnected units and modules distributed throughout a huge network, all operating in parallel—simultaneously.

II. Integration Model and Biological Perspective
Most psychologists currently emphasize an integration of the traditional *three-stage memory model* and the *encoding, storage,* and *retrieval approach.*

We first encode information when we transfer it from sensory memory to short-term memory, and then again during the transfer from STM to LTM. Organization and rehearsal are important to successful encoding. To improve encoding during STM, we can use the organizational method of *chunking* or the rehearsal key of *maintenance rehearsal*. During LTM, we can use the organizational strategy of creating *hierarchies* and the rehearsal key of *elaborative rehearsal*.

Storage in LTM is divided into two major systems—**explicit/declarative** and **implicit/nondeclarative/procedural** memory. Explit/declarative memory can be further subdivided into two parts—**semantic** and **episodic** memory. Retrieval from LTM relies on **retrieval cues** (**recognition** and **recall**) and the **encoding specificity principle.**

The biological perspective of memory focuses on changes in neurons and hormones, as well as searching for the locations of memory in the brain. Hebb's original idea that memory traces consist of specific neural circuits is supported by research on **long-term potentiation (LTP).** When we are stressed or excited, we naturally produce hormones that may enhance memory. Memory tends to be localized *and* distributed throughout the brain—not just the cortex.

III. Why Do We Forget?
Herman Ebbinghaus was one of the first researchers to extensively study forgetting. His famous "curve of forgetting" shows that it occurs most rapidly immediately after learning. However, Ebbinghaus also showed that **relearning** usually takes less time than original learning. Two important factors in forgetting are the **serial position effect** (where material at the beginning and end of the list is remembered better than material in the middle) and spacing of practice (where **distributed practice** is found to be superior to **massed practice**).

The decay theory of forgetting simply states that memory, like all biological processes, deteriorates as time passes. The interference theory of forgetting suggests memories are forgotten because of either proactive or retroactive interference. **Proactive interference** occurs when old information interferes with newly learned information. **Retroactive interference** occurs when new information interferes with previously learned information. The motivated forgetting theory states that people forget things that are painful, threatening, or embarrassing. Some material is forgotten because it was never encoded from STM to LTM. Other forgetting occurs because of retrieval failure, information stored in LTM is not forgotten but may at times be inaccessible.

III. Problems with Memory

Some memory problems are the result of injury and disease (organic pathology). Forgetting as a result of serious brain injuries or trauma is called *amnesia*. In **retrograde amnesia**, memory for events that occurred *before* the accident is lost. In **anterograde amnesia** memory for events that occur *after* an accident is lost. **Alzheimer's disease** is a progressive mental deterioration and severe memory loss occurring most commonly in old age.

Memories are not exact duplicates. We actively shape and build on information as it is encoded, stored, and retrieved**.** There are three major errors that occur during the constructive processes of memory**:** **source amnesia**, the **sleeper effect** and the **misinformation effect**. Two areas of memory problems that have profound legal and social implications are *eyewitness testimony* and *repressed memories.*

IV. Improving Memory

The psychology of memory and key points from this chapter offer concrete strategies for improving memory. These include paying attention and reducing interference; using rehearsal techniques (both maintenance and elaborative rehearsal); improving your organization (by chunking and creating hierarchies); counteracting the serial position effect, managing your time; using the encoding specificity principle; employing self-monitoring and overlearning; and using **mnemonic devices**.

According to Schachter, there are seven sins that affect memory and forgetting. The first three sins are types of *forgetting,* the second three involve memory *distortions,* and the last sin is *persistence.*

SELF-TESTS (<u>R</u>eview & w<u>R</u>ite)

Completing the following SELF-TESTS will provide immediate feedback on how well you have mastered the material. In the *crossword puzzle* and *fill-in exercises*, write the appropriate word or words in the blank spaces. The *matching exercise* requires you to match the terms in one column to their correct definitions in the other. For the *multiple-choice questions* in Practice Tests I and II, circle or underline the correct answer. When you are unsure of any answer, be sure to highlight or specially mark the item and then go back to the text for further review. Correct answers are provided at the end of this study guide chapter.

Crossword Puzzle for Chapter 7

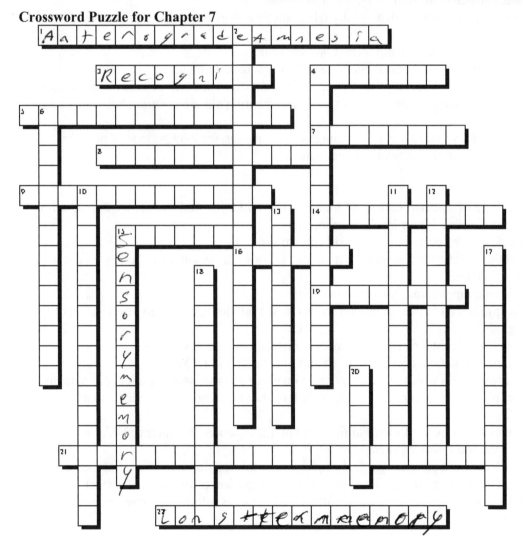

ACROSS

1 The inability to form new memories.

3 The process of recovering information out of memory storage.

4 The process by which an earlier encounter with a stimulus (such as a word or picture) increases the likelihood of that stimulus or a related stimulus being remembered at a later time.

5 The subpart of explicit/declarative memory that stores general knowledge; a mental encyclopedia or dictionary.

7 The process of grouping information into units in order to store more information in short-term memory.

8 A clue or prompt that helps stimulate recall and retrieval of a stored piece of information from long-term memory.

9 Attributing to a wrong source an event that we have experienced, heard about, read about, or imagined. (Also called source confusion or source misattribution.)

14 Learning material a second time, which usually takes less time than original learning; also called the savings method.

15 The process of retaining neural coded information over time.

16 Process of using a very general retreival cue to search the contents of LTM.

19 The process of translating information into neural codes (language) that will be retained in memory.

21 Forgetting in which new information interferes with remembering old information; backward-acting interference.

22 The third stage of memory that functions as storage of information for long periods of time; its capacity is limitless and its duration is relatively permanent.

DOWN

2 An encoding technique of associating new information with already stored knowledge in long-term memory (LTM). Also known as deeper levels of processing.

4 Long-term memories for the performance of skills or actions.

6 The subpart of explicit/declarative memory that stores memories of personally experienced events; a mental diary of a person's life.

10 Difficulty in remembering previously learned material.

11 A learning technique in which time spent learning is massed into long, unbroken intervals; also known as cramming.

12 A memory improvement technique based on encoding items in a special way.

13 Process of matching a specific retrieval cue to an appropriate item in LTM.

15 The first stage of memory in which a relatively exact image of each sensory experience is held briefly until it can be further processed; its capacity is relatively large but its duration is restricted to a few seconds.

17 The initial tendency to discount information from an unreliable source, but later consider it trustworthier because the source is forgotten.

18 A hypothetical process explaining the gradual conversion of information into long-term memories.

20 An internal record or representation of some prior event or experience; also a set of mental processes that receives, encodes, stores, organizes, alters, and retrieves information over time.

FILL-IN EXERCISES

1. The traditional view of memory contains three distinct memory storage systems: the _____, _____, and _____ (p. 238).

2. Keeping information in STM by repeating or reviewing it is known as _____ (p. 239).

3. The capacity of STM can be improved by _____ (p. 239).

4. The third stage of memory that functions as storage of information for long periods of time is known as _____ (p. 240).

5. The second major model of memory, the _____, focuses on memory as a process (p. 241).

6. Factual information is stored in _____ memory; whereas memories for events are stored in _____ memory (p. 247).

7. Taking a multiple-choice test requires use of the _____ retrieval strategy; whereas an essay test requires use of the _____ strategy (p. 249).

8. _____ explains why we remember things at the end of a list but forget things in the middle (p. 255).

9. The decay theory suggests that forgetting is largely due to _____ (p. 258).

10. Memory strategies that help organize or "tag" information are called _____ (p. 269).

MATCHING EXERCISES

Column A

5 a. Distributed Practice
9 b. Motivated Forgetting
1 c. Retrieval
6 d. Zeigarnik Effect
8 e. Mnemonic device
3 f. Alzheimer's Disease
4 g. Semantic Memory
7 h. Constructive Processes
2 i. Consolidation
1 j. Retroactive Interference

Column B

1. _J_ New information interferes with the old.
2. _i_ Gradual conversion of information into LTM.
3. _f_ Progressive mental deterioration with severe memory loss.
4. _g_ Stores general knowledge and facts.
5. _a_ Short study sessions mixed with rest periods.
6. _i_ Recall is better for unfinished tasks.
7. _d_ Can result in errors and distortions of memory.
8. _e_ Method of loci.
9. _b_ Forgetting painful or embarrassing information.
10. _c_ Process of getting information out of LTM.

PRACTICE TEST I

1. A visual image in sensory memory _____.
   a. lasts about 1/2 second
   b. lasts longer than sounds remain in this stage
   c. contains only the image that has been selected for our attention
   d. is always processed into STM

2. Short-term memory is sometimes called _____.
   a. mental imaging
   b. present memory
   c. brief memory
   d. working memory

3. Maintenance rehearsal _____.
   a. causes consolidation
   b. prevents chunking
   c. reenters information in sensory memory
   d. reenters information in STM

4. Chunking enables a person to _____.
   a. select contents from sensory memory
   b. organize contents of STM
   c. organize contents of LTM
   d. use dual coding in sensory memory

5. An encoding technique of associating new information with already stored knowledge in LTM is known as _____.
   a. sensory consolidation
   b. mnemonic techniques
   c. semantic memory
   d. elaborative rehearsal

6. Memory for events are stored in _____.
   a. sensory memory
   b. STM
   c. semantic memory
   d. episodic memory

7. Which of the following is a recognition test of memory?
   a. remembering a name that goes with a face
   b. a multiple choice test
   c. an essay test
   d. reciting the names of the state capitals

8. A relatively permanent change in the strength of synaptic responsiveness believed to be a biological mechanism for learning and memory is called _____.
   a. long-term potentiation (LTP)
   b. an excitatory post-synaptic potential
   c. reverberating circuits
   d. the process of neuron transformation

9. Research on flashbulb memories has found that _____.
   a. once a memory is stored in LTM, it is not changed
   b. stored memories are subject to alteration
   c. inferences or assumptions are not added to information with a strong emotional impact
   d. if a memory is vivid, it is an accurate account of the original experience

10. According to the decay theory of forgetting, we are unable to remember information when it _____.
    a. has been replaced with newer information
    b. has deteriorated with the passage of time
    c. has a negative emotional impact
    d. was learned in an emotional state different from the state we are in when trying to remember it

11. If during a French test in college, you remember some Spanish words you learned in high school, these previously learned words would be causing _____ interference.
    a. retroactive
    b. proactive
    c. chunking
    d. semantic

12. You probably don't remember whose head in on a U.S. penny because of problems with _____.
    a. sensory memory
    b. STM
    c. LTM
    d. encoding failure

13. Alfredo was unable to remember the events occurring just before his automobile accident. This memory loss from brain trauma is known as _____ amnesia.
    a. anterograde
    b. retrograde
    c. proactive
    d. retroactive

14. The patient H. M. was unable to remember information from the last few years before his operation and has difficulty forming new memories. This is because of _____.
    a. anterograde amnesia
    b. removal of portions of his temporal lobes
    c. retrograde amnesia
    d. all of these options

15. _____ processes explain how we actively shape and build on information as it is encoded and retrieved.
    a. Flashbulb
    b. Constructive
    c. Mnemonic
    d. Consolidative

16. Thinking that you heard some bit of information from a friend when you actually heard on TV is known as _____.
    a. retroactive interference
    b. Alzheimer's disease (AD)
    c. source amnesia
    d. senile dementia

17. Remembering your sister's 16th birthday party as your own is an example of _____.
    a. sibling rivalry
    b. reconstructive consolidation
    c. the misinformation effect
    d. decay of flashbulb memory

18. The famous cognitive and developmental psychologist, Jean Piaget, misremembered a childhood story of almost being kidnapped. This is an example of _____.
    a. source amnesia
    b. misinformation effect
    c. constructive processes
    d. all of these options

19. A memory improvement technique based on encoding items in a special way is known as
    _____.
    a.   encoding elaboration
    b.   the encoding specificity principle
    c.   a mnemonic device
    d.   none of these options

20. The method of loci mnemonic system uses _____ to organize information to be learned.
    a.   images of physical locations
    b.   substitute words
    c.   images of objects to represent numbers
    d.   numbers

PRACTICE TEST II

1. This type of memory has a large capacity and short duration.
    a.   semantic
    b.   sensory
    c.   short-term
    d.   working

2. Short-term memory receives information from sensory memory and from _____.
    a.   long-term memory
    b.   working memory
    c.   the perceptual processing network
    d.   maintenance rehearsal

3. The process that allows us to store more information in short-term memory by grouping information
    into units is called _____.
    a.   maintenance rehearsal
    b.   collective organization
    c.   chunking
    d.   proximal closure

4. Researchers believe there are three parts to working memory: visuospatial sketchpad, phonological
    rehearsal loop, and _____.
    a.   Reverberating circuits
    b.   brief sensory storage
    c.   a central executive
    d.   short-term perceptual storage

5. According to the encoding, storage, and retrieval approach, memory is a process that can be compared to the workings of _____.
   a. a board of executives
   b. a flashbulb memory
   c. redintegration
   d. a computer

6. The process of translating information into neural codes (language) that will be retained in memory is known as _____.
   a. the Zeigarnik effect
   b. neural transformation
   c. encoding
   d. consolidation

7. Actively reviewing and relating new information to material previously stored in LTM is called _____.
   a. studying
   b. elaborative rehearsal
   c. deep processing
   d. all of these options

8. A subsystem within LTM that stores facts, information, and personal life experiences is called _____.
   a. procedural memory
   b. explicit/declarative memory
   c. implicit/episodic memory
   d. none of these options

9. A clue or prompt that helps stimulate recall and retrieval of a stored piece of information from LTM is called _____.
   a. redintegration
   b. an encoding specificity prompt
   c. priming
   d. a retrieval cue

10. Recalling interrupted tasks better than completed tasks is known as _____.
    a. the Zeigarnik effect
    b. an insight
    c. redintegration
    d. the Eureka experience

11. Drinking coffee while studying or before an exam may improve your performance because of
    _____.
    a.   the drug elaboration effect
    b.   caffeine priming
    c.   consolidation
    d.   state-dependent retrieval

12. A vivid image of circumstances associated with surprising or emotional events, like the Challenger
    explosion, is known as _____.
    a.   long-term potentiation (LTP)
    b.   a flashbulb memory
    c.   redintegration
    d.   all of these options

13. Relearning occurs when it takes _____ to regain lost information.
    a.   longer
    b.   less time
    c.   more trials
    d.   the same number of trials or amount of time

14. The _____ effect suggests that people will recall information presented at the beginning and end of a
    list better than information from the middle of a list.
    a.   recency
    b.   serial position
    c.   latency
    d.   primacy

15. Memory research suggests that, in comparison to literate cultures, preliterate cultures _____.
    a.   have better short-term, but worse long-term memory abilities
    b.   are better at face-recognition memory tasks
    c.   demonstrate better recall for orally presented stories
    d.   are not affected by the recency effect

16. Forgetting that you fell off the stage during your high school graduation is an example of _____.
    a.   epinephrine overexcitation
    b.   adrenaline synthesis
    c.   interference theory
    d.   motivated forgetting theory

17. Alzheimer's disease (AD) is characterized by _____.
   a.   sudden memory loss
   b.   progressive mental deterioration with severe memory loss
   c.   gradual memory loss without deterioration in other mental functioning
   d.   gradual and severe memory loss accompanied by physical deterioration

18. Hearing a politician discuss problems with global warming and later thinking you read it in your college biology text is an example of the _____.
   a.   Zeigarnik effect
   b.   Newsweek effect
   c.   misinformation effect
   d.   sleeper effect

19. The method of loci, peg-word system, and substitute word system are all _____ devices.
   a.   visually organized
   b.   verbally organized
   c.   mnemonic
   d.   moderately effective

20. When you want to remember a series of words or facts in their appropriate sequence, it would be best to use the mnemonic device called the _____.
   a.   peg-word system
   b.   method of loci
   c.   method of word association
   d.   substitute word system

ANSWERS

The following answers to active learning exercises, fill-ins, matching exercises, and practice tests 1 and 2 provide immediate feedback on your mastery of the material. Try not to simply memorize the answers. When you are unsure of your "guess" or make an error, be sure to go back to the textbook and carefully review. This will greatly improve your scores on classroom exams and quizzes.

FILL-IN EXERCISES

1. sensory memory, short-term memory (STM), long-term memory (LTM); 2. maintenance rehearsal; 3. chunking; 4. long-term memory (LTM); 5. encoding, storage, retrieval approach; 6. semantic, episodic; 7. recognition, recall; 8. serial position effect; 9. biological decay over time; 10. mnemonics.

Crossword Puzzle for Chapter 7

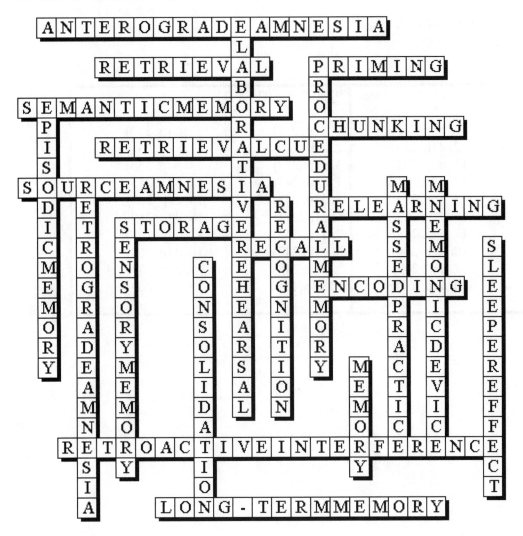

MATCHING EXERCISES

a. 5, b. 9, c. 10, d. 6, e. 8, f. 3, g. 4, h. 7, i. 2, j. 1.

PRACTICE TEST I		PRACTICE TEST II	
1. a (p. 238)	11. b (p. 258)	1. b (p. 238)	11. d (p. 250)
2. d (p. 240)	12. d (p. 259)	2. a (p. 240)	12. b (p. 251)
3. c (p. 239)	13. b (p. 261)	3. c (p. 239)	13. b (p. 255)
4. b (p. 239)	14. d (p. 261,235)	4. c (p. 240)	14. b (p. 255)
5. d (p. 245)	15. b (p. 263)	5. d (p. 241)	15. c (p. 257)
6. d (p. 247)	16. c (p. 263)	6. c (p. 242)	16. d (p. 2599)
7. b (p. 249)	17. c (p. 263)	7. d (p. 245)	17. b (p. 261)
8. a (p. 250)	18. d (p. 264)	8. b (p. 247)	18. d (p. 263)
9. b (p. 253)	19. c (p. 269)	9. d (p. 248)	19. c (p. 269)
10.b (p. 258)	20. a (p.267)	10.a (p. 250)	20. b (p. 269)

8 Thinking, Language and Intelligence

TOPIC	NOTES

I. THINKING

   A. The Thinking Brain

   B. Cognitive Building Blocks

   C. Solving Problems

       Critical Thinking/Active Learning: Solving Problems in College Life

  D. Creativity

II. LANGUAGE

A. Characteristics of Language

B. Language and Thought

C. Animals and Language

Research Highlight: Language and the Brain

III. INTELLIGENCE

A. The Nature of Intelligence

B. Test Construction

C. Assessing Intelligence

D. Explaining Differences in Intelligence

Gender and Cultural Diversity: The Bell Curve, Stereotype Threat, and IQ Tests

Core and Expanded LEARNING OBJECTIVES   (Read, Recite & wRite)

While *reading* the chapter, stop periodically and *recite* (or repeat in your own words) the answers to the following learning objectives. It will also help your retention if you *write* your answer in the space provided. (Page numbers refer to the text <u>Psychology in Action</u>, 6th Ed.)

Core Learning Objectives
These objectives are found at the beginning of each chapter of <u>Psychology in Action</u> (6th ed.).

1. What is thinking and how does the brain do it?

2. What are the building blocks of thought?

3. How do we solve problems?

4. What is creativity and how is it measured?

5. What is language and how is it related to thinking?

6. What is intelligence and how is it measured?

7. How do biology, genetics, and the environment influence intelligence?

Expanded Learning Objectives
These objectives offer more detail and a more intensive way to study the chapter.

Upon completion of CHAPTER 8, the student will be able to:

1. Define cognition and thinking, and describe the use of mental imaging in cognition (pp. 278-280).

2. Define concepts, and describe the three major methods for concept formation (pp. 280-282).

3. List and describe the three stages of problem-solving, including an explanation of the types of thinking that occur in each stage (pp. 283-284).

4. List and describe the three major barriers to problem-solving; discuss the role of incubation in overcoming these barriers (pp. 284-287).

5. Define creativity, and discuss how convergent and divergent thinking, and the investment theory of creativity are related to the creative process (pp. 288-289).

6. Describe how human language differs from patterns of communication used by non-humans (pp. 290-291).

7. Define and provide an example of each of the following building blocks of language: phonemes, morphemes, grammar, syntax, and semantics; describe Chomsky's surface and deep structures of language (pp. 291-292).

8. Describe the interaction between language and thought (pp. 292-293).

9. Describe the research on teaching language to animals, and summarize each side of the "animal language" debate (pp. 293-295).

10. Describe the research on language and the brain (p. 295).

11. Explain why intelligence is difficult to define, and state the text's definition; differentiate between Cattell's fluid and crystallized intelligence (pp. 296-297).

12. Describe Gardner's theory of multiple intelligences and Sternberg's triarchic theory of successful intelligence (pp. 299-301).

13. Define standardization, reliability, and validity, and explain why each is important for intelligence testing (pp. 301-302).

14. Explain how an intelligence quotient (IQ) is determined and differentiate between the Stanford-Binet Intelligence Test and the Wechsler intelligent tests; describe the extremes of mental retardation and mental giftedness (pp. 302-307).

15. Explain how biology, genetics, and the environment impact intelligence (pp. 307-309).

16. Describe what is known about the influence of gender and culture on intelligence (pp. 310-312).

KEY TERMS (Review)

The *review* step in the SQ4R method is very important to your performance on quizzes and exams. Upon completion of this chapter, you should be able to define the following terms.

Algorithm: _____

_____

Cognition: _____

_____

Concept: _____

_____

Confirmation Bias: _____

_____

Convergent Thinking: _____

_____

Creativity: _____

_____

Crystallized Intelligence: _____

_____

Divergent Thinking: _____

_____

Fluid Intelligence: _____

_____

Functional Fixedness: _____

_____

Grammar: _____

_____

Heuristics: _____

_____

Incubation: _____

_____

Intelligence: _____

_____

Intelligence Quotient (IQ): _____

_____

Mental Images: _____

_____

Mental Set: _____

_____

Morpheme: _____

_____

Phoneme: _____

_____

Prototype: _____

_____

Reliability: _____

_____

Semantics: _____

_____

Standardization: _____

_____

Stereotype Threat: _____

_____

Syntax: _____

_____

Validity: _____

_____

ACTIVE LEARNING EXERCISES (Recite)

The *recite* step in the SQ4R method requires you to be an ACTIVE learner. By completing the following exercises, you will test and improve your mastery of the chapter material, which will also improve your performance on quizzes and exams. Answers to some exercises appear at the end of this study guide chapter.

ACTIVE LEARNING EXERCISE I

The text describes two major ways to generate hypotheses during the production stage of problem solving—algorithms and heuristics.

To improve your algorithm strategy, try the following:

There are 1025 tennis players participating in a single's elimination tournament. How many matches must be played before there is one winner and 1024 losers?

To work on your skill in "working backwards" (a type of heuristic), try this problem:

While three watchmen were guarding an orchard, a thief crept in and stole some apples. During his escape, he met the three watchmen one after the other. In exchange for his freedom, he gave each one-half of the apples he had at the time, plus an extra two. After he had shared his apples with each of the three watchmen, he had one left for himself. How many apples had he stolen originally?

Answers can be found at the end of this study guide chapter.

ACTIVE LEARNING EXERCISE II

Metacognition (A Cognitive Skill)

Metacognition, also known as reflective or recursive thinking, involves a review and analysis of your own mental processes-- thinking about your own thinking. Below is a problem that involves this type of active learning. Take a few minutes and work on it.

Problem

There is a bird, Tweety, that likes to perch on the roof of Casey Jones, a locomotive that travels the 200-mile route from Cucamonga to Kalamazoo. As Casey Jones pulls out from Cucamonga, the bird takes to the air and flies to Kalamazoo, the train's destination. Because the train travels at only 50 mph whereas the bird travels at 100 mph, Tweety reaches Kalamazoo before the train and finds that it has nowhere to perch. So the bird flies back to the train and finds it still moving, whereupon Tweety flies back to Kalamazoo, then back to the train, and so on until Casey Jones finally arrives in Kalamazoo, where the bird finally rests on the locomotive's roof. How far has the bird flown?

This exercise helps apply what you've learned in your textbook about steps involved problem solving. To review these steps, fill in the name of the step, then describe the processes you used during each step in solving the above problem. Make sure you include the following terms, if applicable:

algorithm	creating subgoals	evaluation
goal	heuristics	hypothesis
incubation	preparation	production

Step 1: _____

Procedure: _____

_____

_____

_____

Step 2: _____

Procedure: _____

_____

_____

_____

Step 3: _____

Procedure: _____

_____

_____

_____

CHAPTER OVERVIEW (<u>R</u>eview)

The following CHAPTER OVERVIEW provides a narrative overview of the main topics covered in the chapter. Like the Visual Summary found at the end of each chapter in the text, this narrative summary provides a final opportunity to *review* chapter material.

I. The Thinking Brain and Cognitive Building Blocks

Cognition, or thinking, is defined as mental activities involved in acquiring, storing, retrieving, and using knowledge. Thought processes are distributed throughout the brain via neural networks. Almost the entire cerebral cortex is activated when thinking involves forming mental representations. During problem solving and decision-making, our thoughts are localized for special processing within the frontal lobes.

The prefrontal cortex links to other areas of the brain to synthesize information from several senses. It is also connected to the limbic system. Without connecting thoughts to feelings, solving problems and making decisions would be difficult.

The three basic building blocks of cognition are mental images, concepts, and language. **Mental images** are mental representations of a sensory experience, including visual, auditory, gustatory, motor, olfactory, or tactile elements. **Concepts** are mental categories that groups objects, events, activities, or ideas that share similar characteristics. (Language is discussed in a later section.)

There are three ways we learn concepts: 1) Artificial concepts are formed by logical, specific rules or characteristics. 2) Natural concepts are formed by experience in everyday life. When we are confronted with a new item, we compare it with the **prototype** (most typical) of that concept. 3) Concepts are generally organized into hierarchies. We most frequently use the middle, basic-level concepts, when first learning material.

II. Solving Problems

Problem solving entails three steps: *preparation*, *production*, and *evaluation*. During the preparation stage, we identify given facts, separate relevant from irrelevant facts, and define the ultimate goal.

During the production stage, we generate possible situations, called hypotheses. We typically generate hypotheses by using **algorithms** and **heuristics**. Algorithms, as problem solving strategies, are guaranteed to lead to a solution eventually, but they are not practical in many situations. Heuristics, or simplified "rules of thumb" that are based on experience, are much faster but do not guarantee a solution. Three common heuristics are *means-end analysis, working backward,* and *creating subgoals.*

The evaluation step in problem solving involves judging the hypotheses generated during step two (production stage) against the criteria established in step one (preparation stage),

Three major barriers to successful problem solving are **mental sets, functional fixedness,** and **confirmation bias.** Some problems require a period of **incubation**, or time out, before a solution is apparent.

III. Creativity

Creativity is the generation of ideas that are original, novel, and useful. Creative thinking involves *fluency, flexibility,* and *originality.* **Divergent thinking**, trying to generate as many solutions as possible, is a special type of thinking involved in creativity. In contrast, **convergent thinking**, or conventional thinking, works toward a single solution to a problem, and is not related to creativity.

The investment theory of creativity proposes that creative people "buy low" by pursuing promising but unpopular ideas and "sell high" by developing the ideas until they are widely accepted. It also proposes that creativity depends on six specific resources: intellectual ability, knowledge, thinking style, personality, motivation, and environment.

IV. Language

Human language is a creative form of communication consisting of symbols put together according to a set of rules. The three building blocks of language are **phonemes**, **morphemes**, and **grammar**. Phonemes are the basic speech sounds; they are combined to form morphemes, the smallest meaningful units of language. Phonemes, morphemes, words, and phrases are put together by rules of grammar (**syntax** and **semantics**). Syntax refers to the grammatical rules for ordering words in sentences; semantics refers to meaning in language.

Noam Chomsky believes that humans are born with an ability to put words together in a meaningful way. Also, according to Chomsky, every sentence has both a *surface structure* (the words themselves) and a *deep structure* (the actual meaning).

According to Whorf's *linguistic relativity hypothesis*, language shapes thought. Generally, Whorf's hypothesis is not supported. However, our choice of vocabulary can influence our mental imagery and social perceptions.

The most successful animal language studies have been done with apes using American Sign Language. Dolphins have also been taught to comprehend sentences that vary in syntax and meaning. Some psychologists believe that animals can truly learn human language, but others suggest that the animals are merely responding to rewards.

V. The Nature of Intelligence and Test Construction

Today, **intelligence** is commonly defined as the general capacity to profit from experience, to acquire knowledge, and adapt to changes in the environment. However, there are several theorists who have defined it differently: Spearman viewed intelligence as "g," a general intelligence; Thurstone saw it as seven distinct mental abilities; Guilford believed it was composed of 120 or more separate abilities; and Cattell viewed it as two types of "g," which he called **fluid intelligence** and **crystallized intelligence.**

In addition to these early theorists, Gardner's theory of multiple intelligences identifies eight types of intelligence. He believes that both teaching and assessing should take into account people's learning styles and cognitive strengths. Sternberg's triarchic theory of successful intelligence emphasizes the thinking process rather than the end product (the answer). The Triarchic Theory of Successful Intelligence identifies three aspects of intelligence: analytical, creative, and practical intelligences.

For any test to be useful, it must be standardized, reliable, and valid. **Standardization** refers to (a) giving a test to a large number of people in order to determine norms and (b) using identical procedures in administering a test so that everyone takes the test under exactly the same testing conditions. **Reliability** refers to the stability of test scores over time. **Validity** refers to how well the test measures what it is intended to measure.

VI. Assessing Intelligence/ Explaining Differences in Intelligence

Intelligence quotient (IQ) tests do not, and are not intended to, measure overall intelligence. Rather, they are designed to measure verbal and quantitative abilities needed for school success. Several individual IQ tests are in common use. The Stanford-Binet measures primarily verbal abilities of children ages 3 to 16. The Wechsler tests, consisting of three separate tests for three distinct age levels, measure both verbal and nonverbal abilities. People with IQs of 70 and below are identified as mentally retarded, whereas people with IQs of 140 and above are identified as gifted.

Most neuroscientists believe that all mental activity results from neural activity in the brain. Their research on intelligence has focused on three major questions: 1) Does a bigger brain mean greater intelligence? (Answer: "not necessarily.") 2) Is a faster brain more intelligent? (Answer: " a qualified yes." And 3) Does a smart brain work harder? (Answer: "No, the smarter brain is more efficient.")

According to the Minnesota Study of Twins Reared Apart, heredity and environment appear to be important, inseparable factors in intellectual development. Heredity equips each of us with innate capacities, but environment significantly influences whether an individual will reach full potential.

SELF-TESTS (<u>R</u>eview & w<u>R</u>ite)

Completing the following SELF-TESTS will provide immediate feedback on how well you have mastered the material. In the *crossword puzzle* and *fill-in exercises*, write the appropriate word or words in the blank spaces. The *matching exercise* requires you to match the terms in one column to their correct definitions in the other. For the *multiple-choice questions* in Practice Tests I and II, circle or underline the correct answer. When you are unsure of any answer, be sure to highlight or specially mark the item and then go back to the text for further review. Correct answers are provided at the end of this study guide chapter.

Crossword Puzzle for Chapter 8

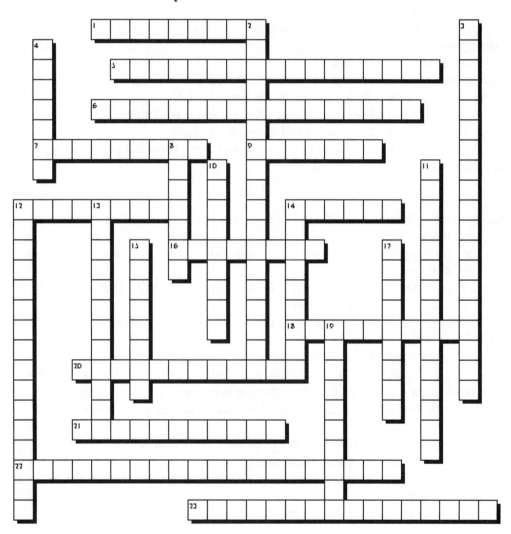

ACROSS

1 Problem-solving strategies, or "rules of thumb," used as shortcuts to complex solutions, which generally, but not always, lead to a solution.

5 Thinking that produces many alternatives or ideas; a major element of creativity (e.g., finding as many uses as possible for a paper clip).

6 The capacity for acquiring new knowledge and solving new problems that is at least partially determined by biological and genetic factors.

7 A typical, highly representative example that serves as a model on which other examples are based or judged (e.g., baseball is a prototype of the concept of sports.)

9 The rules of a language that specify how phonemes, morphemes, words, and phrases should be combined to meaningfully express thoughts.

12 The mental activities involved in acquiring, storing, retrieving, and using knowledge.

14 The grammatical rules that specify in what order the words and phrases should be arranged in a sentence in order to convey meaning.

16 The smallest meaningful unit of language, formed from a combination of phonemes.

18 A period of time during which active searching for a problem's solution is set aside; this is sometimes necessary for a successful solution of the problem.

20 The mind's representation of a sensory experience, including visual, auditory, gustatory, motor, olfactory, or tactile elements (e.g., visualizing a train and hearing its whistle).

21 A measure of the consistency and stability of test scores when the test is readministered.

22 A score on a test that is intended to measure verbal and quantitative abilities.

23 A psychological predicament in which a person experiences doubt about his or her performance, due to negative stereotypes about his or her group's abilities.

DOWN

2 Conventional thinking; thinking directed toward a single correct answer (e.g., standard academic tests generally require convergent thinking).

3 A barrier to problem solving that occurs when people are unable to recognize novel uses for an object because they are so familiar with its common use.

4 A mental category that groups objects, events, activities, or ideas that share similar characteristics.

8 The most basic unit of speech; an individual speech sound.

10 A problem-solving strategy that guarantees a solution if correctly applied; it involves trying out all possible solutions to a problem in a systematic manner.

11 The process of establishing the norms and uniform procedures for giving and scoring a test.

12 The tendency to seek out and pay attention to information that confirms existing positions or beliefs, while at the same time ignoring or not considering contradictory information.

13 The general capacity to profit from experience, to acquire knowledge, and adapt to changes in the environment.

14 Meaning or the study of meaning derived from morphemes, words, and sentences.

15 The ability of a test to measure what it was designed to measure.

17 A mental barrier to problem solving that occurs when people apply only methods that have worked in the past rather than trying innovative ones.

19 The generation of ideas that are original, novel, and useful.

FILL-IN EXERCISES

1. The mental activities involved in acquiring, storing, retrieving, and using knowledge is known as _____ (p. 278).

2. For most Westerners baseball is a _____ of the concept of sports (p. 280).

3. To solve a problem there are three major stages: _____, _____, and _____ (pp. 283-284).

4. The three most common barriers to effective problem solving are _____, _____, _____ (p. 284).

5. Creativity is associated with _____ thinking, which is the opposite of _____ thinking (p. 288).

6. The smallest meaningful unit of language is called a _____ (p. 291).

7. The general capacity to profit from experience, to acquire knowledge, and adapt to changes in the environment _____ (p. 296).

8. As we age our _____ intelligence tends to increase, whereas our _____ intelligence gradually decreses (p. 297).

9. A ten-year-old child with a mental age of seven would have an IQ score of _____ (p. 303).

10. Some psychologists prefer the Wechsler to the Stanford-Binet intelligence test because the Wechsler test gives both a _____ and a _____ score (p. 304).

MATCHING EXERCISES

Column A   Column B

a. Syntax   1. ____ Mental representation of a sensory experience.
b. Convergent Thinking 2. ____ Leads to many solutions.
c. Stanford-Binet   3. ____ Meaning in language.
d. Evaluation   4. ____ Accumulation of knowledge over the life span.
e. Mental Images   5. ____ Order of words in a sentence.
f. Crystallized Intelligence 6. ____ Speed of information processing.
g. Wechsler   7. ____ Measures both verbal and nonverbal abilities.
h. Fluid Intelligence 8. ____ Primarily measures verbal abilities.
i. Divergent Thinking 9. ____ Evaluating hypothesis for goal attainment.
j. Semantics   10. ____ Leads to a single solution.

PRACTICE TEST I

1. A mental _____ is used to categorize things that share similar characteristics.
   a. program
   b. attribute
   c. concept
   d. image

2. When building concepts, we use _____ (p. 280).
   a. artificial concepts
   b. natural concepts
   c. hierarchies
   d. all of these options

3. Preparation, production, and evaluation are the three major steps in _____.
   a. problem solving
   b. cognition
   c. thinking
   d. artificial intelligence

4. What are the two major methods used in generating hypotheses for solving problems?
   a. factor analysis and analysis of variance
   b. insight and meditation
   c. insight and deduction
   d. algorithms and heuristics

5. Which of the following is an algorithm?
   a. a fixed ratio reinforcement schedule
   b. dream analysis
   c. 3 X 10 is 10 + 10 + 10
   d. asking the smartest person in the class

6. _____ is the failure to solve a problem because of an inability to see novel uses for a familiar object.
   a. Problem-solving set
   b. Functional fixedness
   c. Heuristics
   d. Incubation

7. When politicians accept opinion polls that support them and ignore those that don't, this is an example of _____.
    a.   fluid intelligence
    b.   mental set
    c.   confirmation bias
    d.   originality, fluency, experience

8. According to J. P. Guilford, which of the following are the three abilities associated with creativity?
    a.   fluency, vocabulary, experience
    b.   fluency, flexibility, originality
    c.   flexibility, heuristics, algorithms
    d.   originality, fluency, experience

9. According to _____, creative people are willing to "buy low and sell high."
    a.   Guilford
    b.   Sternberg
    c.   investment theory
    d.   connectionism theory

10. The basic building blocks of language are called _____.
    a.   verbalization
    b.   morphemes
    c.   phonemes
    d.   deep structure

11. Benjamin Whorf proposed that _____.
    a.   language is not natural and must be learned
    b.   the structure of language can influence people's thoughts
    c.   American Sign Language is not a natural language
    d.   language development is genetically predetermined

12. Knowledge and skills gained through experience and education is known as _____ intelligence.
    a.   crystallized
    b.   fluid
    c.   general
    d.   specific

13. Howard Gardner proposed a theory of _____.
    a.   language development
    b.   fluid and crystallized intelligence
    c.   culture specificity intelligence
    d.   multiple intelligences

14. Sternberg's triarchic theory of successful intelligence includes analytic intelligence, creative
    intelligence, and _____.
    a.   fluid intelligence
    b.   past and present knowledge to ongoing problems
    c.   fluid and crystallized knowledge to problem-solving
    d.   practical intelligence

15. If a test gives you the same score each time you take the test, that test would be _____.
    a.   reliable
    b.   valid
    c.   standardized
    d.   useless

16. Validity refers to the ability of a test to _____.
    a.   return the same score on separate administrations of the test
    b.   measure what it is designed to measure
    c.   avoid discrimination between different cultural groups
    d.   give a standard deviation of scores

17. Most IQ tests are designed to _____.
    a.   measure general intelligence
    b.   measure achievement
    c.   predict academic grades
    d.   predict crystallized intelligence

18. The first IQ test to be widely used in the United States was the _____?
    a.   Stanford-Binet
    b.   SAT
    c.   ACT
    d.   AFQT

19. An IQ score of _____ is the cutoff for mental retardation.
    a.   50
    b.   70
    c.   80
    d.   none of these options, this term is no longer being used

20. Which of the following persons would be most likely to have similar IQ test scores?
    a.   identical twins raised apart
    b.   identical twins raised together
    c.   fraternal twins raised apart
    d.   brothers and sisters from the same parents

PRACTICE TEST II

1. A mental image is defined as a _____.
    a. delusion
    b. illusion
    c. hallucination
    d. mental representation of a sensory experience

2. A _____ is a model or best example of items belonging to a particular category.
    a. heuristic
    b. attribute
    c. phoneme
    d. prototype

3. As you work a problem, you move from the _____ state to the _____ state.
    a. initial; final
    b. given; goal
    c. query; response
    d. evaluation; product

4. The generation of possible solutions, or hypotheses, during the _____ stage(s) of problem solving.
    a. preparation
    b. production
    c. preparation and production
    d. evaluation

5. _____ is (are) a simple rule of thumb, or an educated guess, that generally lead to a solution.
    a. Heuristics
    b. Mnemonic devices
    c. Algorithms
    d. all of these options

6. _____ is the final stage in problem solving.
    a. Implementation
    b. Hypothesis testing
    c. Evaluation
    d. None of these options

7. With regard to problem solving, incubation is _____.
   a. the generation of possible solutions
   b. a period of time when active work on the problem is set aside
   c. an evaluation of the results of the applied solution
   d. wasted time

8. The practice of "sleeping on a problem" one has been unable to solve is not a bad idea because it allows the process of _____ to occur.
   a. incubation
   b. convergence
   c. divergence
   d. set disintegration

9. _____ is the generation of ideas that are original, novel and useful.
   a. Fluid intelligence
   b. Multiple intelligence
   c. Creativity
   d. Insight

10. Which rule of English is violated by this sentence? <u>The girl Anne is.</u>
    a. deep structure
    b. phonemic structure
    c. semantics
    d. syntax

11. Chomsky is to deep structure as Freud is to _____.
    a. surface structure
    b. manifest content
    c. consciousness
    d. latent content

12. "A screaming bouquet of flowers" is an example of the improper use of _____.
    a. pragmatics
    b. schematics
    c. semantics
    d. morphemes

13. Spearman believed that intelligence was composed of a general cognitive ability, which he called _____.
    a. "g"
    b. IQ
    c. GCA
    d. "I"

14. Cattell proposed that there were two types of intelligence: one that referred to new knowledge and one that referred to accumulated knowledge. He called these _____.
    a. knowledge and wisdom
    b. novel and fixed knowledge
    c. fluid and crystallized intelligence
    d. working and stored information

15. Linguistic, logical, spatial, musical, and interpersonal are five of Gardner's eight multiple intelligences. The other three include _____.
    a. sensory, perceptual, and memory
    b. emotional, affective, and limbic
    c. vestibular, auditory, and parietal
    d. kinesthetic, intrapersonal, and naturalistic

16. _____ is (are) the term used for developing specific procedures for administering and scoring a test, and establishing norms for the test scores in a given population.
    a. Reliability procedures
    b. Validity testing
    c. Specification
    d. Standardization

17. The first successful intelligence test was developed in_____ by _____.
    a. France; Terman
    b. France; Binet
    c. the United States; Terman
    d. the United States; Binet

18. Some psychologists prefer the Wechsler scales to the Stanford-Binet because _____.
    a. the Wechsler scales are revised periodically
    b. the Wechsler scales do not take as long to administer
    c. American children were used to standardize the Wechsler scales
    d. the Wechsler scales have both a verbal scale and a performance scale

19. Which of the following is true regarding the relationship between IQ scores and ethnicity.
    a. Members of every ethnic group have scores at all levels of the IQ scale.
    b. The bell curve applies only to Caucasian test-takers.
    c. Overall, the averages for all ethnic groups fall at the same level on the IQ scale.
    d. Americans as a group consistently average higher IQ scores than other ethnic groups.

20. _____ may significantly depress the test performance of people in some stereotyped groups.
    a. Confirmation bias
    b. The bell curve
    c. Stereotype threats
    d. Functional fixedness

ANSWERS

The following answers to active learning exercises, fill-ins, matching exercises, and practice tests 1 and 2 provide immediate feedback on your mastery of the material. Try not to simply memorize the answers. When you are unsure of your "guess" or make an error, be sure to go back to the textbook and carefully review. This will greatly improve your scores on classroom exams and quizzes.

CROSSWORD PUZZLE FOR CHAPTER 8

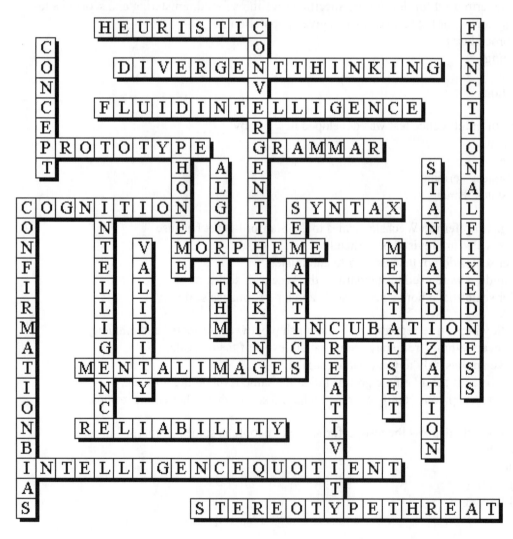

ACTIVE LEARNING EXERCISE I

Algorithm answer 2 players = 1 match, 3 players = 2 matches, 4 players = 5 matches, and so on. The number of required matches is one less than the number of players, so it will take 1024 matches to select a winner.

Working backward—a heuristic answer The thief had one apple after sharing with the third watchman. After sharing with the second watchman, he had 6 apples (1/2 x 2 = 1, X =6). After sharing with the first watchman, he had 16 (1/2 x-2 = 16, x = 36). The thief stole 36 apples.

FILL-IN EXERCISES

1. cognition; 2. prototype; 3. preparation, production, and evaluation; 4. mental sets, functional fixedness, and confirmation bias; 5. divergent, convergent; 6. morpheme; 7. intelligence; 8. crystallized, fluid; 9. 70; 10. verbal, performance.

MATCHING EXERCISES

a. 5, b. 10, c. 8, d. 9, e. 1, f. 4, g. 7, h. 6, i. 2, j. 3.

PRACTICE TEST I		PRACTICE TEST II	
1. c (p. 280)	11. b (p. 293)	1. d (p. 279)	11. d (p. 292)
2. d (p. 280)	12. a (p. 297)	2. d (p. 280)	12. c (p. 292)
3. a (pp. 283,284)	13. d (p. 299)	3. b (p. 283)	13. a (p. 297)
4. d (p. 283)	14. d (p. 300)	4. b (p. 283)	14. c (p. 297)
5. c (p. 283)	15. a (p. 301)	5. a (p. 283)	15. d (p. 299)
6. b (p. 285)	16. b (p. 301)	6. c (p. 284)	16. d (p. 301)
7. c (p. 286)	17. c (p. 302)	7. b (p. 287)	17. b (p. 303)
8. b (p. 288)	18. a (p. 303)	8. a (p. 287)	18. d (p. 304)
9. c (p. 289)	19. b (p. 305)	9. c (p. 288)	19. a (p. 310)
10.c (p. 291)	20. b (p.308)	10.d (p. 291)	20. c (p. 311)

9

Life Span Development I

OUTLINE (Survey & Question)

This outline is intended to help you *survey* the chapter. As you read through the various sections, write down any *questions* or comments that come to mind in the space provided. This is a valuable part of active learning and the SQ4R method. It not only makes your reading time more enjoyable and active, but it also increases retention and understanding of the material.

TOPIC   **NOTES**

I. STUDYING DEVELOPMENT

  A. Theoretical Issues

  B. Research Methods

       Gender and Cultural Diversity: Cultural Psychology's Guidelines for Developmental Research

II. PHYSICAL DEVELOPMENT

A. Prenatal Development and Early Childhood

B. Adolescence and Adulthood

III. LANGUAGE DEVELOPMENT

A. Stages of Language Development

B. Theories of Language Development

IV. SOCIAL-EMOTIONAL DEVELOPMENT

A. Attachment

Research Highlight: Romantic Love and Attachment

V. COGNITIVE DEVELOPMENT

A. Stages of Cognitive Development

Critical Thinking/Active Learning: Assessing Your Knowledge of Piaget

B. Assessing Piaget's Theory

C. Information Processing

Core and Expanded LEARNING OBJECTIVES (Read, Recite & wRite)

While *reading* the chapter, stop periodically and *recite* (or repeat in your own words) the answers to the following learning objectives. It will also help your retention if you *write* your answer in the space provided. (Page numbers refer to the text Psychology in Action, 6th Ed.)

Core Learning Objectives
These objectives are found at the beginning of each chapter of Psychology in Action (6th ed.).

1. How is research in developmental psychology different from research in other areas of psychology?

2. What are the major physical changes that occur throughout the life span?

3. How do children develop language?

4. How do attachment and parenting styles affect life span development?

5. How does cognition, or the way we think about the world, change during the life cycle?

Expanded Learning Objectives
These objectives offer more detail and a more intensive way to study the chapter.

Upon completion of CHAPTER 9, the student will be able to:

1. Define developmental psychology, and discuss the ongoing debates in this field regarding nature versus nurture, continuity versus stages, and stability versus change (pp. 318-319).

2. Differentiate between cross-sectional and longitudinal research, and describe the major advantages and disadvantages of each method (pp. 319-3215).

3. Discuss four ways culture has an impact on the study of human development (pp. 321-322).

4. List and describe the physical changes associated with the three stages of prenatal development (pp. 323-325).

5. Discuss paternal contributions to fetal well-being and the effects of maternal nutrition and exposure to teratogens on prenatal development (pp. 325-326).

6. Describe the major changes in brain, motor, and sensory/perceptual development during the early childhood years; explain how these changes have been measured in newborns and infants (pp. 325-329).

7. Define puberty and adolescence, and describe physical changes associated with puberty, middle age and later adulthood, including menopause and the male climacteric (pp. 329-330).

8. Differentiate between primary and secondary aging, and explain the programmed and damage theories for primary aging (pp. 331-332).

9. Describe the characteristics found in the prelinguistic and linguistic stages of language development (pp. 333-334).

10. Discuss the nativist position regarding language development and contrast it with the position of the "nurturists" (p. 334).

11. Describe the positions and theories of Bowlby, Harlow, and Ainsworth regarding attachment (pp. 335-338).

12. Summarize Baumrind's parenting styles (pp. 338-339).

13. Discuss Piaget's approach to cognitive development; describe the characteristics associated with his four stages of cognitive development and the two major criticisms of his theory (pp. 340-347).

14. Describe the development of attention and memory using the information processing model (pp. 347- 348).

KEY TERMS   (Review)

The *review* step in the SQ4R method is very important to your performance on quizzes and exams. Upon completion of this chapter, you should be able to define the following terms.

Accommodation: *process of*

Assimilation: to respond to a new situation in a familiar way

Attachment: emotional relationship between 2 people

Babbling: The vowel and consonant sounds a baby make at 4 – 6 months

Cooing: vowel sounds made by an infant

Concrete Operational Stage: 3rd piaget stage child can perform mental operational, and concret reversibility and conservation

Conservation: a given quantity can stay constat given change

Critical Period: period of sensitive to learning that shapes capacity for future development

Cross-Sectional Method: _data collection of a group of people of different age at the same point in time_

Developmental Psychology: _The branch of psychology that trys to explain predit age related behaviors_

Egocentrism: _self centered_

Embryonic Period: _the 2nd stage in pregnancy characterised by organ development_

Fetal Alcohol Syndrome (FAS): _birth defects that result from maternal alcohol abuse_

Fetal Period: _3rd stage in pregnancy characterized by weight gains and detailing of organs and systems._

Formal Operational Period: _Piaget 4th stage where a child can think Abstractly_

Germinal Period: _1st stage of pregnancy, rapid cell division_

Imprinting: _____

Language Acquisition Device (LAD): _inborn ability to analyze language and grammatical rules_

Longitudinal Method: _data collection of a single person for an extended time of age related changes_

Maturation: a process of growing in which behavior changes

Object Permanence:

Overextension: a childs tendency to define a word to generaly so some of things don't fit in meaning

Overgeneralize: a childs inproper use of grammer

Preoperational Stage: Second of Piagets stages where children can think symbolicly, uses language and is egocentric and animistic

Puberty: period of life when sex organs mature and reproduction is possible

Schemas: a way of thinking

Sensorimotor Stage: 1st stage where infant explore the world by using their senses and motor skills

Telegraphic Speech: 2-3 word sentences that contain only the simplest words for an infant

Teratogen: any chemical that can enter the placenta and disrupt development.

ACTIVE LEARNING EXERCISES (Recite)

The *recite* step in the SQ4R method requires you to be an ACTIVE learner. By completing the following exercises, you will test and improve your mastery of the chapter material, which will also improve your performance on quizzes and exams. Answers to some exercises appear at the end of this study guide chapter.

ACTIVE LEARNING EXERCISE I

Chapter 9 opens with a discussion of research issues related to developmental psychology. To test your understanding of this material, try the following exercise:

Imagine yourself as a research psychologist who wants to answer the question, "Do feelings of attachment and marital happiness increase over time?" You conduct a longitudinal study of couples married for 5 years, and then reexamine them when they've been married for 10 years. Your research finds couples married only five years rank lowest on these measures, whereas the 10-year couples report increased levels of attachment and higher marital happiness. Before submitting your paper to professional journals for possible publication, what factor(s) should you consider that might explain or contaminate your findings?

_____

_____

_____

_____

Possible answers appear at the end of this study guide chapter.

ACTIVE LEARNING EXERCISE II

Evaluating Arguments: The Pro-Life/Pro-Choice Controversy (A Cognitive Skill)

Evaluation of arguments is important to active learning and critical thinking. Rather than carelessly agreeing or disagreeing, critical thinkers analyze the relative strengths and weaknesses of each position and are especially sensitive to arguments with which they personally disagree.

They recognize a common tendency to ignore or oversimplify opposing information. After carefully evaluating all arguments, a critical thinker develops an independent position.

A contemporary, controversial issue related to material in Chapter 8 is that of abortion. Those who support the pro-life position on abortion believe that abortion is morally and religiously wrong and oppose it in almost all circumstances. On the other side, pro- choice advocates believe the right to an abortion should not be dictated by religion or government, and is a matter of choice for the pregnant woman. To help sharpen your critical thinking skills in this area, try the following:

1. Begin by listing three "points" and three "counterpoints" for each argument. When these points and counterpoints are not explicitly stated, you will need to "read between the lines" and make your best guess.

Point   Counterpoint

_____   _____

_____   _____

_____   _____

2. After clarifying the points and counterpoints, use the following analytical tools to critique each side of the issue:

   a. Differentiating between fact and opinion. The ability to recognize statements of fact versus statements of opinion is an important first step in successful analysis of arguments. After rereading the arguments regarding the pro-life/pro-choice issue, see if you can state at least two facts and two opinions on each side.

   b. Recognizing logical fallacies and faulty reasoning. Several chapters in your text, and their corresponding critical thinking/active learning exercises can help you recognize faulty logic. For example, the problem of "incorrect assumption of cause/effect relationships" is discussed in Chapter 1and the "incorrect and distorted use of statistics" is discussed in Appendix A.

   c. Exploring the implications of conclusions. Questions can help expand your analysis of arguments (e.g., "What are the conclusions drawn by proponents of each side of the issue?" "Are there other logical alternative conclusions?").

   d. Recognizing and evaluating author bias and source credibility. Also ask yourself questions (e.g., "What does the author want me to think or do?" "What qualifications does the author have for writing on this subject?" "Is the author a reliable source for information?").

Although each of these steps requires additional time and energy, the payoff is substantial. Such exercises not only refine your critical thinking skills, but also help make your decisions and opinions more educated and valuable.

CHAPTER OVERVIEW (<u>Review</u>)

The following CHAPTER OVERVIEW provides a narrative overview of the main topics covered in the chapter. Like the Visual Summary found at the end of each chapter in the text, this narrative summary provides a final opportunity to *review* chapter material.

I. Studying Development

Developmental psychology is concerned with describing, explaining, predicting, and modifying age-related behaviors across the entire life span. Three important research issues are nature or nurture, continuity or stages, and stability or change.

Researchers in developmental psychology generally do **cross-sectional** (different participants of various ages at one point in time) or **longitudinal studies** (same participants over an extended period). Each method has its own advantages and disadvantages.

Cultural psychologists suggest that developmental researchers keep the following points in mind: Culture is the most important determinant of development, human development cannot be studied outside its socio-cultural context, each culture's ethnotheories are important determinants of behavior, and culture is largely invisible to its participants.

II. Physical Development

The prenatal period of development consists of three major stages: the **germinal, embryonic,** and **fetal**. Fetal development can be affected by environmental influences. Poor prenatal nutrition is a leading cause of birth defects, and most prescription and over-the-counter drugs are potentially **teratogenic** (capable of producing birth defects). Doctors advise pregnant women to avoid all unnecessary drugs, especially nicotine and alcohol.

During the prenatal period and the first year of life, the brain and nervous system grow faster than all other parts of the body. Early motor development (crawling, standing, and walking) is largely the result of maturation. The sensory and perceptual abilities of newborns are relatively well developed.

At puberty, the adolescent becomes capable of reproduction and experiences a sharp increase in height, weight, and skeletal growth because of the pubertal growth spurt. Both men and women experience bodily changes in middle age. Many female changes are related to the hormonal effects of menopause; similar psychological changes in men are called the male climacteric.

Although many of the changes associated with physical aging (such as decreases in cardiac output and visual acuity) are the result of primary aging, others are the result of abuse, disuse, and disease---secondary aging. Physical aging may be genetically built-in from the moment of conception (programmed theory) or it may result from the body's inability to repair damage (damage theory).

III. Language Development
Children go through two stages in their acquisition of language: prelinguistic (crying, **cooing, babbling**) and linguistic (which includes single utterances, **telegraphic speech**, and the acquisition of rules of grammar).

Nativists believe that language is an inborn capacity and develops primarily from maturation. Noam Chomsky suggests that humans possess a **language acquisition device (LAD)** that needs only minimal environmental input. Nurturists emphasize the role of the environment and suggest that language development results from rewards, punishments, and imitating models

IV. Social-Emotional Development
Nativists believe that **attachment** is innate, whereas nurturists believe it is learned. The Harlow and Zimmerman experiments with monkeys raised by cloth or wire surrogate mothers found that contact comfort might be the most important factor in attachment.
Infants who fail to form attachments may suffer serious effects. When attachments are formed, they may differ in level or degree. Research on securely attached, avoidant, and anxious/ambivalent children found significant differences in behaviors that may persist into adulthood.

Parenting styles fall into three major categories: authoritarian, permissive, and authoritative. Critics suggest that a child's unique temperament, their expectations of parents, and the degree of warmth versus rejection from parents may be the three most important variables in parenting styles.

V. Cognitive Development
Jean Piaget's theories of cognitive development are based on the concept of **schemas,** mental patterns or blueprints used to interpret the world. Sometimes existing schemas can be used "as is" and information is **assimilated**; on other occasions existing schemas must be modified, which calls for **accommodation.**

According to Piaget, cognitive development occurs in an invariant sequence of four stages: **sensorimotor** (birth to 2 years), **preoperational** (from 2 to 7 years), **concrete operational** (from 7 to 11 years), and **formal operational** (from 11 on).

In the sensorimotor stage, children acquire **object permanence**. During the preoperational stage, children are better equipped to use symbols, but their thinking is limited by their lack of operations, **egocentrism**, and animism.

In the concrete operational stage, children learn to perform operations (to think about concrete things, but not actually doing them). They understand the principles of **conservation** and reversibility. During the formal operational stage, the adolescent is able to think abstractly and deal with hypothetical situations, but again, is prone to egotism.

Although Piaget has been criticized for underestimating abilities and genetic and cultural influences, he remains one of the most respected psychologists in modern times.

Psychologists who explain cognitive development in terms of the information processing model have found this model especially useful in explaining attention and memory changes across the life span. In contrast to pessimistic early studies, recent research is much more encouraging about age-related changes in information processing.

SELF-TESTS (Review & wRite)

Completing the following SELF-TESTS will provide immediate feedback on how well you have mastered the material. In the *crossword puzzle* and *fill-in exercises*, write the appropriate word or words in the blank spaces. The *matching exercise* requires you to match the terms in one column to their correct definitions in the other. For the *multiple-choice questions* in Practice Tests I and II, circle or underline the correct answer. When you are unsure of any answer, be sure to highlight or specially mark the item and then go back to the text for further review. Correct answers are provided at the end of this study guide chapter.

Crossword Puzzle for Chapter 9

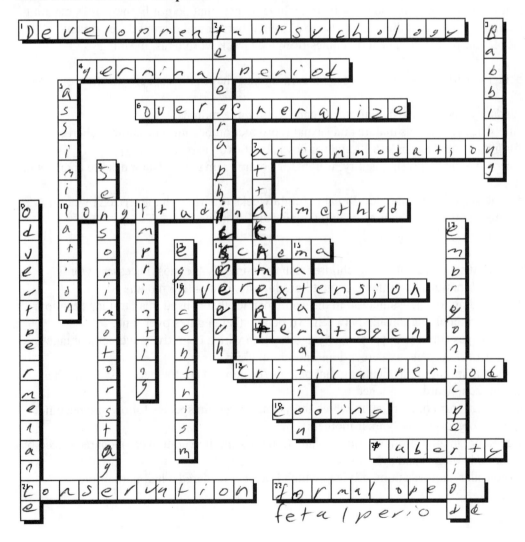

ACROSS

1 The branch of psychology that describes, explains, predicts, and sometimes aims to modify age-related behaviors from conception to death. This field emphasizes maturation, early experiences, and various stages in development.

4 The first stage of pregnancy (conception to two weeks) characterized by rapid cell division.

6 A common error in language acquisition where the child overuses the basic rules of grammar. The rules for past tense and plurals are extended to irregular forms (e.g., they may say "mans" instead of "men.")

7 The process of adjusting existing ways of thinking (reworking schemas) to encompass new information, ideas, or objects.

10 A data collection technique that measures a single individual or group of individuals over an extended period and gives information about age changes.

14 Cognitive structures or patterns consisting of a number of organized ideas that grow and differentiate with experience.

16 A child's tendency to define a word too broadly, to include objects that do not fit the word's meaning.

17 An external, environmental agent that can cross the placental barrier and disrupt development, causing minor or severe birth defects. The term comes from the Greek word teras, meaning malformation.

18 A period of special sensitivity to specific types of learning that shapes the capacity for future development.

19 Vowel-like sounds infants produce beginning around two to three months.

20 The period in life when sex organs mature and sexual reproduction becomes possible. Puberty generally begins for girls around ages 10 to 12 and for boys about two years later.

21 The ability to recognize that a given quantity, weight, or volume remains constant despite changes in shape, length, or position.

22 The third, and final, stage of prenatal development (eight weeks to birth), characterized by rapid weight gain in the fetus and the fine detailing of body organs and systems.

DOWN

2 The two- or three-word sentences of young children that contain only the most necessary words.

3 Vowel/consonant combinations that infants begin to produce at about 4 to 6 months.

5 The process of responding to a new situation in the same manner that is used in a familiar situation.

7 An active, intense, emotional relationship between two people that endures over time.

8 The first of Piaget's stages (birth to approximately age two), in which cognitive development takes place by exploring the world via sensory perceptions and motor skills.

9 A Piagetian term for an infant's understanding that objects (or people) continue to exist even when they cannot directly be seen, heard, or touched.

11 An innate or instinctual form of learning in which the young of certain species follow and become attached to large moving objects (usually their mothers).

12 The second stage of pregnancy (from uterine implantation through the eighth week), characterized by development of major body organs and systems.

13 The inability to consider another's point of view, which Piaget considered a hallmark of the preoperational stage.

13 Biological growth processes that enable orderly changes in behavior, relatively uninfluenced by the environment.

FILL-IN EXERCISES

1. The branch of psychology that describes, explains, predicts, and sometimes aims to modify age-related behaviors from conception to death is known as _____ (p. 318).
    Developmental psychology

2. The three major research issues in developmental psychology are the _____, the _____, and the _____ (pp. 318-319).

3. The *cross sectional* method examines individuals of various ages at one point in time and gives information about age differences; whereas the *longitudinal* method follows a single individual or group of individuals over an extended period of time and gives information about age changes (pp. 319-320).

4. Environmental agents that can cause birth defects are known as *teratogen* (p. 325).

5. Aging that results from disease, disuse, or abuse is known as *secondary aging* (p. 331).

6. *Cooing* includes vowel sounds, whereas *babbling* adds consonants to the vowel sounds (p. 333).

7. In studies of attachment that employed the "strange situation" procedures, infants who used the mother as a safe base for exploration were called _____ (p. 336).

8. Taking in new information that easily fits an existing schema is known as *assimilation*; whereas *accommodation* occurs when old schemas are changed to adapt to the new information (p. 340).

9. During the *Preoperational* stage of development, the child lacks operations and thinking is egocentric and animistic (p. 342).

10. Memory deficits in old age are primarily problems in _____ and _____ (p. 348).

MATCHING EXERCISES

Column A   Column B

3 a. Imaginary Audience   1. _f_ Attaching to first large moving object.
10 b. Schemas   2. _j_ Egocentrism and animism.
8 c. Overextension   3. _a_ Adolescent belief that everyone is watching them.
5 d. Telegraphic Speech   4. _g_ Adding new information to an existing schema.
9 e. Puberty   5. _d_ Omitting unnecessary, connecting words.
1 f. Imprinting   6. _h_ A child saying "I goed to the store."
4 g. Assimilation   7. _i_ Language acquisition device (LAD).
6 h. Overgeneralization   8. _c_ A child calling a "bunny" a "dog."
7 i. Noam Chomsky   9. _e_ When sex organs become capable of reproduction.
2 j. Preoperational Stage   10. _b_ Cognitive structures for organizing ideas.

PRACTICE TEST I

1. Developmental psychologists are **NOT** interested in _____.
    a.   fetal well-being
    b.   age-related differences
    c.   age-related similarities
    d.   life after death

2. Age at crawling, walking, and toilet training is primarily dependent on the _____.
    a.   educational level of the parents
    b.   specific training techniques of the child's caretakers
    c.   maturational readiness of the child
    d.   genetic influences inherited from both the mother and father

3. A _____ is the most appropriate research method for studying age-changes across the life span.
    a.   case study
    b.   natural observation
    c.   longitudinal study
    d.   cross-sectional study

4. In the area of child development, cultures have specific ideas and beliefs regarding how children should be trained. Such a set of ideas and beliefs is referred to as a(n) _____.
    a.   ethnotheory
    b.   cultural bias
    c.   ethnobiography
    d.   cohort effect

5. Conception occurs when a(n) _____.
    a.   fertilized egg implants in the uterine lining
    b.   ovum undergoes its first cell division
    c.   ejaculation occurs
    d.   sperm cell unites with an ovum

6. Rapid cell division from conception to two weeks is known as the _____ period.
    a.   fetal
    b.   germinal
    c.   embryonic
    d.   conceptual

7. Dennis was born with wide-set eyes, a thin upper lip, limb abnormalities, motor and growth
    retardation, and low intelligence. These characteristics are most often related to _____.
    a.   paternal alcoholism
    b.   fetal alcohol syndrome (FAS)
    c.   Down's syndrome
    d.   retardive dyskinesia (RD)

8. At birth, an infant cannot _____.
    a.   see as well as an adult
    b.   recognize the taste or odor of its own mother's milk
    c.   feel pain
    d.   turn its head without help

9. The period of life when an individual first becomes capable of reproduction is known as
    _____.
    a.   the growth spurt
    b.   adolescence
    c.   puberty
    d.   the latency period

10. Menarche is the _____.
    a.   adolescent growth spurt
    b.   end of a woman's reproductive capacity
    c.   end of a man's reproductive capacity
    d.   onset of the menstrual cycle

11. Menopause is _____.
    a.   another name for the onset of the menstrual cycle
    b.   a time of wild mood swings for all women due to fluctuations in hormones
    c.   the cessation of the menstrual cycle
    d.   the result of increases in estrogen levels

12. The physical and psychological changes associated with middle age in men are called the
    _____.
    a.   testosterone crisis
    b.   reproductive decline
    c.   male climacteric
    d.   male refractory period

13. "I goed to the zoo" and "I hurt my foots" are examples of _____.
    a.   prelinguistic verbalizations
    b.   overexposure to adult "baby talk"
    c.   overgeneralization
    d.   Noam Chomsky's theory of language acquisition

14. According to the language theory of Noam Chomsky, _____.
    a.   children are born "prewired" to learn language
    b.   language development is primarily a result of rewards and modeling of adult speech
    c.   overgeneralizations of speech result from faulty development of the language
         acquisition device
    d.   language development is primarily cultural and not biological

15. Harlow's research with infant monkeys and artificial surrogate mothers indicates that _____.
    a.   the most important factor in infant development is a loving environment
    b.   attachment is not essential to normal development
    c.   there is no significant difference in the choice of wire or terrycloth mothers
    d.   the most important variable in attachment may be contact comfort

16. According to Piaget, an infant acquires _____ when he or she understands that people and
    things continue to exist even when they cannot directly be seen, heard, or touched.
    a.   conservation
    b.   reversibility
    c.   egocentrism
    d.   object permanence

17. Piaget used the term egocentrism to describe the fact that _____.
    a.   all children are naturally selfish during the first few years of life
    b.   children view the world from one perspective (their own)
    c.   the child's limited logic impedes his or her understanding of the need to share
    d.   children are unable to conserve.

18. During Piaget's fourth stage of cognitive development, adolescents first become capable of
_____.
   a.   egocentrism
   b.   dealing effectively with transformations
   c.   using language and other symbols
   d.   hypothetical thinking

19. Roberta refuses to go to school today because she's afraid everyone will notice that she is
having a really bad hair day. Her fears most clearly illustrate _____.
   a.   formal operational thinking
   b.   peer pressure
   c.   adolescent egocentrism
   d.   adolescent ethnocentrism

20. The _____ approach to cognitive development draws an analogy between the mind and the
computer.
   a.   human-machine system
   b.   information processing
   c.   mind-matter
   d.   bio-mechanical

PRACTICE TEST II

1.   Maturation refers to development that occurs as a result of _____.
   a.   genetically predetermined signals
   b.   instinctive processes
   c.   homeostatic imbalances
   d.   an interaction between biology and environment

2.   Today, the interactionist approach to development is supported by _____.
   a.   more nativists than empiricists
   b.   more empiricists than nativists
   c.   most psychologists
   d.   more psychiatrists than psychologists

3.   The _____ method of research may confuse genuine age differences with cohort effects, differences
that result from specific histories of the age group studied.
   a.   cross-cultural
   b.   longitudinal
   c.   cross-sectional
   d.   all of these options

4. According to Greenfield, the best predictor of future behavior in a child is _____.
    a.   the parenting style of his or her parents
    b.   his or her intellectual capacity
    c.   the sociocultural context for that child
    d.   his or her health status

5. Pregnant women should avoid all drugs because they are potential _____.
    a.   carcinogens
    b.   DNA disrupters
    c.   chromosomogens
    d.   teratogens

6. A child's brain reaches its full adult weight by _____ of age.
    a.   16 months
    b.   5 years
    c.   10 years
    d.   16 years

7. The psychological development that occurs between childhood and adulthood is called _____.
    a.   adolescence
    b.   puberty
    c.   the phallic stage
    d.   the identity stage

8. The clearest and most dramatic physical sign of puberty is the _____.
    a.   menarche
    b.   spermarche
    c.   growth spurt
    d.   none of these options

9. In the programmed theory of aging, it is believed that cells are genetically programmed to no longer divide once they reach the _____ limit.
    a.   outer
    b.   Hayword
    c.   Harlow
    d.   Hayflick

10. Which of the following is correctly matched?
    a.   babbling = "oooo" and "aaaah"
    b.   cooing = "baa" and "daa-daa"
    c.   telegraphic speech = "No sit there"
    d.   overextension = "I hurted myself"

11. By age _____ most children are capable of communicating adequately in their native language.
    a.   2
    b.   5
    c.   7
    d.   8

12. Chomsky's language acquisition device (LAD) is _____.
    a.   a child's inborn ability to learn language
    b.   a device given to deaf children to help them learn language despite their hearing loss
    c.   learned in infancy when parents use "baby talk" to stimulate its development
    d.   the ability of some children to acquire many languages easily

13. Which of the following is incorrectly matched?
    a.   Lorenz = newly hatched geese will follow the first large moving object they see (imprinting)
    b.   Bowlby = babies elicit caretaker nurturing
    c.   Harlow = contact comfort is more important than care taking in attachment
    d.   all of these options are correctly matched

14. Ainsworth's research suggests that a _____ infant is more likely to be temperamental and anxious that others will not return their affecion.
    a.   securely attached
    b.   avoidant
    c.   anxious/ambivalent
    d.   demanding

15. Schemas are cognitive structures that contain organized ideas about the world and _____.
    a.   expand or differentiate with experience
    b.   may assimilate new information
    c.   may accommodate new information
    d.   all of these options

16. According to Piaget, accommodation means that a schema has _____.
    a.   been changed to fit new information
    b.   been used to understand new information
    c.   reversed itself
    d.   conserved itself

17. Piaget's four stages of cognitive development start with the sensorimotor and preoperational stages, and end with the _____ stages.
    a.   assimilation and accommodation
    b.   operation and abstraction
    c.   concrete and formal operational
    d.   concept testing and deductive reasoning

18. Egocentrism is present in which of Piaget's stages of cognitive development?
    a.   preoperational and formal operational
    b.   preoperational only
    c.   sensorimotor and preoperational
    d.   sensorimotor only

19. A child who believes the sun follows him or her around and that trees have feelings are probably in the _____ stage of development.
    a.   sensorimotor
    b.   animistic
    c.   preoperational
    d.   concrete operational

20. The child who believes that everyone is watching him or her and that no one else can understand and sympathize with him or her is probably in the beginning stages of the _____ stage of development.
    a.   "terrible twos"
    b.   "terrible teens"
    c.   concrete operational
    d.   formal operational

ANSWERS

The following answers to active learning exercises, fill-ins, matching exercises, and practice tests 1 and 2 provide immediate feedback on your mastery of the material. Try not to simply memorize the answers. When you are unsure of your "guess" or make an error, be sure to go back to the textbook and carefully review. This will greatly improve your scores on classroom exams and quizzes.

ACTIVE LEARNING EXERCISE I

Attachment and Marital Happiness Research A major problem with longitudinal research is that people often drop out, and in this study the couples who were most likely to drop out were those who got divorced. After divorcing, they would not be available for your research after ten years of marriage, and they also were more likely to have been unhappy and less attached at the first measurement five years before. To account for this, you could omit those couples divorced after 10 years from the analysis of those married for 5 years. This would help control for the drop out and divorce factor.

FILL-IN EXERCISES

1. developmental psychology; 2. nature or nurture, continuity or stages, stability or change; 3. cross-sectional, longitudinal; 4. teratogens; 5. secondary; 6. cooing, babbling; 7. securely attached; 8. assimilation, accommodation; 9. preoperational; 10. encoding, retrieval.

MATCHING EXERCISES

a. 3; b. 10; c. 8; d. 5; e. 9; f. 1; g. 4; h. 6; i. 7; j. 2.

CROSSWORD PUZZLE FOR CHAPTER 9

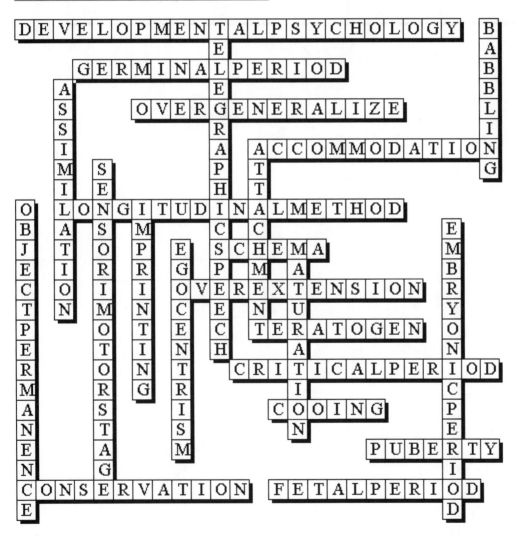

Study and Review Guide

PRACTICE TEST I		PRACTICE TEST II	
1. d (p. 318)	11. c (p. 330)	1. a (p. 318)	11. b (p. 334)
2. c (p. 318)	12. c (p. 330)	2. c (p. 319)	12. a (p. 334)
3. c (p. 319)	13. c (p. 333)	3. c (p. 320)	13. d (p. 335)
4. a (p. 321)	14. a (p. 334)	4. c (p. 321)	14. c (p. 337)
5. d (p. 323)	15. d (p. 335)	5. d (p. 325)	15. d (p. 340)
6. b (p. 324)	16. d (p. 341)	6. d (p. 327)	16. a (p. 340)
7. b (p. 325)	17. b (p. 342)	7. a (p. 329)	17. c (p. 341)
8. a (p. 327)	18. d (p. 343)	8. c (p. 330)	18. a (pp. 342, 343)
9. c (p. 329)	19. c (p. 343)	9. b (p. 332)	19. c (p. 342)
10.d (p. 330)	20. b (p.347)	10.c (p. 333)	20. d (p. 345)

10 Life Span Development II

OUTLINE (Survey & Question)

This outline is intended to help you *survey* the chapter. As you read through the various sections, write down any *questions* or comments that come to mind in the space provided. This is a valuable part of active learning and the SQ4R method. It not only makes your reading time more enjoyable and active, but it also increases retention and understanding of the material.

TOPIC	NOTES

I. MORAL DEVELOPMENT

    A. Kohlberg's Research

       Gender and Cultural Diversity: Insights Into Morality

II. PERSONALITY DEVELOPMENT OVER THE LIFE SPAN

    A. Thomas and Chess' Temperament Theory

    B. Erikson's Psychosocial Theory

Critical Thinking/Active Learning: Applying Erikson's Stages to Your Own Life

III. ADDITIONAL INFLUENCES ON DEVELOPMENT

A. Families

Research Highlight: Children Who Survive Despite the Odds

B. Occupational Choices

Gender and Cultural Diversity: Cultural Differences in Ageism

IV. BEREAVEMENT AND GRIEF

A. Grief

B. Attitudes Toward Death and Dying

C. The Death Experience

Core and Expanded LEARNING OBJECTIVES (Read, Recite & wRite)

While *reading* the chapter, stop periodically and *recite* (or repeat in your own words) the answers to the following learning objectives. It will also help your retention if you *write* your answer in the space provided. (Page numbers refer to the text Psychology in Action, 6th Ed.)

Core Learning Objectives
These objectives are found at the beginning of each chapter of Psychology in Action (6th ed.).

1. How does morality change over the life span?

2. How does personality change from infancy to old age?

3. How do families and career choices influence development?

4. Are there predictable stages for grief and dying?

Expanded Learning Objectives
These objectives offer more detail and a more intensive way to study the chapter.

Upon completion of CHAPTER 10, the student will be able to:

1. List and describe Kohlberg's three levels of moral development, and provide an example of typical reasoning at each stage (pp. 354-357).

2. Describe the relationship between moral reasoning and moral behavior, and discuss the major criticisms of Kohlberg's theory related to political, cultural, and gender biases (pp. 356-357).

3. Describe Thomas and Chess's temperament theory of personality development, including each of their three temperamental styles and the influence of the goodness-of-fit between styles and the environment (pp. 358-359).

4. Describe Erikson's eight stages of psychosocial development, and discuss both the criticisms and contributions of his theory (pp. 359-362).

5. Discuss the three myths of development: adolescent storm and stress, mid-life crisis, and empty nest syndrome (pp. 362-363).

6. Discuss the causes of and treatment for family violence, the consequences and future prevention of teen pregnancy, and the impact of divorce on social and emotional development. List nine predictors for a successful marriage (pp. 364-367).

7. Discuss research regarding factors that can increase resilience in children who are developing in "high-risk" environments (pp. 367-368).

8. Describe how occupational choices affect development, and discuss the activity and disengagement theories of aging (pp. 368-369).

9. Define ageism, and discuss its effects. Describe cultural, gender, and ethnic differences in the status and treatment of the elderly (pp. 369-370).

10. Define grief, and describe the four stages of grieving. List three strategies for coping with grief (pp. 371-372).

11. Describe cultural and age variations in attitudes toward death and dying (pp. 372-373).

12. Describe Kubler-Ross's five-stage theory of death and dying, and discuss both the criticisms and contributions of her theory (pp. 373-374).

KEY TERMS (Review)

The *review* step in the SQ4R method is very important to your performance on quizzes and exams. Upon completion of this chapter, you should be able to define the following terms.

Activity Theory: _____

_____

Ageism: *prejudice against people based on age*

_____

Care Perspective: *Gilligans approach to moral reasoning of that interpersonal w/ others*

Conventional Level: *Kohlbergs 2nd level of moral development Judgments based on rules & value of society*

Disengagement Theory: *individuals and society pull away from each other to prepare for death*

Identity Crisis: *when one questions who they are*

_____

Justice Perspective: *Gilligans approach to moral reasoning that in individuals rights*

Postconventional Level: *Kohlbergs highest level of moral development personal standard of right & wrong*

Preconventional Level: *Kohlbergs 1st level of moral development descions basedon fear & desire*

Psychosocial Stages: *eriksons 8 stages of development adult personality reflects how the distinct crises is resolved*

Resilience: _____

_____

Temperament: _____

_____

Thanatology: *study of death and dying*

_____

ACTIVE LEARNING EXERCISES (<u>R</u>ecite)

The *recite* step in the SQ4R method requires you to be an ACTIVE learner. By completing the following exercises, you will test and improve your mastery of the chapter material, which will also improve your performance on quizzes and exams. Answers to some exercises appear at the end of this study guide chapter.

ACTIVE LEARNING EXERCISE I

One of the best ways for young and middle-aged people to reduce ageism is through increased exposure to the elderly. Try visiting a local senior center, retirement home, and convalescent hospital. Each of these facilities houses people with varying ages, abilities, and levels of activity. When you talk with the people in these facilities, try to really get to know them. Ask important questions about their political, spiritual, or personal beliefs about child rearing, divorce, or the value of a college education. Ask how they think things have changed since they were in their 20s, 30s, and so on. Once you've established a level of comfort, try asking about controversial topics like gun control, abortion, premarital sex, and so on. (You might also try asking similar questions with elderly relatives. Younger people sometimes complain about "having to visit" their relatives, but interest might increase if they asked interesting questions.)

Our stereotypes about aging and the elderly are generally based on lack of information. As you get to know a larger group of older people, you'll realize your previous stereotypes no longer fit. Just as African Americans or Latinos cannot be categorized under a few stereotypical traits or characteristics, the same is true for the elderly.

ACTIVE LEARNING EXERCISE II

<u>Thinking</u> <u>Independently:</u> <u>Making</u> <u>Peace</u> <u>with</u> <u>Your</u> <u>Parents</u>
  (An Affective Skill)

One mark of a critical thinker is the ability to think independently, which requires insight into one's own beliefs. When we feel at peace with people, we can consider their beliefs in an untroubled way and espouse them as our own or reject them freely. The following exercise will help clarify how psychologically independent you are from your parents. Many people consider independence to be merely financial. However, psychological independence is an equally significant mark of adult development. Hopefully, exploring your relationship with your parents will help you become independent of them, as a critical thinker and as a person. In that regard, take a few moments to jot down your answers to the following:

1.   Are you truly free of regrets and resentments from your childhood?

2.   Are you relaxed and do you enjoy spending time with your parents? Or do you resent "having" to visit or interact with them?

3.   Are you able to accept your parents, forgive them their mistakes, and give up trying to change them?

4.   Do you feel loved and accepted by your parents?

5.   Do you still compare yourself and compete with one of your brothers or sisters?

6.   Are you still waiting to escape from your parents' rules, influence, or habits to become your own person?

7. Are you glad you had the parents you did?

8. If your parents are divorced, have you resolved your mixed feelings about this situation?

9. Do you have fears of being trapped or disappointed by a committed love relationship or marriage in your own life?

10. Have you completed your resentments and regrets toward your parent who may no longer be living? Can you accept the reality and inevitability of your own death?

Your answers to each of these questions are an important first step in actually recognizing and eventually working through these long-standing problems. These questions were adapted from the paperback book Making Peace With Your Parents by Harold H. Bloomfield, M.D. and Leonard Felder, Ph.D. (New York: Ballantine Books, 1983). If you desire further information on this topic, this book is a wonderful resource. If problems with your parents are longstanding and too overwhelming, you may want help from professional psychologists or counselors. Your psychology instructor may be willing to recommend someone in your area.

CHAPTER OVERVIEW (Review)

The following CHAPTER OVERVIEW provides a narrative overview of the main topics covered in the chapter. Like the Visual Summary found at the end of each chapter in the text, this narrative summary provides a final opportunity to *review* chapter material.

I. Moral Development

According to Kohlberg, morality progresses through three levels--each level consists of two stages. At the **preconventional level**, morality is self-centered. What is right is what one can get away with (Stage 1) or what is personally satisfying (Stage 2). **Conventional level** morality is based on a need for approval (Stage 3) and obedience to laws because they maintain the social order (Stage 4). **Postconventional** moral reasoning comes from adhering to the social contract (Stage 5), and the individual's own principles and universal values (Stage 6).

Kohlberg's theory has been criticized for being politically, culturally, and gender biased. Carol Gilligan has suggested women tend to take a **care perspective** in their moral reasoning, whereas men favor a **justice perspective**. Research shows that in real life situations, not hypothetical situations, both sexes typically use both the justice and care orientations.

II. Personality Development over the Life Span

Stella Thomas and Alexander Chess emphasize the genetic component of certain traits (such as sociability) and the fact that babies often exhibit differences in **temperament** shortly after birth.

Erik Erikson expanded on Freud's ideas to develop eight **psychosocial stages** that cover the entire life span. The four stages that occur during childhood are trust versus mistrust, autonomy versus shame and doubt, initiative versus guilt, and industry versus inferiority. Erikson believes the major psychosocial crisis of adolescence is the search for identity versus role confusion. During young adulthood, the individual's task is to establish intimacy over isolation, and during middle adulthood, the person must deal with generativity versus stagnation. At the end of life, the older adult must establish ego integrity, or face overwhelming despair at the realization of lost *opportunities*.

Research shows that adolescent storm and stress, the midlife crisis, and the empty nest syndrome may be exaggerated accounts of a few people's experiences and not that of most people.

III. Additional Influences on Personality Development

Resilient children who survive an abusive and stress-filled childhood usually have good intellectual functioning, a relationship with a caring adult, and the ability to regulate their attention, emotions, and behavior.

The kind of work you do and the occupational choices you make can play a critical role in your life. Before making a career decision, it is wise to research possible alternatives and take interest inventories. One theory of successful aging, **activity theory**, says people should remain active and involved throughout the entire life span. The other major theory, **disengagement theory**, says the elderly naturally and gracefully withdraw from life because they welcome the relief from roles they can no longer fulfill. **Ageism** is an important stressor for the elderly, but there are some cultures where aging is revered.

IV. Bereavement and Death

Attitudes about death and dying vary greatly across cultures and among age groups. While adults understand the permanence, universality, and nonfunctionality of death, children often do not master these concepts until around age 7.

Grief is a natural and painful reaction to a loss. For most people, grief consists of four major stages—numbness, yearning, disorganization and despair, and resolution. Elisabeth Kubler-Ross' five-stage theory of dying (denial, anger, bargaining, depression, and acceptance) offers important insights into the last major crisis that we face in life. The study of death and dying, **thanatology,** has become an important topic in human development.

SELF-TESTS (Review & wRite)

Completing the following SELF-TESTS will provide immediate feedback on how well you have mastered the material. In the *crossword puzzle* and *fill-in exercises*, write the appropriate word or words in the blank spaces. The *matching exercise* requires you to match the terms in one column to their correct definitions in the other. For the *multiple-choice questions* in Practice Tests I and II, circle or underline the correct answer. When you are unsure of any answer, be sure to highlight or specially mark the item and then go back to the text for further review. Correct answers are provided at the end of this study guide chapter.

CROSSWORD PUZZLE FOR CHAPTER 10

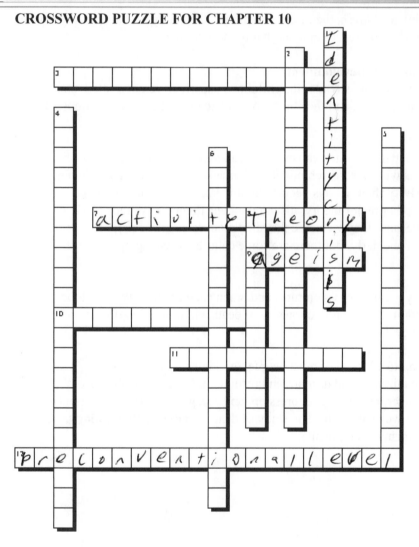

ACROSS

 3 Gilligan's terms for an approach to moral reasoning that emphasizes interpersonal responsibility and interconnectedness with others.

 7 A theory of aging that suggests successful adjustment is fostered by a full and active commitment to life.

 9 Prejudice against people based on their age.

 10 A basic, inborn disposition that appears shortly after birth and characterizes an individual's style of approaching people and situations.

 11 A term referring to a child's good developmental outcome, sustained competence under stress, and recovery from trauma despite high-risk status.

 12 Kohlberg's first level of moral development, characterized by moral judgments based on fear of punishment or desire for pleasure.

DOWN

 1 According to Erikson, a period of inner conflict during which an individual examines his or her life and values and makes decisions about life roles.

 2 A theory of aging suggesting that both the individual and society gradually and naturally pull away from each other in preparation for death.

 4 Kohlberg's highest level of moral development, which occurs when individuals develop personal standards for right and wrong.

 5 Kohlberg's second level of moral development, where moral judgments are based on compliance with the rules and values of society.

 6 Gilligan's term for an approach to moral reasoning that emphasizes individual rights and views people as differentiated and standing alone.

 8 The study of death and dying. The term comes from thanatos, the Greek name for a mythical personification of death, and was borrowed by Freud to represent the death instinct.

FILL-IN EXERCISES

1. According to Kohlberg, individuals at the _____ level make moral judgments based on fear of punishment or desire for pleasure (p. 354),

2. The _____ level of moral development occurs when moral judgments are based on compliance with the rules and values of society (p. 356).

3. According to Gilligan, the _____ perspective emphasizes individual rights and views people as differentiated and standing alone, while the _____ perspective focuses on interpersonal responsibility and interconnectedness with others (p. 357).

4. Erikson's _____ suggest individuals pass through eight developmental stages and that adult personality reflects how the distinct challenges or crises at each stage are resolved (p. 359).

5. According to Erikson, the dominant crisis of _____ is the establishment of an identity (p. 361).

6. The myth of _____ suggests emotional turmoil and rebellion are characteristic of all adolescents (p. 362)

7. Research shows that many _____ are due to poverty and the resulting perception that life options and choices are limited (p. 366).

8. Some children survive and prosper even under the harshest environmental circumstances. They are known as _____ children (p. 367).

9. The _____ theory of aging suggests remaining active and involved as long as possible; whereas the _____ theory says older people should naturally and gracefully withdraw from life (pp. 368, 369).

10. The four stages of grief are called _____, _____, _____ and _____ (p. 372).

MATCHING EXERCISES

Column A		Column B
3 a. Thanatology	1. _e_	Basic inborn disposition.
5 b. Ageism	2. _g_	Time of Erikson's crisis of intimacy versus isolation.
9 c. Activity Theory	3. _a_	The study of death and dying.
10 d. Grief	4. _h_	Good-child and law-and-order moral orientations.
1 e. Temperament	5. _b_	Prejudice against people based on their age.
8 f. Postconventional Level	6. _j_	Care and justice perspective on morality.
2 g. Young Adulthood	7. _i_	Myth of development.
4 h. Conventional Level	8. _f_	Social contract and universal ethics moral orientations.
7 i. Midlife Crisis	9. _c_	Suggests older people should remain active.
6 j. Gilligan	10. _d_	A natural and painful reaction to a loss.

PRACTICE TEST I

1. During Kohlberg's _____ level of moral development, right and wrong are judged on the basis of consequences.
    a.   conventional
    b.   amoral
    c.   postconventional
    d.   preconventional

2. When people have developed their own standards for right and wrong, they are judged by Kohlberg to be at the _____ level of morality.
    a.   adolescent
    b.   postconventional
    c.   nonconventional
    d.   conventional

3. Kohlberg's theory of moral development has been criticized for its _____.
    a.   cultural bias toward Western ideas of morality
    b.   political bias in favor of conservatives
    c.   sexual bias in favor of women
    d.   ethnic bias against Anglo-Saxons

4. Gilligan's _____ perspective suggests that moral reasoning is based on the values of individual rights and independence.
    a.   justice
    b.   care
    c.   differentiated
    d.   independent

5. _____ is the basic, inborn dispositional quality that appears shortly after birth and characterizes an individual's style of approaching people and situations.
    a.   Personality
    b.   Trait theory
    c.   Character
    d.   Temperament

6. The positive or negative resolution of eight developmental challenges is characteristic of _____ theory.
    a.   Freud's psychosexual
    b.   Freud's psychoanalytic
    c.   Maslow's hierarchical
    d.   Erikson's psychosocial

7. According to Erikson, the challenge faced by infants in their first year is _____.
    a. weaning
    b. object permanence
    c. trust versus mistrust
    d. toilet training

8. According to Erikson, the need to develop a sense of identity is the principal task of _____.
    a. the phallic stage of psychosexual development
    b. adolescence
    c. middle adulthood
    d. the generativity versus stagnation stage of development

9. According to Erikson, the inner conflict during which an individual examines his or her life and values and makes decisions about life roles is called a(n) _____ crisis.
    a. midlife
    b. climacteric
    c. integrity
    d. identity

10. In Erikson's final stage of psychosocial development, adults may _____.
    a. regret lost opportunities
    b. become despondent
    c. review their accomplishments
    d. any of these options

11. The belief that most parents experience depression and pain when the last child leaves home is supported by _____.
    a. natural observation across cultures
    b. a few individual cases
    c. controlled experiments
    d. random, large-scale surveys

12. Research on the midlife crisis suggests that it is _____.
    a. typical of most middle-aged males
    b. typical of most middle-aged females
    c. rare in males and females
    d. more likely to occur after middle age

13. Marital conflict, substance abuse, mental disorders, and economic stress are all related to
_____.
   a.   adolescent storm and strife
   b.   family violence
   c.   midlife crisis
   d.   all of these options

14. This is **NOT** a problem related to adolescent pregnancy.
   a.   reduced educational achievement
   b.   fewer children over the life span
   c.   more risks to maternal health
   d.   more risks to the child's health

15. The most common reason for dropping out of high school is _____.
   a.   drug abuse
   b.   family violence
   c.   financial problems
   d.   pregnancy

16 There has been a _____ in the divorce rate since the 1970s in the United States.
   a.   dramatic rise
   b.   modest rise
   c.   dramatic decline
   d.   modest decline

17. _____ children recover from trauma, display competence under stress, and prosper despite a
high-risk status.
   a.   Resilient
   b.   Self-actualized
   c.   Autonomous
   d.   Attached

18. The _____ theory of aging says that one should remain active and involved in
fulfilling activities as long as possible.
   a.   engagement
   b.   activity
   c.   involvement
   d.   life-enhancement

19. Helen has always looked forward to retirement as a time to "sit back and do nothing." She is therefore very surprised at recommendations to the contrary from her company's pre-retirement seminars. Her company apparently accepts the _____ theory of aging, while Helen apparently supports the _____ theory.
    a.   vitality; relaxation
    b.   involvement; retreat
    c.   activity; disengagement
    d.   incentive; drive-reduction

20. In the United States, _____ is one of the greater stresses experienced by the elderly.
    a.   physical decline
    b.   psychological decline
    c.   fear of death
    d.   ageism

PRACTICE TEST II

1.   Moral judgment is self-centered and based on obtaining rewards and avoiding punishment in this stage of moral development.
    a.   preoperational
    b.   preconventional
    c.   conventional
    d.   postoperational

2.   Once an individual accepts, internalizes, and applies the rules of society in making moral decisions, he or she is in the _____ stage.
    a.   formal conventional
    b.   conventional
    c.   informal operational
    d.   social operational

3.   Personal standards of right and wrong are found in Kohlberg's _____ level of moral development.
    a.   lowest
    b.   highest
    c.   middle
    d.   all of these options

4. Jeff is a private in a combat unit during a war. His commanding officer orders him to shoot two young adolescents whom they have taken prisoner. Jeff is LEAST likely to follow the orders if he is in Kohlberg's _____ stage.
   a. lowest
   b. highest
   c. preconventional
   d. postconventional

5. Thomas and Chess suggested that most children were born with one of these three temperament styles.
   a. easy, difficult, slow-to-warm-up
   b. attached, unattached, avoidant
   c. imprinted, attached, anxious
   d. introverted, extroverted, averted

6. You have a child who is a month old and seems to be moody and overreactive to most situations. According to Thomas and Chess's temperament theory, your child might be classified as a(n) _____ child.
   a. extroverted
   b. difficult
   c. imprinted
   d. difficult

7. Trust, initiative, identity, and generativity are the odd-numbered stages in Erikson's psychosocial theory of development. The even-numbered stages include ____.
   a. autonomy, industry, intimacy, and ego integrity
   b. egocentrism, effort, caring, and retirement
   c. attachment, independence, genuineness, and self-actualization
   d. anal, phallic, latent, and genital

8. According to Erikson, intimacy is the result of the successful completion of this stage of development.
   a. infancy and toddlerhood
   b. junior and senior high school
   c. young adulthood
   d. middle adulthood

9. During early childhood, your child will have a growing self-awareness and need for independence. Erikson called this psychosocial crisis the need for _____.
   a. authoritarian discipline
   b. acceptance versus mistrust
   c. autonomy versus shame and doubt
   d. attachment versus autonomy

10. According to Erikson, resolution of the critical conflict of young adulthood leads to a sense of
    _____.
    a.   parental rejection
    b.   strong parental control
    c.   intimacy
    d.   none of these options

11. With regard to community resources for families, primary programs are designed to _____.
    a.   identify and prevent violence
    b.   rehabilitate violent family members
    c.   punish violent family members with jail or prison time
    d.   punish violent family members with mandatory community service

12. According to Everett and Everett, when children are involved, ex-spouses must let go of the marital
    relationship, develop new social ties, and _____.
    a.   gain joint-custody of the children
    b.   spend equal time and money on the children to avoid "favorites"
    c.   decide which parent will be the primary caretaker for the children
    d.   redefine parental roles

13. Satisfaction during retirement is strongly related to good health, community and social activities,
    and _____.
    a.   access to a willing sexual partner
    b.   socioeconomic status
    c.   being closer to 65 than 75 years of age
    d.   control over one's life

14. The _____ theory of aging suggests that it is natural and necessary for people to withdraw from their
    roles in life as they age in order to prepare themselves for death.
    a.   Kubler-Ross
    b.   secondary process
    c.   developmental
    d.   disengagement

15. What do Japan, China, Native-American, and African-American cultures/ethnic groups have in
    common? They each _____.
    a.   support the disengagement theory of aging
    b.   revere the elderly
    c.   exploit the elderly for their wisdom
    d.   have lower life-expectancies than other cultures and ethnic groups

16. Research on aging in the United States indicates that elderly men generally have more _____ than elderly women, but elderly women usually have more_____.
    a. income; sexual partners
    b. income; friends
    c. family relationships; money
    d. friends; sexual partners

17. Which of the following is NOT one of the four stages in the "normal" grieving process?
    a. nonfunctional
    b. yearning
    c. bargaining
    d. resolution

18. As adults we understand death in terms of three general concepts: permanence, universality, and _____.
    a. spirituality
    b. painfulness
    c. nonfunctionality
    d. all of these options

19. According to Elizabeth Kubler-Ross, which of the following is **NOT** one of the stages that people go through while coping with death?
    a. retrenchment
    b. denial
    c. anger
    d. bargaining

20. The acronym "DABDA" is used to remember Kubler-Ross's stages of dying. First comes denial and anger, followed by _____ and depression, then ending with acceptance.
    a. bargaining
    b. begging
    c. believing
    d. borrowing (hope)

ANSWERS

The following answers to active learning exercises, crossword puzzles, fill-ins, matching exercises, and practice tests 1 and 2 provide immediate feedback on your mastery of the material. Try not to simply memorize the answers. When you are unsure of your "guess" or make an error, be sure to go back to the textbook and carefully review. This will greatly improve your scores on classroom exams and quizzes.

CROSSWORD PUZZLE FOR CHAPTER 10

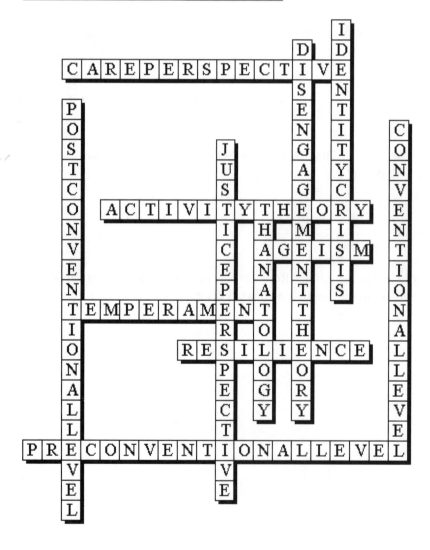

FILL-IN EXERCISES

1. preconventional; 2. conventional; 3. justice, care; 4. psychosocial stages of development; 5. adolescence; 6. adolescent storm and stress; 7. teen pregnancies; 8. resilient; 9. activity, disengagement; 10. numbness, yearning, disorganization/despair, and resolution.

MATCHING EXERCISES

a. 3; b. 5; c. 9; d. 10; e. 1; f. 8; g. 2; h. 4; i. 7; j. 6.

PRACTICE TEST I		PRACTICE TEST II	
1. d (p. 354)	11. b (p. 362)	1. b (p. 354)	11. a (p. 365)
2. b (p. 356)	12. c (p. 362)	2. b (p. 356)	12. d (p. 366)
3. a (pp. 356,357)	13. b (p. 364)	3. b (p. 356)	13. d (p. 368)
4. a (p. 357)	14. b (p. 365)	4. d (p. 356)	14. d (p. 369)
5. d (p. 358)	15. d (p. 365)	5. a (pp. 358,359)	15. b (p. 369)
6. d (p. 359)	16. d (p. 366)	6. d (p. 359)	16. b (p. 370)
7. c (p. 359)	17. a (p. 367)	7. a (p. 360)	17. c (p. 372)
8. b (p. 361)	18. b (p. 368)	8. c (p. 361)	18. c (p. 373)
9. d (p. 361)	19. c (pp. 368,369)	9. c (p. 359)	19. a (p. 374)
10.d (p. 361)	20. d (p.369)	10.c (p. 359)	20. a (p. 374)

Gender and Human Sexuality

OUTLINE (Survey & Question)

This outline is intended to help you *survey* the chapter. As you read through the various sections, write down any *questions* or comments that come to mind in the space provided. This is a valuable part of active learning and the SQ4R method. It not only makes your reading time more enjoyable and active, but it also increases retention and understanding of the material.

TOPIC	NOTES

I. SEX AND GENDER

A. Problems with Definition

B. Gender Role Development

C. Sex and Gender Differences

Research Highlight: The Art and Science of Flirting

II. THE STUDY OF HUMAN SEXUALITY

Gender and Cultural Diversity: A Cultural Look at Sexual Behaviors

III. SEXUAL BEHAVIOR

A. Sexual Arousal and Response

Research Highlight: Are There Evolutionary Advantages to *Female* Nonmonogamy?

C. Sexual Orientation

IV. SEXUAL PROBLEMS

A. Sexual Dysfunction

B. Sexually Transmitted Infections (STIs)

Critical Thinking/Active Learning: Rape Myths and Rape Prevention

Core and Expanded LEARNING OBJECTIVES (Read, Recite & wRite)

While *reading* the chapter, stop periodically and *recite* (or repeat in your own words) the answers to the following learning objectives. It will also help your retention if you *write* your answer in the space provided. (Page numbers refer to the text <u>Psychology in Action</u>, 6th Ed.)

Core Learning Objectives
These objectives are found at the beginning of each chapter of <u>Psychology in Action</u> (6th ed.).

1. How are sex and gender defined, and how do we develop our gender roles? What are the major sex

and gender differences between men and women?

2. How do scientists study a sensitive topic like sex?

3. How are men and women alike and different in sexual arousal and response? What is the latest

research on sexual orientation?

4. What factors contribute to sexual dysfunction and sexually transmitted infections?

Expanded Learning Objectives
These objectives offer more detail and a more intensive way to study the chapter.

Upon completion of CHAPTER 11, the student should be able to:

1. Differentiate between sex and gender, gender identity and sexual orientation, transsexualism and transvestitism, and homosexual and bisexual (pp. 380-382).

2. Define gender role, and describe the two major theories of gender role development: social learning theory and cognitive developmental theory (pp. 383-384).

3. Describe the major sex and gender differences between males and females; and discuss the contributions of nature and nurture on gender differences (pp. 384-386).

4. Define androgyny, and discuss research on the relationship between mental health characteristics and higher scores on masculinity or androgyny (pp. 386-387).

5. Describe the findings of naturalistic studies of human courtship rituals, including the role of the female in initiating and maintaining a flirtatious interaction (pp. 388-389).

6. Briefly discuss the contributions of Havelock Ellis, Kinsey, and Masters and Johnson to the study of human sexuality (pp. 389-391).

7. Briefly describe cultural variations in human sexual behavior, and provide an example of an ethnocentric bias related to a U.S. sexual ritual or procedure (pp. 391-393).

8. List and describe the four stages in Masters and Johnson's sexual response cycle (p. 393-394).

9. Discuss the two major perspectives that explain differences in sexual desire, motivation, and activity between men and women (p. 395).

10. Discuss genetic/biological and psychosocial explanations for homosexuality; define homophobia and state the position of the psychological community regarding homosexuality (pp. 396-397).

11. List the major forms of sexual dysfunction and state their possible organic and/or psychological causes (pp. 398-399).

12. Discuss the role of performance anxiety, the interaction of the sympathetic and parasympathetic nervous systems, and the impact of sexual scripts, hormones, nerve impulses, and emotions on sexual arousal (pp. 399-402).

13. Describe the four major principles of Masters and Johnson's approach to sex therapy. Describe three guidelines for improving sexual functioning (pp. 402-403).

14. State age- and gender-related risk factors for contracting an STI, and list the major sexually transmitted infections (STIs), describing their basic symptoms and the consequences if left untreated. (pp. 403-405).

15. Describe the progression of an HIV infection to "full-blown AIDS," and describe six suggestions for decreasing the chances of contracting HIV/AIDS and other STIs (pp. 404-407).

16. Discuss common rape myths, and state three ways to avoid stranger rape plus three ways to prevent acquaintance rape (p. 406, Appendix B).

KEY TERMS (Review)

The *review* step in the SQ4R method is very important to your performance on quizzes and exams. Upon completion of this chapter, you should be able to define the following terms.

AIDS (Acquired Immune Deficiency Syndrome): _____

_____

Androgyny: _____

_____

Double Standard: _____

_____

Excitement Phase: _____

_____

Gender: _____

_____

Gender Identity: _____

_____

Gender Role: _____

_____

HIV positive: _____

_____

Orgasm Phase: _____

_____

Performance Anxiety: _____

_____

Plateau Phase: _____

_____

Refractory Period: _____

_____

Resolution Phase: _____

_____

Sex: _____

_____

Sexual Dysfunction: _____

_____

Sexual Orientation: _____

_____

Sexual Prejudice: _____

_____

Sexual Response Cycle: _____

_____

Sexual Scripts: _____

_____

ACTIVE LEARNING EXERCISES (Recite)

The *recite* step in the SQ4R method requires you to be an ACTIVE learner. By completing the following exercises, you will test and improve your mastery of the chapter material, which will also improve your performance on quizzes and exams. Answers to some exercises appear at the end of this study guide chapter.

ACTIVE LEARNING EXERCISE I

The Role of Culture and Gender on Personal Sexual Values

One of the most important ingredients of healthy sexuality is the ability to recognize and evaluate one's own values (ideals, mores, standards, and principles that guide behavior). Are the sexual values you hold a simple reflection of the values of your family or peer group? Or are they the result of careful, deliberate choice? Have you carefully examined opposing values and compared them to your own? How do your values reflect your culture and your gender role?   Since values have such a powerful influence on thinking, you should critically evaluate them.

To help you explore your values regarding gender and human sexuality, read the four value statements on the left. Then, in the space to the right, simply check whether you agree or disagree.

                                                                    Agree   Disagree

1. Anyone who wants to prevent pregnancy should have easy
access to reliable methods of contraception; it doesn't matter
whether a person is married or single, young or old.   _____ _____

2. Gay and lesbian couples should be allowed the same legal
protections (property inheritance, shared pension plans,
shared medical benefits) as heterosexual married couples.   _____ _____

3. Abortion in the first four months of pregnancy should be a
private decision between the woman and her doctor.   _____ _____

4. Sex education belongs in the home, not in public schools.   _____ _____

Each person's sexual values come from a host of sources, some internal and others external to the
individual. The second part of this exercise gives you an opportunity to examine these sources.
Review your agree or disagree responses to the previous four statements. Indicate the degree to which
each of the sources listed in the left-hand column has influenced your beliefs by placing a check mark in
the appropriate column.

VS = Very Significant Influence
SS = Somewhat Significant Influence
NS = Not a Significant Influence

Sources	Contraception			Homosexuality			Abortion			Sex Education		
	VS	SS	NS	VS	SS	NS	VS	SS	NS	VS	SS	NS
Personal experience												
Family patterns												
Peer standards												
Historical events												
Religious views												
Research findings												

Now reexamine the checks you made for each of your four sexual values and their source of influence.
Do you notice any patterns in your check marks? Which source has been most influential in the
development of your sexual values? Do you think this source is the most appropriate and most
justifiable? Why or why not? Which source has been least influential in the development of your sexual
values? How do you explain this? Do you notice any inconsistencies in your choice of sources? In what
cases has personal experience played a more significant role than family patterns, peer standards, and so

on? To further clarify your sexual perspective and sharpen your critical thinking skills, share your responses with a close friend, dating partner, or spouse.

ACTIVE LEARNING EXERCISE II

<u>Personal</u> <u>Values</u> <u>Clarification:</u> <u>Exploring</u> <u>Your</u> <u>Own</u> <u>Gender</u> <u>Role</u> <u>Development</u> (An Affective Skill)

To help you explore your values regarding "masculinity and femininity," we offer several critical thinking questions regarding your own gender role socialization. While reading through the questions, jot down your thoughts and try to think of specific examples from your personal history. You will find that sharing these written notes with others often leads to a fascinating discussion of "the proper roles for women and men."

1. During your early childhood, what gender messages did you receive from your favorite fairy tales, books, television shows? How were women and men portrayed? Are the roles of men and women different in the books and television programs you read and watch today?

2. Did anyone ever tell you that you were a "big boy now" or to "act like a lady?" What did they mean? How did you feel?

3. What were the power relationships like in your family? In what situations was your mother powerful? Your father? Do you remember being treated differently from your opposite-sexed brother or sister? What is the division of labor in your family today (breadwinner, housekeeper, etc.)?

4. As a child, what did you want to be when you grew up? Did that change, and if so, when? Why? What career are you now pursuing? Why?

5. What were your favorite subjects in school? Your most hated subjects? Why?

6. Have you ever wished you were born as the opposite sex? If so, why?

7. Have you ever felt competitive with friends of your same sex? If so, over what?

8. In what ways do you express your emotions (crying, slamming doors, etc.), and how is it related to your being a male or female?

9. What kinds of things do you get most rewarded for by others today (attractiveness, strength, intelligence, business success, money earned, family status, etc.)? How does this relate to your gender role?

10. Have you ever deviated from traditional expectations of you as a male or female? If so, what was your own and others' reaction to it? Have you ever felt restricted or pressured by social expectations of you as a man or woman? If so, in what way?

CHAPTER OVERVIEW (<u>R</u>eview)

The following CHAPTER OVERVIEW provides a narrative overview of the main topics covered in the chapter. Like the Visual Summary found at the end of each chapter in the text, this narrative summary provides a final opportunity to *review* chapter material.

I. Sex and Gender

The term **sex** is differentiated along seven dimensions: chromosomal sex, gonadal sex, hormonal sex, external genitals, internal accessory organs, secondary sex characteristics, and sexual orientation. **Gender**, on the other hand, is differentiated according to **gender identity** and **gender role.** Transsexualism is a problem with gender identity; transvestism is cross-dressing for sexual arousal. **Sexual orientation** (gay, lesbian, bisexual, or heterosexual) is unrelated to both transsexualism and transvestism. There are two main theories of gender role development: Social learning theorists focus on rewards, punishments, and imitation, whereas cognitive-developmental theorists emphasize the active, thinking processes of the individual.

Studies of male and female sex differences find several obvious physical differences, such as height, body build, and reproductive organs. There are also important functional and structural sex differences in the brains of human females and males. Looking at gender differences, studies find some differences (such as in aggression and verbal skills), but the cause of these differences (either nature or nurture) is still being debated.

II. The Study of Human Sexuality

Although sex has always been an important part of human interest, motivation, and behavior, it received little scientific attention before the twentieth century. Havelock Ellis was among the first to study human sexuality despite the repression and secrecy of nineteenth-century Victorian times.

Alfred Kinsey and his colleagues were the first to conduct large-scale, systematic surveys and interviews of the sexual practices and preferences of Americans during the 1940s and 1950s. The research team of Masters and Johnson pioneered the use of actual laboratory measurement and observation of human physiological response during sexual activity. Cultural studies are also important sources of scientific information on human sexuality.

III. Sexual Behavior
Masters and Johnson identified a four-stage **sexual response cycle** during sexual activity---*excitement, plateau, orgasm, and resolution*. There are numerous similarities and differences between the sexes in this cycle, but differences are the focus of most research. According to the *evolutionary perspective*, males engage in more sexual behaviors with more sexual partners because it helps the species survive. The *social role approach* suggests this difference results from traditional cultural divisions of labor.

Although researchers have identified several myths concerning the causes of homosexuality, the origins remain a puzzle. In recent studies, the genetic and biological explanation has gained the strongest support. Despite increased understanding, sexual orientation remains a divisive issue in America.

IV. Sexual Problems
Many people experience **sexual dysfunction**. They often fail to recognize the role of biology in both sexual arousal and response. Ejaculation and orgasm are partially reflexive. And the parasympathetic nervous system must be dominant for sexual arousal, whereas the sympathetic nervous system must dominate for orgasm to occur. Several aspects of sexual arousal and response are also learned. Early *gender role training*, the **double standard**, and **sexual scripts** teach us what to consider the "best" sex.

Many sexual problems can be helped with sex therapy. Masters and Johnson emphasize the couple's relationship, combined physiological and psychosocial factors, cognitions, and specific behavioral techniques. Professional sex therapists offer important guidelines for everyone: Sex education should be early and positive, avoid a goal or performance orientation, and keep communication open.

The most publicized STI is **AIDS (acquired immunodeficiency syndrome)**. Although AIDS is transmitted only through sexual contact or exposure to infected blood, many people have irrational fears of contagion. At the same time, an estimated one million North Americans are **HIV positive** and therefore carriers.

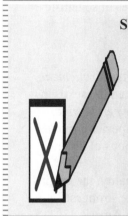

SELF-TESTS (Review & wRite)

Completing the following SELF-TESTS will provide immediate feedback on how well you have mastered the material. In the *crossword puzzle* and *fill-in exercises*, write the appropriate word or words in the blank spaces. The *matching exercise* requires you to match the terms in one column to their correct definitions in the other. For the *multiple-choice questions* in Practice Tests I and II, circle or underline the correct answer. When you are unsure of any answer, be sure to highlight or specially mark the item and then go back to the text for further review. Correct answers are provided at the end of this study guide chapter.

CROSSWORD PUZZLE FOR CHAPTER 11

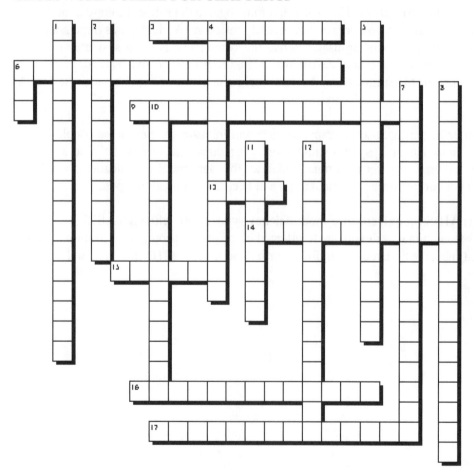

ACROSS

3 The societal expectations for normal and appropriate male and female behavior. When these expectations are based on exaggerated and biased beliefs about differences between the sexes and are rigidly applied to all members of each sex, they are known as gender role stereotypes.

6 Impairment of the normal physiological processes of arousal and orgasm.

9 Final stage of the sexual response cycle when the body returns to its nonaroused state.

13 A catastrophic illness in which human immunodeficiency viruses (HIV) destroy the immune system's ability to fight disease, leaving the body vulnerable to a variety of opportunistic infections and cancers.

14 Third stage of the sexual response cycle when pleasurable sensations peak and orgasm occurs.

15 The psychological and sociocultural meanings added to biological maleness or femaleness.

16 Socially dictated descriptions of the sequences of behavior that are considered appropriate in sexual interactions.

17 How one psychologically perceives oneself as either male or female.

DOWN

1 An individual's primary erotic attraction can be toward members of the same sex (homosexual or gay or lesbian), both sexes (bisexual), or other sex (heterosexual).

2 Second stage of the sexual response cycle, characterized by a leveling off of high arousal.

4 The beliefs, values, and norms that subtly encourage male sexuality and discourage female sexuality.

5 Phase following orgasm during which further orgasm is considered physiologically impossible.

6 Biological maleness and femaleness, including chromosomal sex, gonadal sex, hormonal sex, external genitals, and internal accessory organs. Also, activities related to sexual behaviors, such as masturbation and intercourse.

7 A fear that one will be unable to meet the expectations for sexual "performance" of one's self or one's partner.

8 Masters and Johnson's description of the bodily response to sexual arousal. The four stages are excitement, plateau, orgasm, and resolution.

10 First stage of the sexual response cycle, characterized by increasing levels of arousal and increased engorgement of the genitals.

11 Combining characteristics considered typically male (e.g., assertive, athletic) with characteristics considered typically female (e.g., yielding, nurturant); from the Greek andro meaning male and gyn meaning female.

12 Negative attitudes toward an individual because of her or his sexual orientation.

FILL-IN EXERCISES

1. The psychological and sociocultural meanings added to biological maleness and femaleness is known as _____ (p. 381).

2. _____ refers to having a gender identity opposite that of the biological sex; whereas _____ refers to becoming sexually aroused by wearing the clothing of the other sex (p. 382).

3. _____ refers to a sexual orientation toward the same sex; whereas being sexually attracted to both males and females is referred to as _____ (p. 382).

4. Societal expectations for normal and appropriate female and male behavior are known as _____ (p. 400).

5. _____ individuals combine some characteristics considered typically male with characteristics considered typically female (p. 407).

6. During the 19th century, it was believed that _____ caused brain damage and death (p. 390).

7. During the resolution phase of the sexual response cycle, a male is likely to be in the _____ period (p. 394).

8. According to the _____, sexual differences (such as males having more sexual partners) evolved from an ancient set of mating patterns that helped the species survive (p. 395).

9. An irrational fear of homosexuality in others or oneself is known as _____ (p. 397).

10. Impairment of the normal physiological processes of arousal and orgasm is known as a _____ (p. 398).

MATCHING EXERCISES

Column A

a. Double Standard
b. Havelock Ellis
c. Sex
d. Bisexual
e. Masters and Johnson
f. Plateau Phase
g. Gender Identity
h. Orgasmic Dysfunction

Column B

1.____ Self perception as either male or female.
2.____ Sexual orientation to both men and women.
3.____ Combination of both masculine and feminine.
4.____ Used direct measurement and observation of sex.
5.____ Encourages male sexuality and discourages female's.
6.____ Inability to respond to sexual arousal to point of orgasm.
7.____ Leveling off of sexual arousal.
8.____ Fearing won't meet self or partner's sexual expectations.

i.   Performance Anxiety   9._____ Biological dimensions of maleness or femaleness.
j.   Androgyny   10._____ Based his research on personal diaries.

PRACTICE TEST I

1. _____ refers to a person's biological dimensions of maleness or femaleness.
   a.   The sex chromosome
   b.   The gonads
   c.   Sex
   d.   Gender

2. _____ refers to the psychological perception of oneself as either male or female.
   a.   Sex role conformity
   b.   Assigned sex
   c.   Gender dysphoria
   d.   Gender identity

3. A transsexual is a person who has a _____.
   a.   mismatch between gender identity and his or her gonads, genitals, or internal accessory organs
   b.   mismatch between gender role and his or her gonads, genitals, or internal accessory organs
   c.   homosexual preference for sexual gratification
   d.   need to wear clothing of the opposite sex for sexual gratification

4. A _____ individual is sexually attracted to the same sex.
   a.   lesbian
   b.   gay
   c.   homosexual
   d.   all of the above

5. The _____ theory states that children learn their gender roles by actively processing information about their sex, gender schemas, and social reinforcements.
   a.   mental processing
   b.   cognitive developmental
   c.   information gathering
   d.   cognitive-social

6. Males with _____ levels of intellectual abilities achieve significantly higher math scores on the SAT.
   a.   lower
   b.   average
   c.   the highest
   d.   all of these options

7. Males display more _____ aggression than females.
    a. physical
    b. indirect
    c. relational
    d. all of these options

8. Androgyny is another word for a(n) _____.
    a. combination of both male and female personality traits
    b. adrenogenital syndrome
    c. oversupply of androgens during prenatal development
    d. transvestite

9. A major pioneer in sex research who first used the case study method was _____.
    a. B. F. Skinner
    b. Sigmund Freud
    c. Alfred Kinsey
    d. Havelock Ellis

10. One of the earliest and most extensive surveys of human sexual behavior in the United States was conducted by _____.
    a. Havelock Ellis
    b. William Masters and Virginia Johnson
    c. Emily and John Roper
    d. Alfred Kinsey

11. Limited exposure to the sexual practices of other cultures may lead to _____, the tendency to view our culture's sexual practices as normal.
    a. sexual prejudice
    b. ethnic typing
    c. ethnocentrism
    d. sexual predation

12. Orgasm refers to the _____.
    a. final phase of the sexual response cycle
    b. male refractory period
    c. experiencing a highly intense and pleasurable sense of release of tension
    d. peak of the excitement phase

13. Research on the causes of homosexuality _____.
    a.   has helped overcome many misconceptions and myths
    b.   provides evidence of a biological foundation
    c.   is inconclusive
    d.   all of these options

14. _____ refers to negative attitudes toward an individual because of his or her sexual orientation.
    a.   Homophobia
    b.   Gay pride
    c.   Gay prejudice
    d.   Sexual prejudice

15. The inability to obtain or maintain an erection sufficiently firm for intercourse is _____.
    a.   primarily a psychological problem
    b.   sometimes associated with diabetes, hormonal deficiencies, stress, and anxiety
    c.   experienced only by older males
    d.   associated with long-term relationships

16. Regarding sexuality, the double standard _____.
    a.   encourages male sexuality
    b.   discourages female sexuality
    c.   makes women responsible for stopping male advances
    d.   all of these options

17. _____ teach us "what to do, when, where, how, and with whom."
    a.   Sex surrogates
    b.   Sex therapists
    c.   Sex manuals
    d.   Sexual scripts

18. Painful intercourse in men or women is called _____.
    a.   dyspareunia
    b.   endorphin-deficient syndrome
    c.   sexual aversion disorder
    d.   priapism

19. All of the following are principles of Masters and Johnson's approach to sex therapy except _____.
    a.   setting goals to improve sexual performance
    b.   examination of the relationship between the two people
    c.   use of medical histories and physical examinations
    d.   exploration of individual attitudes and sex education

20. AIDS is the result of an infection by the _____ virus (HIV).
    a.   human incapacitating
    b.   herpes I
    c.   human immunodeficiency
    d.   hepatitis I

PRACTICE TEST II

1. Sex is to biological as _____.
    a.   gender is to psychosocial
    b.   anatomy is to physiology
    c.   intercourse is to making love
    d.   physiological is to psychological

2. Which of the following is **NOT** a gonad?
    a.   ovary
    b.   testicle
    c.   uterus
    d.   all of these are gonads

3. Gender _____ is a term most associated with cognitive developmental theory.
    a.   roles
    b.   identity
    c.   confusion
    d.   schemas

4. Men are more likely to attribute their successes to internal abilities; women are more likely to attribute their successes to _____.
    a.   internal abilities
    b.   external factors
    c.   the men in their lives
    d.   their mothers

5. Lower levels of serotonin in males have been linked to _____.
    a.   sexual arousal
    b.   aggressive behavior
    c.   alertness
    d.   all of these options

6. Androgyny is _____.
    a.   a combination of masculine and feminine traits
    b.   another term for a hermaphrodite
    c.   an intersexed individual
    d.   an intrasexed individual

7. The physiological aspects of human sexual responses were studied by _____.
    a.   Havelock Ellis
    b.   Freud
    c.   Masters and Johnson
    d.   Alfred Kinsey

8. In recent years, _____ have condemned female circumcision, clitoridectomy, and genital infibulation.
    a.   most Middle Eastern countries
    b.   the United Nations
    c.   all African nations
    d.   all of these options

9. In your text's diving analogy for the sexual response model, walking across the diving board is analogous to the _____ phase
    a.   excitement
    b.   plateau
    c.   orgasm
    d.   resolution

10. Which of the following is NOT one of the stages in the human sexual response cycle as described by Masters and Johnson?
    a.   resolution
    b.   orgasm
    c.   foreplay
    d.   excitement

11. The _____ first occurs during the excitement phase of the sexual response cycle.
    a.   spermarche
    b.   woman's refractory period
    c.   man's refractory period
    d.   sex flush

12. The _____ branch of the _____ nervous system is in dominance during orgasm and ejaculation.
    a.   sympathetic; autonomic
    b.   peripheral; somatic
    c.   parasympathetic; autonomic
    d.   somatic; parasympathetic

13. When a male cannot control how quickly he ejaculates in 50% or more of his sexual encounters, he is most likely experiencing a problem called _____.
    a.   spermarche
    b.   dyspareunia
    c.   male orgasmic dysfunction
    d.   premature ejaculation

14. Vaginismus is a sexual disorder that involves fear of _____.
    a.   hormosexuality
    b.   androgyn
    c.   heterosexuality
    d.   intercourse

15. Sexual arousal is dependent on the dominance of the _____ nervous system.
    a.   parasympathetic
    b.   autonomic
    c.   somatic
    d.   sympathetic

16. Based on your answer to the previous question, _____ can therefore interfere with sexual arousal.
    a.   relaxation
    b.   strong emotions
    c.   vaginismus
    d.   foreplay

17. With regard to sexual functioning, tobacco use is associated with _____.
    a.   increased sexual desire
    b.   lowered inhibitions
    c.   inhibited orgasm
    d.   a decrease in the frequency and duration of erections

18. Having AIDS generally refers to being infected with a virus that attacks the _____.
    a.   central nervous system
    b.   peripheral nervous system
    c.   mucous membranes
    d.   immune system

19. With regard to STIs, the use of latex condoms and the practice of monogamy are considered to be
    _____.
    a.   a waste of time
    b.   safe sexual practices
    c.   the only ways to prevent STD transmission
    d.   methods of lessening your chance of contracting an STD

20. Suggested ways to help prevent acquaintance rape include each of the following EXCEPT _____.
    a.   be assertive
    b.   date in groups
    c.   avoid physical resistance
    d.   threaten to call the police

ANSWERS

The following answers to active learning exercises, crossword puzzles, fill-ins, matching exercises, and practice tests 1 and 2 provide immediate feedback on your mastery of the material. Try not to simply memorize the answers. When you are unsure of your "guess" or make an error, be sure to go back to the textbook and carefully review. This will greatly improve your scores on classroom exams and quizzes.

CROSSWORD PUZZLE FOR CHAPTER 11

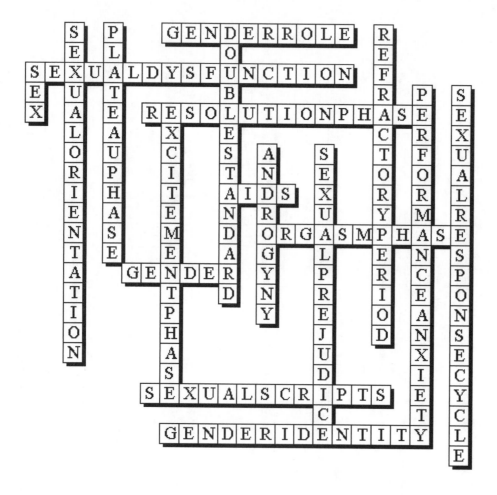

FILL-IN EXERCISES

1. gender; 2. Transsexualism, transvestism; 3. Homosexuality (or gay or lesbian), bisexuality; 4. sexual scripts; 5. Androgynous; 6. nocturnal emissions; 7. refractory; 8. evolutionary perspective; 9. sexual prejudice; 10. sexual dysfunction.

MATCHING EXERCISES

a. 5, b. 10, c. 9, d. 2, e. 4, f. 7, g. 1, h. 6, i. 8, j. 3.

PRACTICE TEST I		PRACTICE TEST II	
1. c (p. 381)	11. c (p. 391)	1. a (p. 381)	11. d (p. 394)
2. d (p. 381)	12. a (p. 394)	2. c (p. 381)	12. a (p. 398)
3. a (p. 382)	13. d (p. 396)	3. d (p. 383)	13. d (p. 399)
4. d (p. 382)	14. d (p. 397)	4. b (p. 385)	14. d (p. 399)
5. b (p. 383)	15. b (p. 399)	5. b (p. 386)	15. a (p. 398)
6. c (p. 386)	16. d (p. 400)	6. a (p. 386)	16. b (p. 398)
7. a (p. 386)	17. d (p. 400)	7. c (p. 390)	17. d (p. 402)
8. a (p. 386)	18. a (p. 399)	8. b (p. 393)	18. d (p. 404)
9. d (p. 390)	19. a (p. 402)	9. b (p. 394)	19. b (p. 407)
10.d (p. 390)	20. c (p. 404)	10.c (p. 393)	20. c (p. 406)

12 Motivation and Emotion

OUTLINE (Survey & Question)

This outline is intended to help you *survey* the chapter. As you read through the various sections, write down any *questions* or comments that come to mind in the space provided. This is a valuable part of active learning and the SQ4R method. It not only makes your reading time more enjoyable and active, but it also increases retention and understanding of the material.

TOPIC	NOTES

I. UNDERSTANDING MOTIVATION

A. Hunger and Eating

B. Arousal

C. Achievement

Critical Thinking/Active Learning: Measuring Your Own Need for Achievement

II. GENERAL THEORIES OF MOTIVATION

   A. Biological Theories

   B. Psychosocial Theories

   C. Interactionism

III. UNDERSTANDING EMOTION

   A. Components of Emotion

   Gender and Cultural Diversity: How Culture and Evolution Affect Emotional Expression

   B. The Polygraph

   C. Emotional Intelligence (EQ)

IV. GENERAL THEORIES OF EMOTION

   A. James-Lange Theory

   B. Cannon-Bard Theory

   C. Facial Feedback Hypothesis

   D. Schachter's Two-Factor Theory

   Research Highlight: Are Abused Children More Alert to Negative Emotions?

Core and Expanded LEARNING OBJECTIVES   (Read, Recite & wRite)

While *reading* the chapter, stop periodically and *recite* (or repeat in your own words) the answers to the following learning objectives. It will also help your retention if you *write* your answer in the space provided. (Page numbers refer to the text Psychology in Action, 6th Ed.)

Core Learning Objectives
These objectives are found at the beginning of each chapter of Psychology in Action (6th ed.).

1. Why do we feel hungry, search for stimulation, and need to achieve?

2. Are we motivated by biological or psychosocial factors? Or both?

3. What major concepts do I need to know to understand emotion?

4. How are emotional states produced?

Expanded Learning Objectives
These objectives offer more detail and a more intensive way to study the chapter.

Upon completion of CHAPTER 12, the student should be able to:

1. Define motivation and emotion, and discuss how they overlap (p. 412).

2. Describe how internal and external factors trigger hunger or eating behavior, and state the safest, most reliable method of weight loss (pp. 412-415).

3. Define anorexia nervosa and bulimia nervosa, and state the causes and risk factors for the development of these eating disorders (pp. 415-416).

4. Describe the arousal motive, the effects of under- or over-arousal, and the four factors that characterize sensation-seeking (pp. 416-419).

5. Describe the achievement motive, possible causal factors, and the traits that characterize people with a high need for achievement. Define intrinsic and extrinsic motivation, and describe their relationship to achievement (pp. 419-424).

6. Describe the biological theories of motivation: instinct and drive-reduction (pp. 424-426).

7. Describe the psychosocial theories of motivation: incentive, cognitive, and Maslow's hierarchy of needs (pp. 426-428).

8. Describe the cognitive, physiological, and behavioral components of emotion (pp. 428-431).

9. Describe the evolutionary theory of emotional development, culturally universal emotions, and culturally different display rules (pp. 432-434).

10. Describe the use of the polygraph in measuring sympathetic arousal; discuss the effectiveness of the polygraph in lie detection (pp. 434-435).

11. Describe how emotional intelligence combines the cognitive, physiological, and behavioral components of emotion, and discuss the controversy regarding this concept (p. 436).

12. Compare and contrast the James-Lange, Cannon-Bard, facial-feedback, and two-factor theories of emotion; discuss the research regarding each of these theories (pp. 437-442).

13. Describe research findings on the abused child's heightened reactivity to anger (pp. 441).

KEY TERMS (Review)

The *review* step in the SQ4R method is very important to your performance on quizzes and exams. Upon completion of this chapter, you should be able to define the following terms.

Achievement Motivation (nAch): _____

_____

Anorexia Nervosa: _____

_____

Bulimia Nervosa: _____

_____

Cannon-Bard Theory: _____

_____

Drive-Reduction Theory: _____

_____

Emotion: _____

_____

Emotional Intelligence: _____

_____

Extrinsic Motivation: _____

_____

Facial-Feedback Hypothesis: _____

_____

Hierarchy of Needs: _____

_____

Incentive Theory: _____

_____

Instincts: _____

_____

Intrinsic Motivation: _____

_____

James-Lange Theory: _____

_____

Motivation: _____

_____

Polygraph: _____

_____

Schachter's Two-Factory Theory: _____

_____

Set Point: _____

_____

ACTIVE LEARNING EXERCISES (Recite)

The *recite* step in the SQ4R method requires you to be an ACTIVE learner. By completing the following exercises, you will test and improve your mastery of the chapter material, which will also improve your performance on quizzes and exams. Answers to some exercises appear at the end of this study guide chapter.

ACTIVE LEARNING EXERCISE I

Charting Your Moods and Emotions (An Affective Skill)

Self-understanding requires the ability to recognize and analyze your own emotions and to recognize the external factors that affect your emotions. From this place of self-understanding you will, hopefully, be able to be more in control of your own moods and needs, gain insight into the moods and needs of others, and improve your relationships.

One of the best ways to understand the three basic components of emotions and to understand your own daily or monthly "mood swings" is to chart your emotions for at least one week. Each morning when you first wake up or each night before retiring, complete your daily mood evaluation chart. Describe your primary mood at the time of your writing, how your body physiologically registers that emotion or mood, the thoughts, expectations, or beliefs surrounding that mood, and give a number or word to rank or evaluate the pleasure or intensity of that emotion. Charting your moods or emotions helps you to recognize your own fluctuations and helps you to explain yourself to others.

	Primary Mood	Physiological Description	Cognitive (Thoughts)	Behavioral Description	Subjective Evaluation
Day					
(1)					
(2)					
(3)					
(4)					

(5)

(6)

(7)

ACTIVE LEARNING EXERCISE II

Having practiced identifying your mood or emotional states in the previous active learning exercise, now we can explore a related topic, that of *subjective well being*. Researchers in this area often ask participants to evaluate either their overall life satisfaction or their feelings of happiness (sometimes defined as a high ratio of positive to negative feelings). Stop for a moment and write down your own life satisfaction and happiness scores (on a scale from one to 100 with one as the lowest) in the space provided. Life Satisfaction score _____ Happiness score _____

Now circle true or false to the following items:

1. Among all age groups, America's senior citizens are the least happy and most dissatisfied with their life. True or False?
2. People who have complete quadriplegia (with both arms and both legs paralyzed) feel their lives are below average in happiness. True or False?
3. Having children is life's greatest joy; thus, parents report more overall happiness than those who do not have children. True or False?
4. Most people would be happier if they had more money. True or False?
5. People with a college education are happier and report more life satisfaction than people with only a high school diploma. True or False?

The answers to this exercise can be found at the end of this study guide chapter—and they may surprise you!

CHAPTER OVERVIEW (Review)

The following CHAPTER OVERVIEW provides a narrative overview of the main topics covered in the chapter. Like the Visual Summary found at the end of each chapter in the text, this narrative summary provides a final opportunity to *review* chapter material.

I. Understanding Motivation

Motivation is the study of the "whys" of behavior, whereas emotion is the study of feelings. Because motivated behaviors are often closely related to emotions, these two topics are frequently studied together. A variety of motives are discussed throughout this text. In this chapter, we focus on hunger, arousal, and **achievement motivation**.

Both internal (stomach, blood chemistry, the brain) and external (cultural conditioning) factors affect hunger and eating. A large number of people have eating disorders. Obesity seems to result from biological factors, such as the individual's genetic inheritance, and from psychological factors. Anorexia nervosa (extreme weight loss due to self-imposed starvation) and bulimia nervosa (excessive consumption of food followed by purging) are both related to an intense fear of obesity.

According to the arousal motive, people seek an optimal level of arousal that maximizes their performance. There are, however, individual differences in this need. According to Zuckerman, high sensation seekers are biologically "prewired" to need a higher level of stimulation, whereas the reverse is true for low sensation seekers.

Achievement involves the need for success, for doing better than others, and for mastering challenging tasks. Research with **intrinsic** versus **extrinsic motivation** shows that extrinsic rewards can lower interest and achievement motivation.

II. General Theories of Motivation

There are three approaches explaining motivation: biological theories (including **instinct** theory and **drive-reduction theory**) and psychosocial theories (including incentive and cognitive), and interactionist (Maslow's **hierarchy of needs**).

Instinct theories suggest there is some inborn, genetic component to motivation. Drive-reduction theory suggests that internal tensions (produced by the body's demand for homeostasis) "push" the organism toward satisfying basic needs. According to incentive theory, motivation results from the "pull" of external environmental stimuli. Cognitive theories emphasize the importance of thoughts, attributions, and expectations. Maslow's hierarchy of needs or motives incorporates both biological and psychological theories. He believed that basic physiological and survival needs must be satisfied before a person can attempt to satisfy higher needs. Critics question the importance of sequentially working up through these steps.

III. Understanding Emotion

All emotions have three basic components: cognitive (thoughts, beliefs, and expectations); physiological (increased heart rate, respiration rate, and so on); and behavioral (facial expressions and bodily gestures). Self-report techniques, such as paper-and-pencil tests, surveys, and interviews, are used to study the cognitive component of emotions.

Studies of the physiological component of emotion find that most emotions involve a general, nonspecific arousal of the nervous system. This arousal involves the cerebral cortex, the limbic system, and the frontal lobes of the brain. The most obvious signs of arousal (trembling, increased heart rate, sweating, and so on) result from activation of the sympathetic nervous system, a subdivision of the autonomic nervous system. The parasympathetic system restores the body to the "status quo."

The behavioral component of emotions refers to how we express our emotions. Facial expressions and body movements are two major forms of nonverbal communication. Most psychologists believe that emotions result from a complex interplay between evolution and culture. Studies have identified 7 to 10 basic emotions that are universal ---experienced and expressed in similar ways across almost all cultures. Display rules differ across cultures and between men and women.

A polygraph measures changes in emotional arousal (increased heart rate, blood pressure, and so on). Although the **polygraph** is used in police work and for employment purposes, psychologists have found it a poor predictor of guilt or innocence or of truth or lies. **Emotional intelligence** involves knowing and managing emotions, empathy, and maintaining satisfying relationships.

IV. General Theories of Emotion

There are four major theories to explain what causes emotion: The **James-Lange theory** suggests we interpret the way we feel on the basis of physical sensations such as increased heart rate, trembling, and so on. The **Cannon-Bard theory** suggests feelings are created from independent and simultaneous stimulation of both the cortex and the autonomic nervous system.

According to the **facial feedback hypothesis**, facial movements elicit specific emotions. **Schachter's two-factor theory** suggests that emotions depend on two factors---physical arousal and a cognitive labeling of the arousal. In other words, people notice what is going on around them, as well as their own bodily responses, and then label the emotion accordingly.

SELF-TESTS (<u>R</u>eview & w<u>R</u>ite)

Completing the following SELF-TESTS will provide immediate feedback on how well you have mastered the material. In the *crossword puzzle* and *fill-in exercises*, write the appropriate word or words in the blank spaces. The *matching exercise* requires you to match the terms in one column to their correct definitions in the other. For the *multiple-choice questions* in Practice Tests I and II, circle or underline the correct answer. When you are unsure of any answer, be sure to highlight or specially mark the item and then go back to the text for further review. Correct answers are provided at the end of this study guide chapter.

CROSSWORD PUZZLE FOR CHAPTER 12

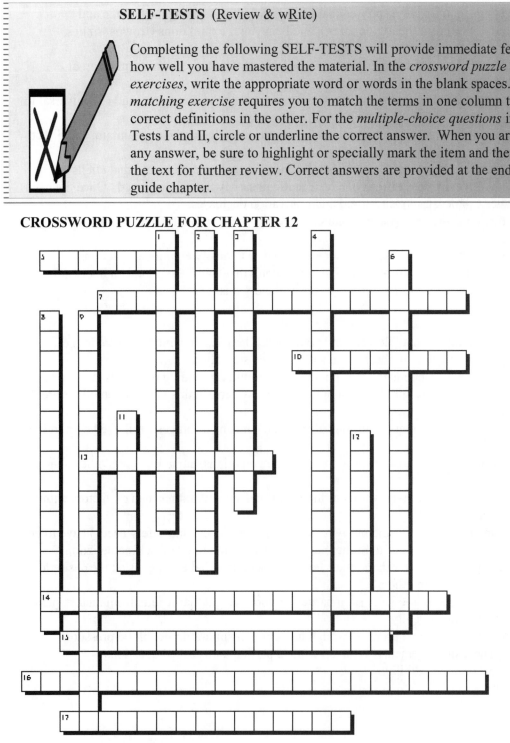

ACROSS

5 An individual's feelings or affective responses that include cognitions (thoughts, beliefs, and expectations), physiological arousal (heart pounding), and behavioral expressions (frowns, smiles, running, and so on).

7 Motivation that comes from personal enjoyment of a task or activity, rather than from external rewards or fear of punishment.

10 Behavioral patterns that are (1) unlearned, (2) always expressed in the same way, and (3) universal in a species.

13 Factors within an individual (such as needs, desires, and interests) that activate, maintain, and direct behavior toward a goal.

14 The theory that motivation begins with a physiological need (a lack or deficiency) that elicits a psychological energy or drive directed toward behavior that will satisfy the original need. Once the need is met, a state of balance (homeostasis) is restored and motivation decreases.

15 The theory that emotion is the perception of one's own bodily reactions and that each emotion is physiologically distinct.

16 The proposal that movements of the facial muscles produce or intensify emotional reactions.

17 The theory that motivation results from environmental stimuli that "pull" the organism in certain directions, as opposed to internal needs that drive or "push" the organism.

DOWN

1 An eating disorder, seen mostly in adolescent and young adult females, in which a severe loss of weight results from an obsessive fear of obesity and self-imposed starvation.

2 The theory that the thalamus responds to emotion-arousing stimuli by sending messages simultaneously to the cerebral cortex and the autonomic nervous system. In this view, all emotions are physiologically similar.

3 An eating disorder in which enormous quantities of food are consumed (binges), followed by purging through vomiting or taking laxatives.

4 According to Goleman, the ability to know and manage one's emotions, empathize with others, and maintain satisfying relationships.

6 Motivation based on obvious external rewards or threats of punishment, rather than on factors within the individual or the behavior itself.

8 Maslow's theory of motivation, that some motives (such as physiological and safety needs) have to be satisfied before an individual can advance to higher needs (such as belonging and self-actualiztion).

9 The need for success, for doing better than others, and for mastering challenging tasks; the desire to excel, especially in competition with others.

11 An organism's personal homeostatic level for a particular body weight that results from factors such as early feeding experiences and heredity.

12 Instrument that measures emotional arousal through heart rate, respiration rate, blood pressure, and skin conductivity. These measurements are taken while a participant is asked questions designed to determine his or her credibility.

FILL-IN EXERCISES

1. _____ refers to factors within an individual that activate, maintain, and direct behavior toward a goal; whereas _____ refers to feelings or affective responses that result from physiological arousal, thoughts and beliefs, subjective evaluation, and bodily expression (p. 412).

2. If the _____ of a rat is destroyed, the rat will overeat to the point of extreme obesity (p. 414).

3. Consuming enormous quantities of food (binges) followed by purging with laxatives or vomiting is referred to as _____ (p. 415).

4. The _____ motive causes us to look for a certain amount of stimulation and complexity from our environment (p. 416).

5. _____ refers to the need for success, for doing better than others, and for mastering challenging tasks (p. 419).

6. Whereas _____ says internal factors *push* us in certain directions, _____ says external stimuli *pull* us (p. 426).

7. Maslow's _____ suggests basic survival and security needs must be satisfied before moving on to higher needs such as self-actualization (p. 427).

8. There are three basic components of emotions: the _____, _____, and _____ (pp. 429-430).

9. Research on the _____ suggests that smiling can actually make you happier (p. 438).

10. Research finds that people across a variety of cultures express emotions in strikingly similar ways. This supports _____ theories of emotion (p. 432).

MATCHING EXERCISES

Column A   Column B

a. Motivation   1.____ Measures changes in emotional arousal.
b. Drive-Reduction Theory   2.____ Can sometimes lower interest and achievement.
c. Anorexia Nervosa   3.____ Facial movements elicit specific emotions.
d. Polygraphs   4.____ Knowing and appropriately managing emotions.
e. James-Lange Theory   5.____ Study of the "whys" of behavior.
f. Emotional Intelligence   6.____ Cultural norms governing emotional expressions.
g. Facial Feedback Hypothesis 7.____ A smile of real joy.
h. Display Rules   8.____ Feelings interpreted from physical sensations.
i. Duchenne Smile   9.____ Internal tensions "push" organism toward basic needs.
j. Extrinsic Motivation   10.____ Extreme weight loss due to self-imposed starvation.

PRACTICE TEST I

1. _____ activates and directs behavior; _____ represents the feeling responses to thoughts, situations, or behaviors.
    a. Motivation; emotion
    b. Incentives; needs
    c. Motives; drives
    d. Motivation; compulsions

2. Hunger is least likely to be motivated by _____.
    a. glucose uptake
    b. stomach contractions
    c. the hypothalamus
    d. cultural conditioning

3. Belinda appears to be starving herself, and has obviously lost a lot of weight in just a few months. You suspect she might have _____.
    a. a compulsive dieting disorder
    b. an obesity phobia
    c. anorexia nervosa
    d. bulimia nervosa

4. According to the _____theory, there is an ideal or optimal level of arousal that organisms are motivated to achieve and maintain.
    a. sensory arousal
    b. arousal motive
    c. sensation seeking
    d. achievement

5. Henry prefers moderately difficult tasks, wants a career that involves competition, and personal responsibility, and will persist until a task is done. He most likely has a _____.
    a.   high need for arousal
    b.   moderate need for achievement
    c.   high nAch
    d.   moderate need for arousal

6. If you studied for this test solely to avoid a bad grade, it is most likely that you are _____.
    a.   extrinsically motivated to study
    b.   intrinsically motivated to study
    c.   an above average student
    d.   a typical student

7. This is **NOT** characteristic of instincts.
    a.   unlearned
    b.   uniform
    c.   universal
    d.   unique

8. According to the drive-reduction theory, motivation begins with a _____.
    a.   goal
    b.   physiological need
    c.   cognitive need
    d.   motivational need

9. Nest building is an example of _____.
    a.   drive-reduction
    b.   an incentive motive
    c.   an instinct
    d.   all of these options

10. This is **NOT** associated with the incentive theory of motivation.
    a.   external stimuli
    b.   an external "push"
    c.   obtaining reinforcement
    d.   avoiding punishment

11. Cognitive theories of motivation focus on _____.
    a.   attributions for the causes of behavior
    b.   biological factors in thought processes
    c.   previous learning experience
    d.   the role of external stimuli

12. The psychologist associated with a hierarchy of needs is _____.
    a.   Murray
    b.   Freud
    c.   Skinner
    d.   Maslow

13. The _____ component of emotions involves active changes in the body, such as pupil dilation or increased heart rate.
    a.   cognitive
    b.   psychological
    c.   physiological
    d.   behavioral

14. Across cultures, people can reliably identify at least _____ basic emotions from a person's facial expression.
    a.   32
    b.   15
    c.   9
    d.   6

15. The apparatus commonly used as a "lie detector" is called a(n) _____.
    a.   electroencephalograph
    b.   EEG
    c.   polygraph
    d.   galvanograph

16. You suddenly see an oncoming car in your lane. You swerve to miss it, and your car finally comes to a bouncing halt in the ditch at the side of the road. At this point you notice your high level of fear. This reaction best supports the _____ theory of emotions.
    a.   Cannon-Bard
    b.   James-Lange
    c.   two-factor
    d.   common sense

17. You are kissing your dating partner good night and notice that you are physiologically aroused. You think about your feelings and decide that you are probably in love with this individual. This response best supports the_____ theory of emotions.
    a.   Cannon-Bard
    b.   James-Lange
    c.   Schachter's two-factor
    d.   companionate love

18. The _____ theory (hypothesis) suggests that an emotional experience and a body reaction occur simultaneously.
    a.   James-Lange
    b.   Schachter's two-factor
    c.   Cannon-Bard
    d.   facial feedback

19. You grin broadly while your best friend tells you she was just accepted to Harvard Medical School. The facial feedback hypothesis predicts that you will feel _____.
    a.   happy
    b.   envious
    c.   lonely
    d.   all of these emotions

20. According to research, abused children _____.
    a.   are more alert to angry faces
    b.   exhibit negative emotional expressions earlier
    c.   have difficulty in responding to distress
    d.   all of the above

PRACTICE TEST II

1.   _____ energizes and directs behavior.
    a.   Emotion
    b.   Motivation
    c.   Serotonin
    d.   Melatonin

2.   What do glucose and and insulin have in common? They both _____.
    a.   motivate arousal
    b.   are released during stressful events
    c.   affect satiety
    d.   are secreted by the hypothalamus

3.   The arousal motive causes us to _____ for no apparent reason.
    a.   seek novel and complex stimuli
    b.   become sexually excited
    c.   wake up
    d.   get excited

4.   Advance preparation and hard work are the most important ways to combat _____.
     a.   boredom
     b.   obesity
     c.   test anxiety
     d.   all of these options

5.   Homeostasis is associated with which of the following theories of motivation?
     a.   instinct
     b.   incentive
     c.   Maslow's hierarchy of needs
     d.   drive-reduction

6.   Maslow's theory of motivation suggests that, compared to physiological needs and needs for safety, needs for belonging and self-esteem _____.
     a.   differentiate us from other species
     b.   are satisfied first
     c.   are stronger
     d.   cannot be considered until the physiological and safety needs are met

7.   The cortex, reticular formation, and limbic system are all involved in _____.
     a.   the experience of emotion
     b.   motivation and desire
     c.   reflexes and instincts
     d.   sham rage experiments

8.   During an "emergency," epinephrine and norepinephrine help maintain the activation of the _____ system.
     a.   limbic
     b.   sympathetic nervous
     c.   parasympathetic nervous
     d.   emotional motivation

9.   Senate legislation in 1988 severely restricted the use of _____ in the courts, government, and private industry.
     a.   rational thinking
     b.   democracy
     c.   consensus
     d.   polygraph tests

10. Which of the following is TRUE about the polygraph?
    a.   It does in fact measure sympathetic nervous system arousal
    b.   It cannot tell which emotion is being felt
    c.   Error rates range between 25 and 75 percent
    d.   all of the above

11. Research on emotional intelligence suggests those students with a higher "EQ" _____.
    a.   have lower overall intelligence
    b.   have higher IQs as well
    c.   are more likely to be athletes
    d.   none of the above

12. In the _____ theory, physiological responses are distinctly different for each basic emotion.
    a.   Cannon-Bard
    b.   James-Lange
    c.   two-factor
    d.   all of these options

13. You feel anxious because you are sweating and your heart is beating rapidly. This statement illustrates the _____ theory of emotion.
    a.   James-Lange
    b.   two-factor
    c.   Cannon-Bard
    d.   physiological feedback

14. Which of the following research findings supports the Cannon-Bard theory of emotion?
    a.   Animals who are surgically prevented from experiencing physiological arousal still demonstrate emotional behaviors.
    b.   Smiling improves self-ratings of positive mood-states.
    c.   Misinformed or uninformed research participants take on the emotional reactions of others around them.
    d.   There are distinct, though small, differences in the physiological response of several basic emotions.

15. A therapist who believes in the facial feedback hypothesis regarding emotions might prescribe this if you were depressed.
    a.   Prozac
    b.   record your thoughts whenever you feel depressed
    c.   smile at least 3 times a day
    d.   get a PET scan to see if your thalamus is functioning properly

16. _____ theorists suggested emotions evolved before thought and are important to survival.
    a.   Sociobiological
    b.   Psychobiological
    c.   Behavioral
    d.   Evolutionary

17. Schachter's two factor theory claims that we identify our emotions on the basis of _____.
    a.   physiological changes, specifically changes related to epinephrine
    b.   external, environmental cues
    c.   genetic predispositions
    d.   homeostatic counterbalance

18. Schacter's two factor theory emphasizes the _____ component of emotion.
    a.   stimulus-response
    b.   cognitive
    c.   behavioral-imitation
    d.   physiological

19. Which of the following children will be more alert and responsive to facial expressions of anger?
    a.   non-abused children
    b.   abused children
    c.   all children
    d.   the vast majority of children pay no attention to parental anger

20. Complex emotions, like jealousy and depression, seem to require_____.
    a.   input from higher cortical areas of the brain
    b.   subtle changes in facial expressions
    c.   complex cognitive processing
    d.   the interpretation of environmental stimuli

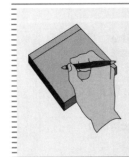

ANSWERS

The following answers to active learning exercises, crossword puzzles, fill-ins, matching exercises, and practice tests 1 and 2 provide immediate feedback on your mastery of the material. Try not to simply memorize the answers. When you are unsure of your "guess" or make an error, be sure to go back to the textbook and carefully review. This will greatly improve your scores on classroom exams and quizzes.

CROSSWORD PUZZLE FOR CHAPTER 12

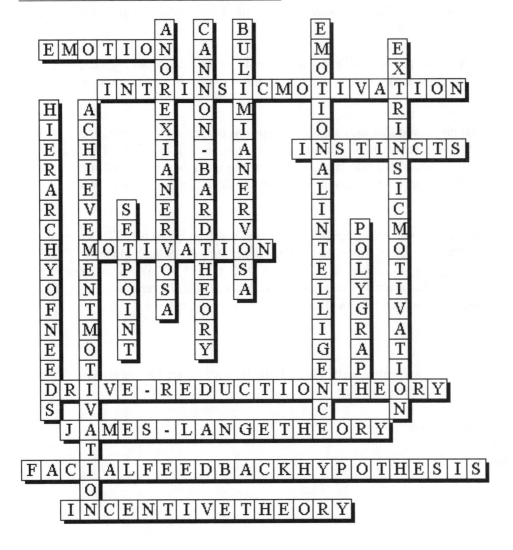

ACTIVE LEARNING EXERCISE II

Subjective well-being exercise It may surprise you to learn that all five statements are false! This is a repeat of the questions and the research answers.

1. Among all age groups, America's senior citizens are the least happy and most dissatisfied with their life. True or False?
2. People who have complete quadriplegia (with both arms and both legs paralyzed) feel their lives are below average in happiness. True or False?
3. Having children is life's greatest joy; thus, parents report more overall happiness than those who do not have children. True or False?
4. Most people would be happier if they had more money. True or False?
5. People with a college education are happier and report more life satisfaction than those with only a high school diploma. True or False?

#'s 1, 3, and 5. Factors such as age, parenthood, and educational level (as well as race, gender, and physical attractiveness) do NOT play a measurable role in either overall life satisfaction or happiness.

#2 People who have serious physical disabilities are just as happy as others. For example, in one survey of 128 people who had suffered an injury causing quadriplegia, most acknowledged having considered suicide in the beginning. Yet, a year later only 10 percent rated their quality of life as poor (Whiteneck et al., 1985). In general, people seem to overestimate the long-term emotional consequences of tragic events.

#4 Does it surprise you that subjective well being (life satisfaction and happiness) is NOT strongly correlated with income? Research shows that as long as people have enough money to buy essentials, extra money does not buy happiness (Myers and Diener, 1995, 1996). For example, in the past 40 years the average U.S. citizen's buying power has doubled; yet, the reported happiness has remained almost unchanged (Niemi et al., 1989).

So what factors *are* correlated with subjective well being? Here the answers are less surprising:
• Having close friendships or a satisfying marriage
• Being optimistic and outgoing
• Having a challenging, satisfying job
• A meaningful religious faith
• Having high self-esteem
• Sleeping well and exercising

References:

Myers, D. G., & Diener, E. (1995). Who is happy? <u>Psychological Science, 6,</u> 10-19.

Myers, D. G., & Diener, E. (1996, May). The pursuit of happiness. <u>Scientific American</u>, pp. 70-72.

Niemi, R. G., Mueller, J., & Smith, T. W. (1989). <u>Trends in public opinion: A compendium of survey data</u>. New York: Greenwood Press.

Whiteneck, G. G., et al. (1985). A collaborative study of high quadriplegia. Englewood, CO: Rocky Mountain Regional Spinal Cord Injury System for the National Institute of Handicapped Research.

<u>FILL-IN</u> <u>EXERCISES</u>

1. Motivation, emotion; 2. ventromedial hypothalamus; 3. bulimia nervosa; 4. arousal; 5. Achievement motivation (nAch); 6. drive theory, incentive theory; 7. hierarchy of needs; 8. cognitive, physiological, behavioral; 9. facial feedback hypothesis; 10. evolutionary.

<u>MATCHING</u> <u>EXERCISES</u>

a. 5, b. 9, c. 10, d. 1, e. 8, f. 4, g. 3, h. 6, i. 7, j. 2.

<u>PRACTICE</u> <u>TEST</u> <u>I</u>		<u>PRACTICE</u> <u>TEST</u> <u>II</u>	
1. a (p. 412)	11. a (p. 426)	1. b (p. 412)	11. d (p. 436)
2. b (p. 413)	12. d (p. 427)	2. c (p. 413)	12. b (p. 437)
3. c (p. 415)	13. c (p. 429)	3. a (p. 416)	13. a (p. 437)
4. b (p. 416)	14. d (p. 432)	4. c (p. 418)	14. c (p. 437)
5. c (p. 420)	15. c (p. 434)	5. d (p. 425)	15. c (pp. 438,439)
6. a (p. 420)	16. b (p. 437)	6. d (p. 427)	16. d (p. 439)
7. d (p. 425)	17. c (p. 440)	7. a (p. 429)	17. b (p. 440)
8. b (p. 425)	18. c (p. 437)	8. b (p. 430)	18. b (p. 440)
9. c (p. 425)	19. a (p. 438)	9. d (p. 434)	19. b (p. 441)
10.b (p. 426)	20. d (p. 441)	10.d (pp. 434, 435)	20. c (p. 442)

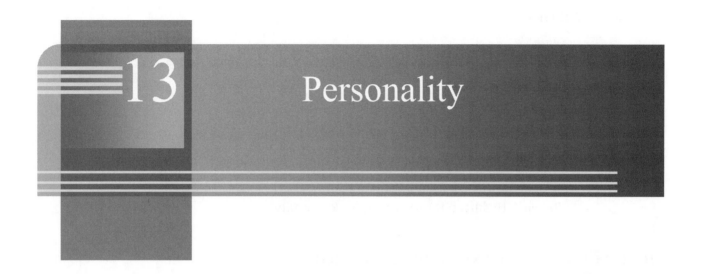

OUTLINE (Survey & Question)

This outline is intended to help you *survey* the chapter. As you read through the various sections, write down any *questions* or comments that come to mind in the space provided. This is a valuable part of active learning and the SQ4R method. It not only makes your reading time more enjoyable and active, but it also increases retention and understanding of the material.

TOPIC	NOTES

I. PERSONALITY ASSESSMENT

    A. How We Measure Personality

    B. Are Personality Measurements Accurate?

        Critical Thinking/Active Learning: Why Are "Pseudo" Personality Tests So Popular?

II. TRAIT THEORIES

A. Early Trait Theorists

B. The "Big 5" Model

C. Evaluating Trait Theories

Research Highlight: Do Animals Have Personality?

III. PSYCHOANALYTIC/PSYCHODYNAMIC THEORIES

A. Freud's Psychoanalytic Theory

B. Neo-Freudian/Psychodynamic Theories

Gender and Cultural Diversity: Horney, Freud, and Penis Envy

C. Evaluating PsychoanalyticTheories

IV. HUMANISTIC THEORIES

A. Carl Rogers

B. Abraham Maslow

C. Evaluating Humanistic Theories

V. SOCIAL/COGNITIVE PERSPECTIVE

A. Bandura's and Rotter's Approaches

B. Evaluating Social/Cognitive Theory

VI. BIOLOGICAL THEORIES

A. Three Major Contributors

B. Interactionism

Gender and Cultural Diversity: Cultural Concepts of "Self"

Core and Expanded LEARNING OBJECTIVES (Read, Recite & wRite)

While *reading* the chapter, stop periodically and *recite* (or repeat in your own words) the answers to the following learning objectives. It will also help your retention if you *write* your answer in the space provided. (Page numbers refer to the text Psychology in Action, 6th Ed.)

Core Learning Objectives
These objectives are found at the beginning of each chapter of Psychology in Action (6th ed.).

1. How do psychologists measure personality?

2. What are the trait theories of personality?

3. What is Freud's psychoanalytic theory, and how did his followers build on his theory?

4. What do humanistic theorists believe about personality?

5. What is the social/cognitive perspective on personality?

6. How does biology contribute to personality?

Expanded Learning Objectives
These objectives offer more detail and a more intensive way to study the chapter.

Upon completion of CHAPTER 13, the student should be able to:

1. Define personality and describe how interviews and observations are used to assess personality (pp. 448-449).

2. List two multitrait objective tests; briefly describe the characteristics of the MMPI/MMPI-2; and differentiate between vocational interest, aptitude, and achievement tests (pp. 449-450).

3. Briefly describe the characteristics of the Rorschach inkblot test and the Thematic Apperception Test (pp. 450-452).

4. Discuss the relative strengths and weaknesses of the four major methods of personality assessment (pp. 452-453).

5. Discuss three logical fallacies that explain the widespread acceptance of "pseudo" personality tests (p. 452).

6. Describe the evolution of the trait theories of personality from Allport to Cattell to Eysenck, ending with the five-factor model (pp. 454-455).

7. Discuss research findings regarding the five-factor model of personality and three major criticisms regarding trait theories in general (pp. 455-459).

8. Describe research findings regarding animal personality (p. 458).

9. Differentiate among Freud's three levels of consciousness (pp. 460-461).

10. Define and discuss Freud's concept of the id, ego, and superego. Define and explain the role of the defense mechanisms employed by the ego (pp. 461-464).

11. Discuss Freud's five stages of psychosexual development and the effects of successful or unsuccessful completion at each stage (pp. 463-467).

12. Compare Freud's original theories to the approaches of the Neo-Freudians: Adler, Jung, and Horney (pp.467-469).

13. Discuss five major criticisms of psychoanalytic theories (pp. 469-470).

14. Discuss humanistic theories of personality, comparing the approaches of Rogers and Maslow; state three major criticisms of humanistic theories (pp. 471-474).

15. Discuss social-cognitive theories of personality, comparing the approaches of Bandura and Rotter; state two strengths and two weaknesses of these theories (pp. 474-476).

16. Describe the role of brain structures, neurochemistry, and genetics advanced in biological theories of personality, and state how the interactionist approach to personality is blending views based on research findings (pp. 476-478).

17. Describe how cultural variations in the concept of "self" affect the study of personality (pp. 478-479).

KEY TERMS (Review)

The *review* step in the SQ4R method is very important to your performance on quizzes and exams. Upon completion of this chapter, you should be able to define the following terms.

Archetypes: _____

_____

Basic Anxiety: _____

_____

Collective Unconscious: _____

_____

Conscious: _____

_____

Ego: _____

_____

Factor Analysis: _____

_____

Five-Factor Model: _____

_____

Id: _____

_____

Inferiority Complex: _____

_____

Minnesota Multiphasic Personality Inventory (MMPI-2): _____

_____

Oedipus Complex: _____

_____

Personality: _____

_____

Pleasure Principle: _____

_____

Preconscious: _____

_____

Projective Tests: _____

_____

Psychosexual Stages: _____

_____

Reality Principle: _____

_____

Reciprocal Determinism: _____

_____

Repression: _____

_____

Rorschach Inkblot Test: _____

_____

Self-Actualization: _____

_____

Self-Concept: _____

_____

Self-Efficacy: _____

_____

Superego: _____

_____

Thematic Apperception Test (TAT): _____

_____

Trait: _____

_____

Unconditional Positive Regard: _____

_____

Unconscious: _____

_____

ACTIVE LEARNING EXERCISES   (Recite)

The *recite* step in the SQ4R method requires you to be an ACTIVE learner. By completing the following exercises, you will test and improve your mastery of the chapter material, which will also improve your performance on quizzes and exams. Answers to some exercises appear at the end of this study guide chapter.

ACTIVE LEARNING I

One way to understand personality and its assessment is to practice testing your friends and family members. In Chapter 13, you were given the following "Try This Yourself" exercise:

Before going on, answer "true" or "false" to the following:

1 People get ahead in this world primarily by luck and connections rather than their own hard work and perseverance.

2 When someone doesn't like you there is little you can do about it.

3 No matter how hard I study; I can't get high grades in most classes.

4 I sometimes keep a rabbit's foot or other special objects as good-luck charms.

5 I sometimes refuse to vote because little can be done to control what politicians do in office.

Using these same five statements, ask at least 10 women and 10 men from your family and friends to complete this test. Be sure NOT to introduce it as an "internal versus external" scale, which could bias their responses. Once you collect their answers and analyze the data, you will probably find female scores are slightly more *external* than males (i.e., they are more likely to answer true to each of the five statements). Can you explain this? Would there also be an age or ethnicity difference? Why or why not? If you would like to read more about this topic and see the original full-length version of Rotter's internal external scale, check out the following reference:

Rotter, J. B. (1966). Generalized expectancies for internal versus external control of reinforcement. Psychological Monographs, 80, 1-28.

ACTIVE LEARNING II

Employing Precise Terms: Defense Mechanisms   (A Behavioral Skill)

A critical thinker is capable of reading a description of an event and determining if this event matches a given situation or individual. Thus, if presented with a number of behavioral descriptions of an individual, such as defense mechanisms, the critical thinker should be able to determine which mechanism best applies in a given situation.

By Freud's definition, defense mechanisms operate at the unconscious level; thus, we are not aware when we are using them. If, however, we practice observing their use by others, we may improve our self-insight. This also may help us replace inappropriate defense mechanisms with more appropriate behaviors.

Identify the following defense mechanisms (answers are at the end of this study guide chapter).

1. A woman who was assaulted and raped several years ago in a terrifying attack has forgotten the incident. _____

2. John told his fiancée Susan about his ongoing sexual involvement with other women, but Susan refuses to believe it even when she's seen him kissing other women. _____

3. Laleh has just read several articles describing danger signals for skin cancer. She carefully examines a dangerous looking mole on her own neck, and then with her doctor she calmly and

academically discusses the pros and cons of various treatment strategies and the fact that her mother died from skin cancer. _____

4. Matt received notice that he is on academic probation. Because he will not be playing football while on probation, he decides to drop out of college "to do something worthwhile." _____

5. The President of Parents Against Pornography was extremely active in campaigning against the "filth" our children are exposed to on the Internet. He was later arrested and convicted of 40 counts of soliciting minors on the Internet. _____.

CHAPTER OVERVIEW (Review)

The following CHAPTER OVERVIEW provides a narrative overview of the main topics covered in the chapter. Like the Visual Summary found at the end of each chapter in the text, this narrative summary provides a final opportunity to *review* chapter material.

I. Personality Assessment
Personality is defined as an individual's relatively stable and enduring pattern of thoughts, emotions, and actions. Psychologists assess, describe, explain, and predict personality according to different theoretical orientations.

Psychologists use four methods to measure or assess personality: interviews, observations, objective tests, and projective techniques. Reliability and validity are the major criteria for evaluating the accuracy of personality tests. Personality is most commonly measured through objective tests (such as the **MMPI-2**), which ask test-takers to respond to paper-and-pencil questionnaires or inventories. These tests provide objective standardized information about a large number of personality traits, but they have their limits, including deliberate deception and social desirability bias, diagnostic difficulties, and inappropriate use.

Projective techniques ask test-takers to respond to ambiguous stimuli (such as the **Rorschach** "inkblot" or the **TAT** pictures). Though these tests are said to provide insight into unconscious elements of personality, they are not very reliable or valid.

II. Trait Theories
Trait theorists believe personality consists of relatively stable and consistent characteristics. Early theorists like Allport, Cattell, and Eysenck used **factor analysis** to identify the smallest number of identifying traits. More recently, researchers identified a **Five-Factor Model (FFM)** that can be used to

describe most individuals. The "Big 5" traits are openness, conscientiousness, extroversion, agreeableness, and neuroticism.

III. Psychoanalytic Theories

Freud founded the psychoanalytic approach to personality, which emphasized the power of the unconscious. The mind (or psyche) reportedly functions on three levels (**conscious, preconscious,** and **unconscious**), and the personality has three distinct structures (**id, ego,** and **superego**). The ego struggles to meet the demands of the id and superego, and when these demands are in conflict the ego may resort to defense mechanisms to relieve the resultant anxiety.

According to Freud, all human beings pass through five **psychosexual stages**: oral, anal, phallic, latency, and genital. How specific conflicts at each of these stages are resolved is important to personality development.

Three influential followers of Freud who broke with him were Adler, Jung, and Horney. Known as neo-Freudians, they emphasized different issues. Adler emphasized the **inferiority complex'** and the compensating *will-to-power.* Jung introduced the **collective unconscious** and **archetypes**. Horney stressed the importance of **basic anxiety** and refuted Freud's idea of *penis envy,'* replacing it with *power envy.*

Critics of the psychoanalytic approach, especially Freud's theories, argue that it is difficult to test, overemphasizes biology and unconscious forces, has inadequate empirical support, is sexist, and lacks cross-cultural support. Despite these criticisms, Freud remains a notable pioneer in psychology.

IV. Biological Theories

Biological theories emphasize the brain, neurochemistry, and inherited genetic components of personality. Research on specific traits such as sensation seeking and extroversion support the biological approach.

The interactionist approach suggests that the major theories overlap and each contributes to our understanding of personality. Most theories of personality are biased toward Western, individualistic cultures and their perception of the "self." Recognizing and understanding this bias helps keep our study of personality in perspective.

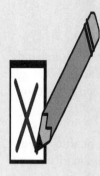

SELF-TESTS (Review & wRite)

Completing the following SELF-TESTS will provide immediate feedback on how well you have mastered the material. In the *crossword puzzle* and *fill-in exercises*, write the appropriate word or words in the blank spaces. The *matching exercise* requires you to match the terms in one column to their correct definitions in the other. For the *multiple-choice questions* in Practice Tests I and II, circle or underline the correct answer. When you are unsure of any answer, be sure to highlight or specially mark the item and then go back to the text for further review. Correct answers are provided at the end of this study guide chapter.

CROSSWORD PUZZLE FOR CHAPTER 13

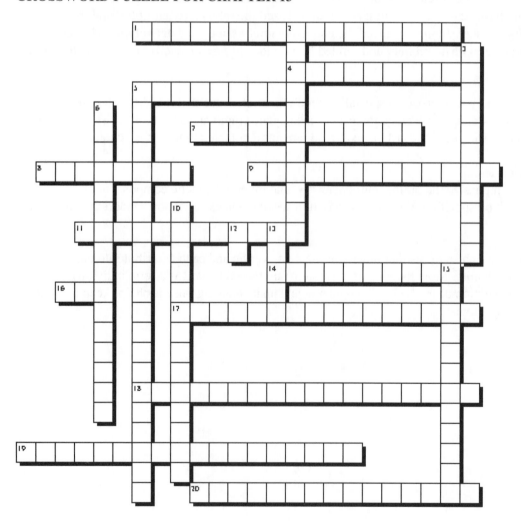

ACROSS

1 In Freud's theory, the principle on which the id operates---that immediate pleasure is the sole motivation for behavior.

4 Freud's first and most basic defense mechanism because it blocks unacceptable impulses from coming into awareness.

5 In Freudian terms, thoughts or information that a person is currently aware of or is remembering.

7 Freud's term for thoughts or information that one can become aware of easily.

8 In psychoanalytic theory, the part of the personality that incorporates parental and societal standards for morality.

9 According to Bandura, a person's learned beliefs that he or she is capable of producing desired results, such as mastering new skills and achieving personal goals.

11 According to Horney, the feelings of helplessness and insecurity that adults experience because as children they felt alone and isolated in a hostile environment.

14 According to Jung, the images or patterns of thoughts, feelings, and behavior that reside in the collective unconscious.

16 In Freud's theory, the rational part of the psyche that deals with reality and attempts to control the impulses of the id while also satisfying the social approval and self-esteem needs of the superego.

17 According to Freud, the principle on which the conscious ego operates as it tries to meet the demands of the unconscious id and the realities of the environment.

18 According to Maslow, an innate tendency toward growth that motivates all human behavior and results in the full realization of a person's highest potential.

19 Adler's idea that feelings of inferiority develop from early childhood experiences of helplessness and incompetence.

20 Psychological tests using ambiguous stimuli, such as inkblots or drawings. The ambiguity of the stimuli reportedly allows the test taker to project his or her true, unconscious conflicts, motives, psychological defenses, and personality traits onto the test material.

DOWN

2 An individual's relatively stable and enduring pattern of thoughts, feelings, and actions.

3 Freud's term for thoughts, motives, impulses, or desires that lie beyond a person's normal awareness, but that can be made available through psychoanalysis.

5 Jung's concept of an inherited unconscious that all humans share.

6 A trait theory that explains personality in terms of a "Big Five" model---openness, conscientiousness, extroversion, agreeableness, and neuroticism.

10 A statistical procedure used to determine the most basic units or factors in a large array of data.

12 According to Freud, the source of instinctual energy, which works on the pleasure principle and is concerned with immediate gratification.

13 A relatively stable and consistent characteristic that can be used to describe someone.

15 In Rogers' theory, all the information and beliefs individuals have about their own nature, qualities, and behavior.

FILL-IN EXERCISES

1. An individual's relatively stable and enduring pattern of thoughts, feelings, and actions is known as _____; whereas a relatively stable and consistent characteristic that can be used to describe someone is known as a _____ (pp. 448, 454).

2. Two important criteria for evaluating the usefulness of tests used to assess personality are _____ and _____ (p. 453).

3. The _____ is an objective, self-report test that was developed for the purpose of psychiatric diagnosis (p. 449).

4. If you are imaginative, curious, open to new ideas, and interested in cultural pursuits, on the "Big 5" model of personality you would score high on _____ (p. 454).

5. _____ theories attempt to *explain* personality by examining unconscious forces, whereas _____ theories tend to *describe* personality as it currently exists (p. 457, 460).

6. According to Freud, thoughts or information we are currently aware of or are remembering are part of our _____, whereas the _____ contains thoughts or information we can become aware of easily, and the _____ contains our hidden thoughts, motives, impulses, and desires (p. 461).

7. The id is often described as operating on the _____, whereas the ego operates on the _____ (p. 462).

8. According to Rogers, all the information and beliefs individuals have about their own nature, qualities, and behavior are known as their _____ (p. 471).

9. According to Bandura, an individual's cognitions, behaviors, and the learning environment interact to produce personality. This is known as _____ (p. 474).

10. The _____ approach represents a blending of several theories of personality (p. 478).

MATCHING EXERCISES

Column A   Column B

a. Bandura   1.____ Self-concept and unconditional positive regard.
b. Rorschach   2.____ Major personality theories overlap and contribute.
c. Five-Factor Model   3.____ Focuses on self-actualization.
d. Interactionism   4.____ Focuses on unconscious forces.
e. Rotter   5.____ Phenomenological perspective.
f. Maslow   6.____ OCEAN.
g. Humanistic Theories   7.____ Cognitive expectancies and locus of control.
h. Jung   8.____ Collective unconscious and archetypes.
i. Psychoanalytic Theory   9.____ Self-efficacy and reciprocal determinism.
j. Rogers   10.____ Projective "inkblot" test.

PRACTICE TEST I

1. The MMPI is an example of a(n) _____.
    a. projective test
    b. personality interview
    c. objective personality test
    d. multiple-measure of personality

2. The _____ is a widely used self-report test designed to detect disturbed personality characteristics.
    a. 16 PF
    b. MMPI
    c. Internal-External Locus of Control Test
    d. structured interview

3. Which of the following is a projective test?
    a. 16 PF
    b. MMPI
    c. TAT
    d. Internal-External Locus of Control Test

4. The Rorschach tests a person's responses to _____.
    a. pictures
    b. movies
    c. sentences
    d. inkblots

5. According to Hans Eysenck, personality is a relationship between all but which one of these traits?
    a.   extraversion-introversion
    b.   neuroticism
    c.   trustworthiness
    d.   psychotism

6. _____ is **NOT** associated with trait theories of personality.
    a.   Cattell
    b.   Allport
    c.   Rorschach
    d.   Eysenck

7. This is **NOT** one of the "Big 5" personality traits.
    a.   openness
    b.   conscientiousness
    c.   egoism
    d.   agreeableness

8. According to Freudian theory, the _____ is the part of the psyche that provides instinctual motivation for behavior.
    a.   id
    b.   superego
    c.   ego
    d.   ego-ideal

9. The first and most basic defense mechanism that keeps unacceptable impulses out of conscious awareness is _____.
    a.   repression
    b.   denial
    c.   rationalization
    d.   displacement

10. The Oedipus Complex is the major conflict during the _____ stage in Freud's theory of psychosexual development.
    a.   oral
    b.   latent
    c.   genital
    d.   phallic

11. Compared with Freudian theory, neo-Freudian approaches tend to emphasize the _____.
    a.   importance of the superego
    b.   unconscious mind
    c.   impact of social and cultural influences
    d.   importance of sexual impulses

12. The concept of the "inferiority complex" was formulated by _____.
    a.   Freud
    b.   Erikson
    c.   Adler
    d.   Jung

13. The collective unconscious contains _____.
    a.   a personal unconscious
    b.   your conscience
    c.   the ego-ideal
    d.   archetypes

14. Rogers believes all but one of the following are innate biological capacities in all human beings.
    a.   self-efficacy
    b.   mental health
    c.   congruence
    d.   self-esteem

15. This term is most associated with Maslow.
    a.   will to power
    b.   basic anxiety
    c.   self-actualization
    d.   congruence

16. Humanistic approaches to personality emphasize the importance of _____.
    a.   intrapsychic conflicts
    b.   archetypes
    c.   observational learning
    d.   the basic goodness in human nature

17. The _____ theory suggests personality is unique because of an individual's history of interaction with the environment.
    a.   social learning
    b.   phenomenological
    c.   Gestalt
    d.   social/cognitive

18. According to Carl Rogers, it is important to receive _____ in order to develop their full potential.
    a.   psychological help
    b.   personal intervention
    c.   empathy reduction
    d.   unconditional positive regard

19. The _____ approach to personality is most likely to analyze self-talk.
    a.   phenomenological
    b.   social/cognitive
    c.   Neo-Freudian
    d.   collective unconscious

20. Rotter's concept of locus of control and Bandura's concept of self-efficacy share the belief that _____ influence(s) behavior.
    a.   reciprocal determinism
    b.   archetypes
    c.   emotions
    d.   expectancies

PRACTICE TEST II

1. The use of handwriting analysis to assess your personality is probably _____.
    a.   unreliable
    b.   invalid
    c.   non-standardized
    d.   all of these options

2. Projective tests measure your _____.
    a.   potential abilities
    b.   current knowledge and abilities
    c.   your interests and aptitudes
    d.   unconscious processes

3. This is an illustration of the Fallacy of Positive Instances.
    a.   offering "something for everyone"
    b.   offering information that maintains a positive self-image
    c.   failing to notice when a characteristic or prediction does not confirm expectations
    d.   all of these options

4. Cheerful, honest, friendly, and optimistic are all _____.
    a. personality traits
    b. motives
    c. emotions
    d. all of these options

5. Which of the following acronyms can help you remember the "Big 5" personality traits?
    a. OCEAN
    b. BEACH
    c. SHORE
    d. WAVES

6. The main problem with all trait theories is that they _____.
    a. are unreliable
    b. cannot explain personality
    c. are invalid descriptions of personality
    d. have not been standardized

7. The id, ego, and superego are _____.
    a. located in the unconscious
    b. three mental structures in the psyche
    c. present at birth
    d. the first three psychosexual stages of development

8. Perfection is a problem that is most associated with the _____.
    a. id
    b. ego
    c. superego
    d. ego and superego

9. The problem with the excessive use of defense mechanisms is that they _____.
    a. distort reality
    b. increase anxiety
    c. become ineffective
    d. become fixated

10. The genitals are the primary erogenous zones in which stage(s) of Freud's psychosexual theory of development?
    a. latency
    b. phallic
    c. phallic and genital
    d. latency, phallic, and genital

11. Basic anxiety is associated with which of the following Neo-Freudians?
    a.   Horney
    b.   Adler
    c.   Jung
    d.   Rogers

12. The good and bad feelings you have about yourself are called _____.
    a.   self-actualization
    b.   self-esteem
    c.   identity
    d.   superiority-inferiority complex

13. A major criticism of humanistic psychology is that most of its concepts and assumptions _____.
    a.   are invalid
    b.   are unreliable
    c.   cannot be tested empirically
    d.   lack a theoretical foundation

14. Self-efficacy is associated with _____.
    a.   Bandura
    b.   Rogers
    c.   Rotter
    d.   Maslow

15. A criticism of the social-cognitive approach is that it overlooks or ignores the contribution of emotion, development, and _____ in understanding personality.
    a.   scientific research
    b.   the role of the unconscious
    c.   motivation
    d.   expectancies

16. Dopamine is involved in the personality trait(s) of _____.
    a.   sensation-seeking
    b.   extroversion
    c.   aggression and altruism
    d.   extroversion and sensation-seeking

17. Based on heritability studies, 40% to 50% of personality appears to be related to _____.
    a.   the environment
    b.   the family
    c.   family, friends, and the environment
    d.   genetic factors

18. An interactionist approach that explains introversion might suggest that this trait is caused by _____.
    a.   high levels of cortical arousal
    b.   conditioning
    c.   cognitive processes
    d.   all of these options

19. The concept of _____ is essential to all Western theories of personality.
    a.   the unconscious
    b.   self
    c.   behavior
    d.   all of these options

20. In Asia, people are defined in terms of their _____.
    a.   enduring traits
    b.   short-term traits
    c.   social relationship
    d.   submissiveness

ANSWERS

The following answers to active learning exercises, crossword puzzles, fill-ins, matching exercises, and practice tests 1 and 2 provide immediate feedback on your mastery of the material. Try not to simply memorize the answers. When you are unsure of your "guess" or make an error, be sure to go back to the textbook and carefully review. This will greatly improve your scores on classroom exams and quizzes.

CROSSWORD PUZZLE FOR CHAPTER 13

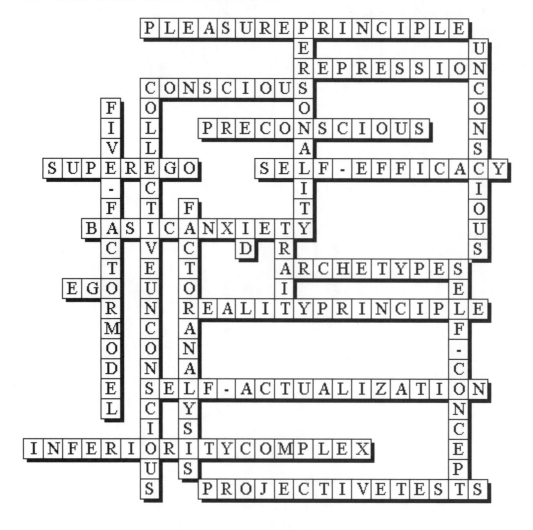

ACTIVE LEARNING EXERCISE II

1. repression; 2. denial; 3. intellectualization; 4. rationalization; 5. projection.

FILL-IN EXERCISES

1. personality, trait; 2. reliability, validity; 3. Minnesota Multiphasic Personality Inventory (MMPI); 4. openness; 5. Psychoanalytic, trait; 6. conscious, preconscious, unconscious; 7. pleasure principle, reality principle; 8. self-concept; 9. reciprocal determinism; 10. interactionist.

MATCHING EXERCISES

a. 9, b. 10, c. 6, d. 2, e. 7, f. 3, g. 5, h. 8, i. 4, j. 1.

PRACTICE TEST I		PRACTICE TEST II	
1. c (p. 449)	11. c (p. 467)	1. d (p. 448)	11. a (p. 469)
2. b (p. 450)	12. c (p. 468)	2. d (p. 450)	12. b (p. 472)
3. c (p. 450)	13. d (p. 468)	3. c (p. 452)	13. c (p. 473)
4. d (p. 450)	14. a (p. 472)	4. a (p. 454)	14. a (p. 474)
5. c (p. 454)	15. c (p. 473)	5. a (p. 454)	15. b (p. 475)
6. c (p. 454)	16. d (p. 473)	6. b (p. 457)	16. d (p. 477)
7. c (pp. 454, 455)	17. d (p. 474)	7. b (p. 462)	17. d (p. 477)
8. a (p. 462)	18. d (p. 472)	8. c (p. 462)	18. d (p. 478)
9. a (p. 463)	19. b (p. 474)	9. a (p. 463)	19. b (p. 478)
10.d (p. 465)	20. d (p 475)	10.c (p. 465)	20. c (p. 479)

14 Psychological Disorders

OUTLINE   (Survey & Question)

This outline is intended to help you *survey* the chapter. As you read through the various sections, write down any *questions* or comments that come to mind in the space provided. This is a valuable part of active learning and the SQ4R method. It not only makes your reading time more enjoyable and active, but it also increases retention and understanding of the material.

TOPIC   **NOTES**

I. STUDYING PSYCHOLOGICAL DISORDERS

   A. Identifying Abnormal Behavior

       Gender and Cultural Diversity: A Cultural Look at Disorders

   B. Explaining Abnormality

   C. Classifying Abnormal Behaviors

II. ANXIETY DISORDERS

A. Unreasonable Anxiety

B. Causes of Anxiety Disorders

III. MOOD DISORDERS

A. Understanding Mood Disorders

B. Causes of Mood Disorders

Gender and Cultural Diversity: Gender, Culture, and Depression

C. Suicide

IV. SCHIZOPHRENIA

A. Symptoms of Schizophrenia

B. Types of Schizophrenia

C. Causes of Schizophrenia

Gender and Cultural Diversity: Culture and Schizophrenia

V. OTHER DISORDERS

A. Dissociative Disorders

B. Personality Disorders

Critical Thinking/Active Learning: Testing Your Knowledge of Abnormal Behavior

Core and Expanded LEARNING OBJECTIVES   (Read, Recite & wRite)

While *reading* the chapter, stop periodically and *recite* (or repeat in your own words) the answers to the following learning objectives. It will also help your retention if you *write* your answer in the space provided. (Page numbers refer to the text <u>Psychology in Action</u>, 6th Ed.)

Core Learning Objectives
These objectives are found at the beginning of each chapter of <u>Psychology in Action</u> (6th ed.).

1. How do psychologists identify, explain, and classify abnormal behavior?

2. What are anxiety disorders and what causes them?

3. When do disturbances in mood become abnormal?

4. What are the symptoms and causes of schizophrenia?

5. How are the dissociative disorders and personality disorders identified?

<u>Expanded</u> Learning <u>Objectives</u>
These objectives offer more detail and a more intensive way to study the chapter.

Upon completion of CHAPTER 14, the student should be able to:

1. Define the medical student's disease, and describe five common myths regarding mental health and illness (p.484).

2. Define abnormal behavior, and describe the four basic standards for identifying such behavior, and the limitations for each standard (pp. 485-486).

3. Differentiate between culture-general and culture-bound symptoms.   State at least five culture-general symptoms (pp. 486-488).

4. Summarize the historical progression in the definition of abnormality from the demonological to the medical model; describe Szasz's criticism of the medical model of mental illness (pp. 488-489).

5. Briefly describe and explain the importance of Rosenhan's classic experiment regarding the consequences of being labeled and treated for mental illness (pp. 489-490).

6. Describe the development of the Diagnostic and Statistical Manual (DSM), including the DSM-IV-TR's classification system, purpose, and limitations. Differentiate between neurosis, psychosis, and insanity (pp. 490-494).

7. Describe five major anxiety disorders and their possible causes (pp. 494-499).

8. Describe two major mood disorders and their possible biological and psychosocial causes (pp. 500-502).

9. Describe similarities and differences in depression across cultures and between genders (pp. 502-503).

10. Discuss ten common myths regarding suicide, list warnings signs for teen suicide, and describe what steps to take if someone is suicidal (pp. 503-504).

11. Define schizophrenia, and describe its five characteristic areas of disturbance; differentiate between positive and negative symptoms (pp. 504-509).

12. Discuss biological and psychosocial theories that attempt to explain schizophrenia (pp. 509-512).

13. Describe similarities and differences in symptoms of schizophrenia across cultures (pp. 512-513).

14. Identify the common characteristic for all dissociative disorders, and differentiate between dissociative amnesia, fugue, depersonalization, and identity disorder (pp. 514-516).

15. Describe the essential characteristics for all personality disorders; describe the four hallmark symptoms for an antisocial personality disorder and the core features of borderline personality disorder; discuss the possible causes of these personality disorders (pp. 516-517).

16. Define comorbidity and describe why alcohol use disorders often overlap with other mental disorders (p. 518).

KEY TERMS (_Review_)

The _review_ step in the SQ4R method is very important to your performance on quizzes and exams. Upon completion of this chapter, you should be able to define the following terms.

Abnormal Behavior: _Pattern of emotion, thought, action considered pathological because of statistics disability dysfunction, violation of norms_

Antisocial Personality: _egocentric, manipulative_

Anxiety Disorder: _____

Bipolar Disorder: _periods of Manic and then of depression_

Borderline Personality Disorder: _unstable mood, relationships, self image_

Comorbidity: _when there are 2 or more disorders present at the same time_

Delusions: Thought ~~Thought~~ true but false w/ evidence

_____

Diagnostic and Statistical Manual of Mental Disorders (DSM-IV-TR): _____

_____

Dissociative Disorder: amnesia or mpd because person trys to escape a memory

Dissociative Identity Disorder (DID): multipul Personality disorder

_____

Dopamine Hypothesis: Theory that schizophrenia is caused by to much dopamine

Generalized Anxiety Disorder: Chronic symptoms of worry no focus of object or situation

Hallucinations: perceptions w/o stimulus

_____

Insanity: legal Term for people w/ mental disorder

_____

Learned Helplessness: Seligmans theory that pain is inescapable

_____

Major Depressive Disorder: long term depression

_____

Medical Model: assumes that all mental illness is physically based

Neurosis: *group of disorders w/ anxiety and other problems*

_____

Obsessive-Compulsive Disorder (OCD): *Obsessive repetitive behavior*

_____

Panic Disorder: _____

_____

Personality Disorder: *inflexable maladaptive personality*

_____

Phobia: *irrational fear*

_____

Post-traumatic Stress Disorder (PTSD): *anxiety that follows traumatic experience flash backs and night mares*

Psychiatry: *medical diagnosis of mental illness*

_____

Psychosis: _____

_____

Schizophrenia: *Thought disorder*

_____

ACTIVE LEARNING EXERCISES (Recite)

The *recite* step in the SQ4R method requires you to be an ACTIVE learner. By completing the following exercises, you will test and improve your mastery of the chapter material, which will also improve your performance on quizzes and exams. Answers to some exercises appear at the end of this study guide chapter.

ACTIVE LEARNING EXERCISE I

HOW YOUR THOUGHTS CAN MAKE YOU DEPRESSED

Events have many causes, but if the following situations really happened to you, what do you think would be the most likely cause? Will the cause change in the future? Is the cause unique? Respond to these questions by circling the number that most closely describes how you would feel in this same situation. Answering carefully and truthfully will provide insight into how your thoughts may cause depression.

SITUATION 1

You are introduced to a new person at a party and are left alone to talk. After a few minutes, the person appears bored.

1. Is this outcome caused by you? Or is it something about the other person or the circumstances?

   1   2   3   4   5   ⑥   7
   Other person or   Me
   circumstances

2. Will the cause of this outcome also be present in the future?

   1   2   3   4   5   ⑥   7
   No   Yes

3. Is the cause of this outcome unique to this situation, or does it also affect other areas of your life?

   1   2   3   ④   5   6   7
   Affects just this   Affects all situations
   situation   in my life

SITUATION 2

You receive an award for a project that is highly praised.

4. Is this outcome cause by you or something about the circumstances?

   1   2   3   4   ⑤   6   7
   Circumstances   Me

5. Will the cause of this outcome also be present in the future?

   1   2   3   ④   5   6   7
   No   Yes

6. Is the cause of this outcome unique to this situation, or does it also affect other areas of your life?

   1   2   3   4   5   ⑥   7
   Affect just this   Affects all situations
   situation   in my life

You have just completed a modified version of the *Attributional Style Questionnaire,* which measures people's explanations for the causes of good and bad events. If you have a *depressive explanatory style,* you tend to explain *bad* events--Situation 1--in terms of internal factors ("It's my fault"), a stable cause ("it will always be this way"), and a global cause ("It's this way in many situations"). In contrast, if you have an *optimistic explanatory style,* you tend to make external ("It's someone else's fault"), unstable ("It won't happen again"), and specific ("It's just in this one area") explanations.

When *good* things happen, however, the opposite occurs. People with a depressive explanatory style tend to make external, unstable, specific explanations, wheras those with an optimistic style tend to make internal, stable, global explanations.

	Depressive Explanatory Style	Optimistic Explanatory Style
Bad Events	Internal, stable, global	External, unstable, specific
Good Events	External, unstable, specific	Internal, stable, global

If you had mostly high scores (5-7) on questions 1, 2, and 3 and low scores (1-3) on questions 4, 5, and 6, you probably have a depressive explanatory style. If the reverse is true (low scores on the first three questions and high scores on the last three), you tend to have an optimistic explanatory style.

What difference does your explanatory style make? Research shows that people who attribute bad outcomes to themselves and good outcomes to external factors are more prone to depression than people who do the opposite (Abramson, Seligman, & Teasdale, 1978; Seligman, 1991, 1994). If you have a bad experience and then blame it on your personal (internal) inadequacies, interpret it as unchangeable (stable), and draw far-reaching (global) conclusions, you are obviously more likely to feel depressed. This self-blaming, pessimistic, and overgeneralizing explanatory style results in a sense of hopelessness (Abramson, Metalsky, & Alloy, 1989; Metalsky et al., 1993).

As expected, the idea that depression can be caused by attributional style has its critics. The problem lies in separating cause from effect. Does a depressive explanatory style cause depression, or does depression cause a depressive explanatory style? Or could another variable, such as neurotransmitters or other biological factors cause both? Evidence suggests that both thought patterns and biology interact and influence depression. Although biological explanations undoubtedly play an important role in major depressive disorders and professional help is needed, you may find that changing your explanatory style can help dispel mild or moderate depression.

ACTIVE LEARNING EXERCISE II

Distinguishing Fact from Opinion   (A Behavioral Skill)

To critically analyze controversial issues, it helps to distinguish between statements of fact and statements of opinion. A fact is a statement that can be proven true. An opinion is a statement that expresses how a person feels about an issue or what someone thinks is true. Although it is also important to determine whether the facts are true or false, in this exercise simply mark "O" for opinion and "F" for fact. After you have responded to each of the items, try discussing your answers with friends and classmates.

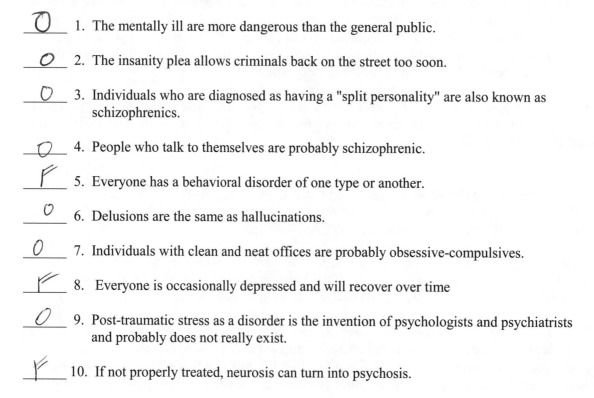

___O___ 1. The mentally ill are more dangerous than the general public.

___O___ 2. The insanity plea allows criminals back on the street too soon.

___O___ 3. Individuals who are diagnosed as having a "split personality" are also known as schizophrenics.

___O___ 4. People who talk to themselves are probably schizophrenic.

___F___ 5. Everyone has a behavioral disorder of one type or another.

___O___ 6. Delusions are the same as hallucinations.

___O___ 7. Individuals with clean and neat offices are probably obsessive-compulsives.

___F___ 8. Everyone is occasionally depressed and will recover over time

___O___ 9. Post-traumatic stress as a disorder is the invention of psychologists and psychiatrists and probably does not really exist.

___F___ 10. If not properly treated, neurosis can turn into psychosis.

CHAPTER OVERVIEW (Review)

The following CHAPTER OVERVIEW provides a narrative overview of the
main topics covered in the chapter. Like the Visual Summary found at the end
of each chapter in the text, this narrative summary provides a final opportunity
to *review* chapter material.

I. Studying Psychological Disorders

Abnormal behavior refers to patterns of emotion, thought, and action considered pathological for one or
more of these reasons: statistical infrequency, disability or dysfunction, personal distress, or violation of
norms.

The belief that demons cause abnormal behavior was common in ancient times. The **medical model**,
which emphasizes diseases and illness, replaced this demonological model. During the Middle Ages,
demonology returned, and exorcisms were used to treat abnormal behavior. Toward the close of the
Middle Ages, the medical model returned in the form of hospitals known as asylums. The medical model
and biological theories still dominate modern times. According to critics, this overlooks the importance
of psychological factors, such as unconscious conflicts, inappropriate learning, faulty cognitive
processes, and negative self-concepts.

The **Diagnostic and Statistical Manual of Mental Disorders (DSM-IV-TR)** categorizes disorders
according to major similarities and differences in the way disturbed people behave. DSM-IV
classification provides detailed descriptions of symptoms, which in turn allows standardized diagnosis
and treatment, and improved communication among professionals and between professionals and
patients. The DSM-IV has been criticized for not paying sufficient attention to cultural factors, for
continuing to support the medical model, and for labeling people. Misdiagnosis also occurs, and the label
"mentally ill" can lead to social and economic discrimination.

II. Anxiety Disorders

People with **anxiety disorders** have persistent feelings of threat in facing everyday problems. **Phobias**
are exaggerated fears of specific objects or situations, such as agoraphobia, a fear of being in open
spaces. In **generalized anxiety disorders**, there is a persistent free-floating anxiety. In **panic disorder**,
anxiety is concentrated into brief or lengthy episodes of panic attacks. In **obsessive-compulsive
disorder**, persistent anxiety-arousing thoughts (obsessions) are relieved by ritualistic actions
(compulsions) such as hand washing. In **post-traumatic stress disorder (PTSD),** a person who has
experienced an overwhelming trauma, such as rape, has recurrent maladaptive emotional reactions, such
as exaggerated startle responses, sleep disturbances, and flashbacks.

Three common explanations for anxiety disorders are learning, biology, and cognitive processes.
Learning theorists suggest anxiety disorders result from classical and operant conditioning, as well as
modeling and imitation; whereas the biological perspective emphasizes genetic predisposition, brain

abnormalities, and biochemistry. The cognitive approach proposes that distorted thinking causes an amplification of ordinary threats.

III. Mood Disorders

Mood disorders are disturbances of affect (emotion) that may include psychotic distortions of reality. In **major depressive disorder**, individuals experience a long-lasting depressed mood, feelings of worthlessness, and loss of interest in most activities. The feelings are without apparent cause and the individual may lose contact with reality. In **bipolar disorder**, episodes of mania and depression alternate with normal periods. During the manic episode, speech and thinking are rapid, and the person may experience delusions of grandeur and act impulsively.

Biological theories of mood disorders emphasize disruptions in neurotransmitters (especially dopamine and serotonin). There is also evidence of a genetic predisposition for both major depression and bipolar disorder. Psychosocial theories of mood disorders emphasize disturbed interpersonal relationships, faulty thinking, poor self-concept, and maladaptive learning. **Learned helplessness** theory suggests that depression results from repeatedly failing to escape from a source of stress.

Depression involves several culture-general symptoms, such as feelings of sadness and loss of enjoyment in daily activities. Women are more likely than men to suffer depressive symptoms in many countries. Suicide is a serious problem associated with depression. By becoming involved and showing concern, we can help reduce the risk of suicide.

IV. Schizophrenia

Schizophrenia is a serious psychotic mental disorder that afflicts approximately one out of every 100 people. The five major symptoms are disturbances in perception (impaired filtering and selection, **hallucinations**); language (word salad, neologisms); thought (impaired logic, **delusions**); emotion (either exaggerated or blunted emotions); and behavior (social withdrawal, bizarre mannerisms, catalepsy, waxy flexibility).

Schizophrenic symptoms can be divided into a two-type classification system: Distorted or excessive mental activity (e.g., delusions and hallucinations) are classified as *positive symptoms*, whereas symptoms involving behavioral deficits (e.g., toneless voice, flattened emotions) are classified as *negative symptoms*.

Biological theories of the causes of schizophrenia propose genetics (people inherit a predisposition), disruptions in neurotransmitters (the **dopamine hypothesis**), and brain function (such as enlarged ventricles and lower levels of activity in the frontal and temporal lobes). Psychosocial theories of schizophrenia focus on stress and disturbed family communication.

Schizophrenia is the most culturally universal mental disorder in the world. Many symptoms are culturally general (such as delusions), but significant differences also exist across cultures in prevalence, form, onset, and prognosis.

V. Other Disorders

In **dissociative disorders**, critical elements of personality split apart. This split is manifested in failing to recall or identify past experiences (dissociative amnesia), by leaving home and wandering off (dissociative fugue), or by developing completely separate personalities (**dissociative identity disorder [DID]** or multiple personality disorder).

Personality disorders involve inflexible, maladaptive personality traits. The best-known type is the antisocial personality, characterized by egocentrism, lack of guilt, impulsivity, and superficial charm. Research suggests this disorder may be related to defects in brain waves, genetic inheritance, or disturbed family relationships. **Borderline personality disorder (BPD)** is the most commonly diagnosed personality disorder. It is characterized by impulsivity and instability in mood, relationships, and self-image.

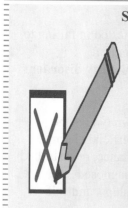

SELF-TESTS (Review & wRite)

Completing the following SELF-TESTS will provide immediate feedback on how well you have mastered the material. In the *crossword puzzle* and *fill-in exercises*, write the appropriate word or words in the blank spaces. The *matching exercise* requires you to match the terms in one column to their correct definitions in the other. For the *multiple-choice questions* in Practice Tests I and II, circle or underline the correct answer. When you are unsure of any answer, be sure to highlight or specially mark the item and then go back to the text for further review. Correct answers are provided at the end of this study guide chapter.

CROSSWORD PUZZLE FOR CHAPTER 14

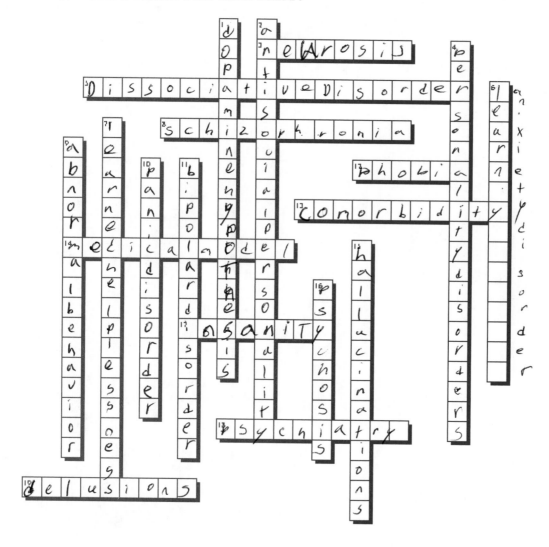

ACROSS

3 A large group of disorders characterized by unrealistic anxiety and other associated problems.

5 Stress-related disorder characterized by amnesia, fugue, or multiple personality. In all cases, though, the person is trying to escape from the memory of a painful experience.

8 Group of psychotic disorders involving major disturbances in perception, language, thought, emotion, and behavior. The individual withdraws from people and reality, often into a fantasy life of delusions and hallucinations.

12 Type of anxiety disorder characterized by intense, irrational fear and avoidance of a specific object or situation.

13 The co-occurrence of two or more disorders in the same person at the same time, as when a person suffers both depression and alcoholism.

14 Perspective that assumes diseases have physical causes that can be diagnosed, treated, and possibly cured. Using this perspective, abnormal behaviors also have physical causes that can be diagnosed by their symptoms and treated and cured through therapy, including drugs, hospitalization, and so on.

17 A legal term for people with a mental disorder that implies a lack of responsibility for their behavior and an inability to manage their affairs.

18 The specialized branch of medicine dealing with the diagnosis, treatment, and prevention of mental

19 Mistaken beliefs maintained in spite of strong evidence to the contrary.

DOWN

1 A theory suggesting that schizophrenia is caused by an overactivity of dopamine neurons in a specific region of the brain.

2 Personality disorder characterized by egocentrism, lack of conscience, impulsive behavior, and manipulation of others.

4 A DSM-IV-TR category that describes individuals with inflexible, maladaptive personality traits. The best-known type is the antisocial personality.

6 Type of abnormal behavior characterized by unrealistic, irrational fear.

7 In Seligman's theory, a state of helplessness or resignation in which people or animals learn that escape from something painful is impossible and depression results.

9 Patterns of emotion, thought, and action considered pathological (diseased or disordered) for one or more of these reasons: statistical infrequency, disability or dysfunction, personal distress, or violation of norms.

10 Type of anxiety disorder characterized by sudden and inexplicable attacks of intense fear. Symptoms include difficulty breathing, heart palpitations, dizziness, trembling, terror, and feelings of impending doom.

11 A diagnostic term in DSM-IV-TR for individuals who experience episodes of mania or of both mania and depression. Excessive and unreasonable elation and hyperactivity characterize manic episodes.

15 Sensory perceptions that occur without an external stimulus.

16 Serious mental disorders characterized by loss of contact with reality and extreme mental disruption. Because daily functioning is often impaired, psychotic individuals are more likely to need hospitalization.

FILL-IN

1. _Psychiatry_ is defined in your text as patterns of emotion, thought, and action considered pathological for one or more of these reasons: statistical infrequency, disability or dysfunction, personal distress, or violation of norms (p. 485).

2. Victims of "windigo psychosis," a malady that occurs among the Chippewa, Cree, and Montagnais-Naskapi Indians, have a compulsion to _____ (p. 486).

3. In early treatment of abnormal behavior, _____ was used to allow evil spirits to escape; whereas _____ was designed to make the body so uncomfortable it would be uninhabitable by the devil (pp. 488-489).

4. David Rosenhan and his colleagues were admitted to a psychiatric hospital with a diagnosis of _____ because they claimed to hear voices, officially known as _____ (p. 489).

5. _Obsessive compulsive disorder_ is a type of anxiety disorder characterized by intrusive thoughts and urges to perform repetitive, ritualistic behaviors (p. 496).

6. The two main types of mood disorders are _Mdd_ and _bipolar_ (p. 500).

7. According to <u>Seligman</u>, people who feel they are unable to control or escape from pain and sadness may develop _____ (p. 502). _learned helplessness_

8. Schizophrenia is also a form of _____, a term describing a general lack of contact with reality (p. 505). _thought disorder_

9. The most severe dissociative disorder is _Did_, previously known as multiple personality disorder, in which at least two separate and distinct personalities exist within the same person (p. 514).

10. The co-occurrence of two or more disorders in the same person at the same time is known as _____ (p. 518). _Comorbility_

MATCHING EXERCISES

Column A   Column B

a. Negative Symptoms   1. _e_ Exaggerated fear of specific objects or situations.
b. Bipolar Disorder   2. _i_ Legal term implying a diminished responsibility.
c. Schizophrenia   3. _b_ Mania and depression alternate with normal periods.
d. DSM-IV-TR   4. _j_ Early term describing anxiety type disorders.
e. Phobias   5. _h_ Also known as psychopath or sociopath.
f. OCD   6. _f_ Persistent thoughts are relieved by ritualistic actions.
g. PTSD   7. _d_ Categorizes mental disorders and their symptoms.
h. Antisocial Personality 8. _c_ Serious psychotic disorder affecting 1:100 people.
i. Insanity   9. _a_ Behavioral deficits in schizophrenia.
j. Neurosis   10. _g_ Anxiety disorder following a traumatic event.

PRACTICE TEST I

1. People may be considered abnormal if their _____ interfere with their ability to function.
    a.   emotions
    b.   thoughts
    c.   behaviors
    d.   any of these options

2. According to the _____ model, someone who worries obsessively and wishes to stop may be experiencing a type of abnormal behavior.
    a.   psychosocial
    b.   sociocultural
    c.   medical
    d.   personal distress

3. The DSM-IV-TR provides _____ for mental disorders.
    a.   categorical descriptions
    b.   treatment recommendations
    c.   theoretical causes
    d.   research suggestions

4. _____ is a legal term indicating that a person cannot be held responsible for his or her actions because of mental illness.
    a.   Psychosis
    b.   Diminished capacity
    c.   Custodianship
    d.   Insanity

5. This type of anxiety is associated with a generalized anxiety disorder.
    a.   phobia
    b.   free-floating
    c.   panic attack
    d.   nervous breakdown

6. In the Japanese social phobia called TKS, people fear that they will _____.
    a.   evaluate others negatively
    b.   embarrass themselves
    c.   embarrass others
    d.   be embarrassed by others

7. Repetitive, ritualistic behaviors such as handwashing, counting, or putting things in order that are associated with an anxiety state are called _____.
    a.   obsessions
    b.   compulsions
    c.   ruminations
    d.   phobias

8. Rape or assault victims who continue to feel unpleasant emotional reactions would be diagnosed as having a(n) _____.
    a.   obsessive-compulsive disorder
    b.   phobia
    c.   generalized anxiety disorder
    d.   post-traumatic stress disorder

9. A major difference between major depressive and bipolar disorder is that only in bipolar disorders do people have _____.
    a.   hallucinations or delusions
    b.   depression
    c.   a biochemical imbalance
    d.   manic episodes

10. This is **NOT** a possible explanation for depression
    a.   imbalances of serotonin or norepinephrine
    b.   genetic predisposition
    c.   lithium deficiency
    d.   learned helplessness

11. Hallucinations and delusions are symptoms of _____.
    a.   mood disorders
    b.   personality disorders
    c.   anxiety disorders
    d.   schizophrenia

12. Antipsychotic drugs can decrease the symptoms of schizophrenia by decreasing the activity of
    _____.
    a.   dopamine synapses
    b.   serotonin synapses
    c.   the frontal lobes
    d.   the autonomic nervous system

13. Family studies have shown that when it comes to schizophrenia, children are more similar to their
    _____.
    a.   biological parents than their adoptive parents
    b.   adoptive parents than their biological parents
    c.   friends than their families
    d.   aunts/uncles than their brothers/sisters

14. Amnesia, fugue, and dissociative identity disorder share this characteristic.
    a.   a separation of experience and memory
    b.   anxiety
    c.   a split personality
    d.   wandering away from home or work

15. Multiple personality disorder is now called _____.
    a.   schizophrenia
    b.   dissociative identity disorder
    c.   amnesiatic personality disorder
    d.   none of these options; this diagnosis is no longer considered real

16. Inflexible, maladaptive personality traits that disrupt occupational and social functioning are _____.
    a.   related to a personality disorder
    b.   common in all of us
    c.   found mostly in Western, individualistic cultures
    d.   related to psychopathic deviation

17. Impulsive behavior, egocentrism, lack of a conscience, and _____ are all characteristic of an antisocial personality disorder.
    a.   manipulation of others
    b.   lack of social skills
    c.   sympathy for victims
    d.   lack of intelligence

18. Impulsivity and instability in mood, relationships, and self-image are part of the _____ personality disorder.
    a.   manic depressive
    b.   bipolar
    c.   borderline
    d.   none of the above

19. People with _____ frequently have a childhood history of neglect and abuse, and as adults tend to see themselves and everyone else in absolutes.
    a.   dissociative identity disorder
    b.   schizophrenia
    c.   generalized anxiety disorder
    d.   borderline personality disorder

20. Your coworker is depressed and using alcohol and amphetamines. This is an example of _____.
    a.   suicidal behavior
    b.   comorbidity
    c.   a death wish
    d.   bipolar personality disorder

PRACTICE TEST II

1. The tendency to think you may have a psychological disorder after reading this chapter is called _____.
    a.   paranoia
    b.   hypochondriasis
    c.   medical student's disease
    d.   a delusion

2. Shortness of breath, headaches, fullness in the head, and problems with memory: Nishimoto found that all of these symptoms are _____.
    a.   cultural universals
    b.   culture-bound
    c.   signs of mental illness
    d.   symptoms of the medical student's disease

3. This was a Freudian term for the causes of anxiety.
    a.   neurosis
    b.   psychosis
    c.   insanity
    d.   hysteria

4. In the DSM-IV-TR, this category describes a person's psychosocial and environmental stressors.
    a.   Axis I
    b.   Axis II
    c.   Axis IV
    d.   Axis V

5. The most frequently occurring category of mental disorders in the general population is _____.
    a.   psychosis
    b.   personality disorders
    c.   depressive disorders
    d.   anxiety disorders

6. In _____ disorder, the individual suffers brief attacks of intense apprehension.
    a.   phobic
    b.   posttraumatic stress
    c.   panic
    d.   dissociative fugue

7. According to _____ theory, classical conditioning, operant conditioning, modeling, and imitation are the causes of anxiety.
    a.   learning
    b.   psychobiological
    c.   sociobiological
    d.   cognitive-behavioral

8. Distorted thinking that magnifies ordinary threats or failures is the _____ explanation for anxiety disorders.
    a.   social learning
    b.   cognitive
    c.   humanistic
    d.   psychoanalytic

9. Mood disorders are treated by _____, which affect the amount or functioning of norepinephrine and serotonin in the brain.
    a.   antidepressants
    b.   antipsychotics and antidepressants
    c.   lithium
    d.   antidepressants and lithium

10. If your _____ has a mood disorder, you have a 50% chance of developing the disorder as well.
    a.   mother
    b.   father
    c.   sibling
    d.   identical twin

11. Internal, stable, and global attributions for failure or unpleasant circumstances are associated with _____.
    a.   anxiety disorders
    b.   delusional disorders
    c.   depression
    d.   all of these options

12. Socialization towards activity, independence, and the suppression of emotions may explain why fewer men than women are diagnosed with _____.
    a.   depression
    b.   anxiety
    c.   schizophrenia
    d.   antisocial personality disorder

13. Auditory hallucinations are most common in _____.
    a.   schizophrenia
    b.   posttraumatic stress disorder
    c.   bipolar disorder
    d.   dissociative identity disorder

14. Believing you are the Queen of England or Jesus Christ would be a symptom called _____.
    a.   hallucinations
    b.   mania
    c.   delusions
    d.   all of these options

15. Delusions, hallucinations, and disorganized speech are _____ symptoms of schizophrenia.
    a.   negative
    b.   positive
    c.   deficit
    d.   undifferentiated

16. The frontal and temporal lobes appear to be less active in people with _____.
    a.   dissociative identity disorder
    b.   personality disorders
    c.   schizophrenia
    d.   all of these options

17. The prognosis for people with schizophrenia is better in _____.
    a.   nonindustrialized societies
    b.   families with expressed emotionality
    c.   stressful situations
    d.   none of these options

18. A history of child abuse, and severe trauma may explain the origins of _____.
    a.   dissociative identity disorder
    b.   schizophrenia
    c.   personality disorders
    d.   phobias

19. Even though emotional deprivation, harsh and inconsistent discipline, and modeling are all highly correlated with antisocial personality disorder, you cannot conclude that these are the causes of this disorder because _____.
    a.   these same behaviors cause schizophrenia in some people
    b.   the correlations are not high enough
    c.   researchers did not look at biological correlations
    d.   correlation does not mean causation

20. The co-occurrence of two or more disorders in the same person at the same time is called _____.
    a.   the synergistic effect
    b.   multiple personality disorder
    c.   comorbidity
    d.   borderline personality disorder

ANSWERS

The following answers to active learning exercises, crossword puzzles, fill-ins, matching exercises, and practice tests 1 and 2 provide immediate feedback on your mastery of the material. Try not to simply memorize the answers. When you are unsure of your "guess" or make an error, be sure to go back to the textbook and carefully review. This will greatly improve your scores on classroom exams and quizzes.

CROSSWORD PUZZLE FOR CHAPTER 14

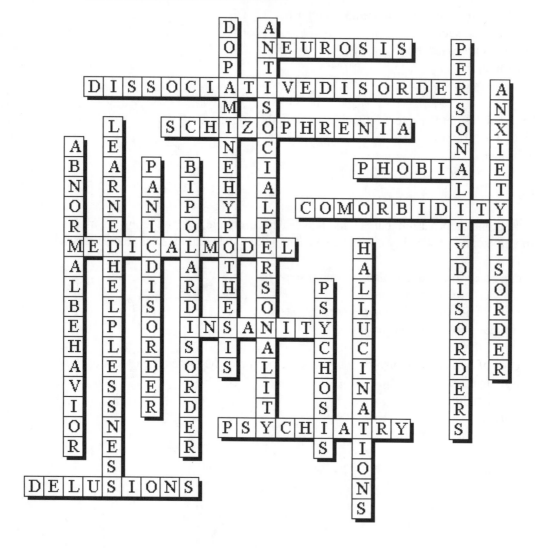

FILL-IN EXERCISES

1. abnormal behavior; 2. consume human flesh; 3. trephining, exorcism; 4. schizophrenia, auditory hallucinations; 5. obsessive-compulsive disorder (OCD); 6. major depressive disorder, bipolar disorder; 7. learned helplessness; 8. psychosis; 9. dissociative identity disorder (DID); 10. comorbidity.

MATCHING EXERCISES

a. 9 b. 3 c. 8 d. 7 e. 1 f. 6 g. 10 h. 5 i. 2 j. 4

PRACTICE TEST I		PRACTICE TEST II	
1. d (p. 485)	11. d (pp.506, 507)	1. c (p. 484)	11. c (p. 502)
2. d (p. 485)	12. a (p. 510)	2. b (p. 487)	12. a (p. 502)
3. a (p. 490)	13. a (p. 510)	3. a (p. 491)	13. a (p. 506)
4. d (p. 491)	14. b (p. 514)	4. c (p. 492)	14. c (p. 507)
5. b (p. 495)	15. b (p. 514)	5. d (p. 495)	15. b (p. 508)
6. c (p. 496)	16. a (p. 516)	6. c (p. 495)	16. c (p. 510)
7. b (p. 496)	17. a (p. 516)	7. a (p. 498)	17. a (p. 513)
8. d (p. 497)	18. c (p. 517)	8. b (p. 499)	18. a (p. 514)
9. d (p. 501)	19. d (p. 517)	9. d (p. 501)	19. d (p. 517)
10.c (pp. 501, 502)	20. b (p.518)	10.d (p. 501)	20. c (p. 518)

15

Psychotherapy

OUTLINE (<u>S</u>urvey & <u>Q</u>uestion)

This outline is intended to help you *survey* the chapter. As you read through the various sections, write down any *questions* or comments that come to mind in the space provided. This is a valuable part of active learning and the SQ4R method. It not only makes your reading time more enjoyable and active, but it also increases retention and understanding of the material.

TOPIC   **NOTES**

I. THERAPY ESSENTIALS

II. BIOMEDICAL THERAPIES

    A. Drug Therapy

    B. Electroconvulsive Therapy and Psychosurgery

    C. Evaluating Biomedical Therapies

III. PSYCHOTHERAPY

A. Psychoanalysis/Psychodynamic Therapies

B. Cognitive Therapies

C. Humanistic Therapies

D. Behavior Therapies

E. Group and Family Therapies

Critical Thinking/Active Learning: Synthesizing Multiple Forms of Psychotherapy

IV. ISSUES IN THERAPY

A. Institutionalization

B. Evaluating Therapy

Research Highlight: Therapy in the Electronic Age

Gender and Cultural Diversity: Cultural Variations and the Special Needs of Women in Therapy

Core and Expanded LEARNING OBJECTIVES (Read, Recite & wRite)

While *reading* the chapter, stop periodically and *recite* (or repeat in your own words) the answers to the following learning objectives. It will also help your retention if you *write* your answer in the space provided. (Page numbers refer to the text Psychology in Action, 6th Ed.)

Core Learning Objectives

These objectives are found at the beginning of each chapter of Psychology in Action (6th ed.).

1. What do all therapies have in common?

2. What are the major biomedical therapies?

3. What is Freudian psychoanalysis? Are there more modern forms of this therapy?

4. What are the major cognitive therapies?

5. What is different about humanistic therapies?

6. How are learning principles used in behavior therapy?

7. How is psychotherapy done in groups and families?

8. What are some of the major issues in therapy?

<u>Expanded</u> <u>Learning</u> <u>Objectives</u>
These objectives offer more detail and a more intensive way to study the chapter.

Upon completion of CHAPTER 15, the student should be able to:

1. Define biomedical therapy, psychotherapy, and eclectic therapy; and discuss the five goals of therapy (pp.524-526).

2. Differentiate between the five types of therapists (psychologists, psychiatrists, psychoanalysts, social workers, and counselors); and describe four common misconceptions about psychotherapy and therapists (p. 526).

3. Describe the advantages and limitations of drug therapy, electroconvulsive therapy, and psychosurgery (pp.527-532).

4. Define psychoanalysis, and describe its major goals and methods of practice (pp. 533-535).

5. Discuss the two major criticisms of psychoanalysis; and differentiate between psychoanalysis of the past and modern psychodynamic therapy (pp. 535-536).

6. Define cognitive therapy, and describe its emphasis on changing self-talk via cognitive restructuring (p. 537).

7. Compare Ellis's rational-emotive behavior therapy with Beck's cognitive-behavior therapy; describe the successes and criticisms of cognitive therapies (pp. 538-540).

8. Define humanistic therapy; describe Rogers' client-centered therapy, the four qualities of client-therapist communication he advocated, and criticisms of humanistic therapy (pp. 541-543).

9. Define behavior therapy, and describe how classical conditioning, operant conditioning, and observational learning are applied to increase adaptive behaviors and decrease maladaptive ones (pp. 543-548).

10. Describe the successes reported for behavioral therapy, and discuss the three major criticisms of this method (p. 548-549).

11. Discuss three advantages of group therapy, and describe self-help groups and family therapy (pp. 549-551).

12. Discuss the controversies regarding deinstitutionalization and involuntary commitment; discuss community mental health centers as an alternative to institutionalization (pp. 552-553).

13. Describe the results of controlled research regarding the effectiveness of therapy; state several strategies for finding an appropriate therapist (pp. 553-555).

14. Describe similarities and differences in therapy across cultures, and the five major areas of concern for women in therapy (pp. 556-558).

KEY TERMS (Review)

The *review* step in the SQ4R method is very important to your performance on quizzes and exams. Upon completion of this chapter, you should be able to define the following terms.

Active Listening: _____

_____

Antianxiety Drugs: _____

_____

Antidepressant Drugs: _____

_____

Antipsychotic Drugs: _____

_____

Aversion Therapy: _____

_____

Behavior Therapy: _____

_____

Biomedical Therapy: _____

_____

Catharsis: _____

_____

Client-Centered Therapy: _____

_____

Cognitive-Behavior Therapy: _____

_____

Cognitive Restructuring: _____

_____

Cognitive Therapy: _____

_____

Deinstitutionalization: _____

_____

Drug Therapy: _____

_____

Eclectic Approach: _____

_____

Electroconvulsive Therapy (ECT): _____

_____

Empathy: _____

_____

Family Therapy: _____

_____

Free Association: _____

_____

Genuineness: _____

_____

Group Therapy: _____

_____

Humanistic Therapy: _____

_____

Interpretation: _____

_____

Lobotomy: _____

_____

Modeling Therapy: _____

_____

Psychoanalysis: _____

_____

Psychodynamic Therapy: _____

_____

Psychosurgery: _____

_____

Psychotherapy: _____

_____

Rational-Emotive Therapy (RET): _____

_____

Resistance: _____

_____

Self-help Group: _____

_____

Self-talk: _____

_____

Systematic Desensitization: _____

_____

Transference: _____

_____

Unconditional Positive Regard: _____

_____

ACTIVE LEARNING EXERCISES (Recite)

The *recite* step in the SQ4R method requires you to be an ACTIVE learner. By completing the following exercises, you will test and improve your mastery of the chapter material, which will also improve your performance on quizzes and exams. Answers to some exercises appear at the end of this study guide chapter.

ACTIVE LEARNING EXERCISE I

Confronting Your Own Faulty Reasoning

Albert Ellis' approach to psychotherapy is based on his belief that most human suffering results from illogical thinking. To improve *logical,* critical thinking skills, try the following exercise. Part I discusses two basic tests for sound reasoning, whereas Part II gives you practice applying these principles to your own irrational beliefs.

Part I
Consider the following syllogism:

Premise 1:	*All dogs are animals.*
Premise 2:	*All animals are blue.*
Conclusion:	*Therefore, all dogs are blue.*

Is this sound and logical reasoning? To determine whether an argument is sound and whether the conclusions should be accepted, critical thinkers ask two major questions: "Is the argument valid?" and "Are all premises true?" An argument is considered valid *if* the conclusion logically follows from the premises. The previous syllogism, for example, would be considered valid because *if* all dogs are animals, and all animals are blue, then *logically* all dogs *must* be blue. The second step in evaluating the soundness of arguments does require an examination of the content of argument. For an argument to be sound, each premise must also be true. This is where the previous syllogism falls apart. All dogs are obviously not blue.

The same faulty reasoning that underlies the blue-dog syllogism underlies the irrational beliefs that Ellis' form of cognitive therapy seeks to dispel. See if you can identify the problems with the following misconception.

Premise 1:I must have love or approval from all the people I find significant (in order to be happy).
Premise 2: I don't have approval from my mother, whom I consider significant.
Conclusion: Therefore, I am unhappy.

Is this argument valid? If not, why not? Are the premises of this argument true? If not, which ones are false and why?

Part II

Now, think carefully about your own irrational misconceptions (e.g., "I must make everyone happy," "Life must be fair," etc.). In the following spaces, analyze your "self-talk" about one of your misconceptions and try to put it in syllogism form--identify your two basic premises and your conclusion.

Premise 1: _____

Premise 2: _____

Conclusion: _____

Now answer the following questions: Is my argument valid? If not, why not?

_____

Are the premises of my argument true? If not, which one is false and why?

_____

For further practice (and self-insight), try using this same procedure on your other irrational misconceptions. By actively applying logical skills to your own thought processes, you will not only improve your basic critical thinking skills, but, according to Ellis you will also be in a better position to change these self-destructive thought patterns and resultant behaviors.

ACTIVE LEARNING EXERCISE II

<u>Expressing</u> <u>Empathy</u>   (An Affective Skill)

According to Dr. Thomas Gordon, people who wish to express empathy must avoid asking questions or giving advice. It is almost always more appropriate to explore the other person's emotional state. He recommends the technique of "active listening," which uses open-ended statements that encourage the expression of feelings. Three basic active listening techniques are:

  a. Repeating what was said as a statement rather than a question.

  b. Slightly rewording (or paraphrasing) the statement.

  c. Stating the feeling you assumed was being expressed.

To practice this technique, use either "b" or "c" for each of the following statements:

Sample Statement = "I had the worst day of my life today at work."

Sample Active Listening Response = "Do you mean that everything you did at work today seemed to go wrong?"

1. "I feel like a nobody. No one ever pays attention to me or seems to care about me."

_____

_____

2. "You always seem to hurt my feelings."

_____

_____

CHAPTER OVERVIEW (Review)

The following CHAPTER OVERVIEW provides a narrative overview of the main topics covered in the chapter. Like the Visual Summary found at the end of each chapter in the text, this narrative summary provides a final opportunity to *review* chapter material.

I. Therapy Essentials

Therapy is a general term for the various approaches to improving psychological functioning and promoting adjustment to life. There are numerous forms of psychotherapy, but they all focus treatment on five basic areas of disturbance---thoughts, emotions, behaviors, interpersonal and life situations, and biomedical.

II. Biomedical Therapies

Biomedical therapies use biological techniques to relieve psychological disorders. **Drug therapy** is the most common form by far. **Antianxiety drugs** (Valium, Xanax) are used to treat anxiety disorders; **antipsychotic drugs** (Haldol, Navane) can relieve the symptoms of schizophrenia, **antidepressants** (Prozac, Zoloft) are used to treat depression, and mood stabilizers (lithium) can stabilize bipolar disorders. Although drug therapy has been responsible for major improvements in many disorders, there are also problems with dosage levels, side effects, and patient cooperation.

Electroconvulsive therapy (ECT) is used primarily to relieve serious depression, when medication has not worked. **Psychosurgeries**, such as lobotomy, have been used in the past but are rarely used today.

III. Psychoanalysis/Psychodynamic Therapies

Sigmund Freud developed the psychoanalytic method of therapy to uncover unconscious conflicts and bring them into conscious awareness. The five major techniques of **psychoanalysis** are **free association, dream analysis,** analyzing **resistance,** analyzing **transference,** and **interpretation.**

Like psychoanalytic theories of personality, psychoanalysis is the subject of great debate. It is primarily criticized for its limited availability (it is time-consuming, expensive, and suits only a small group of people) and its lack of scientific credibility. Modern **psychodynamic therapies** overcome some of these limitations.

III. Cognitive and HumanisticTherapies

Cognitive therapy emphasizes the importance of faulty thought processes, beliefs, and negative **self-talk** in the creation of problem behaviors. Ellis' **rational-emotive therapy** aims to replace a client's irrational beliefs with rational beliefs and accurate perceptions of the world. Beck's **cognitive-behavior therapy** takes a more active approach with clients by emphasizing changes in both thought processes and behavior.

Evaluations of cognitive therapies find Beck's procedures particularly effective for relieving depression; Ellis has had success with a variety of disorders. Both Beck and Ellis, however, are criticized for ignoring the importance of unconscious processes and the client's history. Some critics also attribute any success with cognitive therapies to the use of behavioral techniques.

Humanistic therapies are based on the premise that problems result when an individual's normal growth potential is blocked. In Rogers' **client-centered** approach, the therapist offers **empathy, unconditional positive regard, genuineness,** and **active listening** as means of facilitating personal growth. Perls' Gestalt therapy emphasizes awareness and personal responsibility to help the client integrate present experiences into a "whole" or gestalt. Humanistic therapies are difficult to evaluate scientifically, and research on specific therapeutic techniques has had mixed results.

IV. Behavior Therapies

Behavior therapies use learning principles to change maladaptive behaviors. Classical conditioning principles are used to change associations. In **systematic desensitization**, the client replaces anxiety with relaxation, and in **aversion therapy**, an aversive stimulus is paired with a maladaptive behavior.

Shaping, reinforcement, punishment, and *extinction* are behavioral therapy techniques based on operant conditioning principles. In **modeling therapy**, clients watch and imitate positive role models. Behavior therapies have been successful with a number of psychological disorders. But they are also criticized for lack of generalizability, the chance of symptom substitution, and the questionable ethics of controlling behavior.

V. Group and Family Therapies

In addition to being less expensive and more available than individual therapy, **group therapy** has three other advantages: It provides group support, feedback, information, and opportunities for behavior rehearsal. A variation on group therapy is the **self-help group** (like Alcoholics Anonymous), which is not guided by a professional.

The aim of **family therapy** is to change maladaptive family interaction patterns. Because a family is a system of interdependent parts, the problem of any one member unavoidably affects all the others.

VI. Issues In Therapy

People believed to be mentally ill and dangerous to themselves or others can be involuntarily committed to mental hospitals for diagnosis and treatment. Abuses of involuntary commitments and other problems associated with state mental hospitals have led many states to practice **deinstitutionalization**---discharging as many patients as possible and discouraging admissions. Community services such as *Community Mental Health (CMH)* centers try to cope with the problems of deinstitutionalization. Research on the effectiveness of psychotherapy has found that 40 to 80 percent of those who receive treatment are better off than those who do not receive treatment.

Therapies in all cultures share six culturally universal features: naming a problem, qualities of the therapist, establishing credibility, placing the problems in a familiar framework, applying techniques to bring relief, and a special time and place.

Important cultural differences in therapies also exist. For example, therapies in individualistic cultures emphasize the ""self" and control over one's life, whereas therapies in collectivist cultures emphasize interdependence. Japan's Naikan therapy is a good example of a collectivist culture's therapy. Therapists must take five considerations into account when treating women clients: higher rate of diagnosis and treatment of mental disorders, stresses of poverty, stresses of multiple roles, stresses of aging, and violence against women.

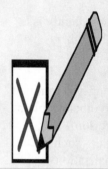

SELF-TESTS (Review & wRite)

Completing the following SELF-TESTS will provide immediate feedback on how well you have mastered the material. In the *crossword puzzle* and *fill-in exercises*, write the appropriate word or words in the blank spaces. The *matching exercise* requires you to match the terms in one column to their correct definitions in the other. For the *multiple-choice questions* in Practice Tests I and II, circle or underline the correct answer. When you are unsure of any answer, be sure to highlight or specially mark the item and then go back to the text for further review. Correct answers are provided at the end of this study guide chapter.

CROSSWORD PUZZLE FOR CHAPTER 15

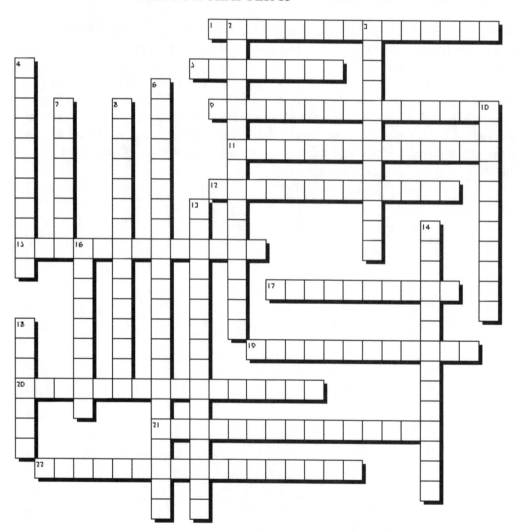

ACROSS

1 A group of techniques based on learning principles that are used to change maladaptive behaviors.

5 Internal dialogue; the things people say to themselves when they interpret events.

9 According to Rogers, the ability to listen with total attention to what another is saying. This involves reflecting, paraphrasing, and clarifying what the person says and means.

11 A psychoanalyst's explanation of a patient's free associations, dreams, resistance, and transference; more generally, any statement by a therapist that presents a patient's problem in a new way.

12 A psychological treatment that attempts to change maladaptive interaction patterns among members of a family.

15 Operative procedures on the brain designed to relieve severe mental symptoms that have not responded to other forms of treatment.

17 A stage in psychoanalysis when the patient avoids (resists) the analyst's attempts to bring threatening unconscious material to conscious awareness.

19 Treatment method in which multiple people meet together to work toward therapeutic goals.

20 Medications used to treat anxiety disorders.

21 Behavior therapy technique that pairs an aversive (unpleasant) stimulus with a maladaptive behavior.

22 Therapy involving physiological interventions (drugs, electroconvulsive therapy [ECT], and psychosurgery) to reduce symptoms associated with psychological disorders.

DOWN

2 An approach to therapy in which the therapist combines techniques from various theories to find the appropriate treatment for the client.

3 In psychoanalysis, the patient may displace (or transfer) thoughts, feelings, fears, wishes and conflicts from past relationships, particularly from childhood, onto new relationships, especially with the therapist.

4 Use of chemicals (drugs) to treat physical and psychological disorders.

6 The policy of discharging as many people as possible from state hospitals and discouraging admissions.

7 A brain operation in which the nerve pathways between the frontal lobes and the thalamus and hypothalamus are cut in hopes of treating psychological disorders.

8 In psychoanalysis, reporting whatever comes to mind without monitoring its contents--regardless of how painful, embarrassing, or irrelevant it may seem. Freud believed that the first thing to come to a patient's mind was often an important clue to what the unconscious mind wants to conceal.

10 In Rogerian terms, authenticity or congruence; the awareness of one's true inner thoughts and feelings and being able to share them honestly with others.

13 Therapy that focuses on faulty thought processes and beliefs to treat problem behaviors.

14 A system of therapy developed by Freud that seeks to bring unconscious conflicts, which usually date back to early childhood experiences, into consciousness. Psychoanalysis is also Freud's theoretical school of thought, which emphasizes the study of unconscious processes.

16 In psychoanalytic theory, the release of tension and anxiety through the reliving of a traumatic incident.

18 In Rogerian terms, an insightful awareness and ability to share another person's inner experience.

FILL-IN EXERCISES

1. ECT is used primarily to treat _____ (p. 529).

2. A system of therapy developed by Sigmund Freud that seeks to bring _____ conflicts into conscious awareness is known as _____ (p. 534).

3. The five major techniques of psychoanalysis are _____, _____, _____, _____, and _____ (pp. 534-535).

4. In modern psychoanalytic therapies known as _____, treatment is briefer, face to face, and more directive (p. 536).

5. _____ therapy was developed by Albert Ellis to eliminate self-defeating beliefs through rational examination (p. 538).

6. Aaron Beck's cognitive-behavior therapy has been successful in the treatment of _____ (p. 539).

7. _____ therapy helps people become creative and unique through affective restructuring (or emotional readjustment) (p. 541).

8. A group of therapies based on learning principles that are used to change maladaptive behaviors is known as _____ (p. 543).

9. _____ is a gradual process of extinguishing a learned fear by associating a hierarchy of fear-evoking stimuli with deep relaxation (p. 544).

10. The policy of discharging as many people as possible from state hospitals and discouraging admissions is known as _____ (p. 553).

MATCHING EXERCISES

Column A   Column B

a. Family Therapy   1.____ Internal dialogue when interpreting events.
b. Antipsychotic Drugs   2.____ Alcoholics Anonymous.
c. ECT   3.____ Reporting whatever comes to mind without censoring.
d. Gestalt Therapy   4.____ Clients watch and imitate positive role models.
e. Self-Help Group   5.____ Relieve symptoms of schizophrenia.
f. Carl Rogers   6.____ Client-centered therapy to facilitate personal growth.
g. Aversion Therapy   7.____ Attempts to change maladaptive family interactions.
h. Modeling Therapy   8.____ Emphasizes awareness and personal responsibility.
i. Free Association   9.____ Treatment for severe depression when medication fails.
j. Self-Talk   10.____ Aversive stimulus is paired with maladaptive behavior.

PRACTICE TEST I

1. _____ therapies act directly on the brain and nervous system; whereas _____ is a collection of techniques to improve psychological functioning and promote adjustment to life.
    a. Drug; psychoanalysis
    b. Medical; psychology
    c. Biomedical; psychotherapy
    d. None of the above

2. Dr. Baker treats patients with mental disorders. Which of the following is least likely to indicate her degree?
    a. Ph.D.
    b. M.D.
    c. D.D.S.
    d. MFT

3. Biomedical therapy does **NOT** use _____ to reduce symptoms associated with psychiatric disorders.
    a. ECT
    b. EST
    c. trephining
    d. lobotomy

4. How do antipsychotic drugs, like Thorazine, work?
    a. They sedate the patient
    b. They appear to decrease activity at the dopamine synapses
    c. They lower the sympathetic activity of the brain
    d. All of the above

5. ECT is now used primarily in the treatment of _____.
   a. depression
   b. anxiety
   c. phobias
   d. schizophrenia

6. The original form of psychosurgery developed by Egaz Moniz disconnected the _____ lobes from the midbrain structures where emotional experiences are relayed.
   a. occipital
   b. parietal
   c. temporal
   d. frontal

7. Tardive dyskinesia is thought to be a side effect of treatment with _____ medication.
   a. mood-altering
   b. psychoactive
   c. antianxiety
   d. antipsychotic

8. Catharsis is the _____.
   a. reporting of psychic contents without censorship
   b. release of tensions and anxieties
   c. attachment process that occurs between patient and therapist
   d. therapist's educated explanations for a patient's behavior

9. In psychoanalytic dream interpretation, the actual events of the dream are known as the _____ content.
   a. manifest
   b. latent
   c. subconscious
   d. transference

10. Free association and dream interpretation are psychoanalytic therapy techniques that are used to _____.
    a. analyze intrapsychic conflicts
    b. keep unconscious conflicts out of awareness
    c. restructure the self-concept
    d. countercondition behavior

11. In _____, mistaken beliefs or misconceptions are actively disputed.
   a. client-centered therapy
   b. psychoanalysis
   c. rational-emotive therapy
   d. systematic desensitization

12. According to rational emotive therapy, a consequence such as depression or anxiety occurs as a result of a(n) _____.
   a. activating experience
   b. stimulus event
   c. conditioning experience
   d. belief

13. A client-centered therapist emphasizes the importance of empathy, unconditional positive regard, genuineness, and _____.
   a. catharsis
   b. self-efficacy
   c. appropriate role models
   d. active listening

14. Sharing another person's inner experience is known as _____.
   a. unconditional positive regard
   b. genuineness
   c. empathy
   d. sympathy

15. _____ pairs relaxation with a graduating hierarchy of anxiety-producing situations to extinguish the anxiety.
   a. Classical conditioning
   b. Shaping
   c. Systematic desensitization
   d. Maslow's pyramid training

16. Aversion therapy applies the principle of _____ by pairing an unpleasant stimulus with a maladaptive behavior to extinguish the behavior.
   a. classical conditioning
   b. operant conditioning
   c. positive punishment
   d. negative punishment

17. One of the most frequently used methods of negative punishment is _____.
    a.   time out
    b.   aversion therapy
    c.   electroconvulsive shock treatment
    d.   token economies

18. Asking clients with snake phobias to watch other (nonphobic) people handle snakes is an example of _____ therapy.
    a.   time out
    b.   aversion
    c.   modeling
    d.   unethical

19. This is **NOT** one of the usual benefits of group therapy.
    a.   support from others with similar problems
    b.   multiple resources
    c.   opportunities for behavioral rehearsal
    d.   group sympathy for a patient complaints

20. A family therapist believes that the family's scapegoat _____.
    a.   should be treated first
    b.   is being blamed for deeper family issues
    c.   requires hospitalization
    d.   is the reason for the family's dysfunction

PRACTICE TEST II

1. Which of the following may actually alter brain functioning?
    a.   electroconvulsive therapy
    b.   drug therapy
    c.   psychotherapy
    d.   all of these options

2. Disturbed behaviors are most likely to be the focus in _____.
    a.   cognitive therapy
    b.   biomedical therapy
    c.   psychoanalysis
    d.   behavior therapy

3. When a therapist combines techniques from various therapies, it is called _____.
   a. psychosynthetic therapy
   b. biomedical therapy
   c. managed care
   d. the eclectic approach

4. Someone with severe, vegetative depression and suicidal ideation that has not been successfully managed with other treatment methods might require _____.
   a. a frontal lobotomy
   b. ECT
   c. combination drug and modeling therapy
   d. none of these options

5. Tardive dyskinesia is associated with _____.
   a. prolonged use of antipsychotic drugs
   b. Parkinson's disease
   c. Alzheimer's disease
   d. too many electroconvulsive shock treatments

6. Transference is the process of _____.
   a. changing therapists
   b. changing therapeutic techniques or strategies
   c. displacing associations from past relationships onto new relationships
   d. replacing maladaptive patterns with adaptive ones

7. According to some critics, traditional psychoanalysis is appropriate only for _____ clients.
   a. young and attractive
   b. verbal
   c. intelligent and successful
   d. YAVIS

8. If you are unhappy because you believe you must be perfect or must get straight A's, Ellis might point out the source of your unhappiness by saying, "You're _____!"
   a. musterbating
   b. already perfect, and just don't know it yet
   c. an overachiever
   d. lying

9. _____ believes selective perception and other distorted thinking patterns cause depression.
   a.   Bandura
   b.   Beck
   c.   Rogers
   d.   Perls

10. Cognitive therapy is effective for treating _____.
   a.   depression
   b.   anxiety
   c.   eating and substance-related disorders
   d.   all of these options

11. The client is responsible for discovering his or her own maladaptive patterns in _____ therapy.
   a.   biomedical
   b.   psychoanalytic
   c.   humanistic
   d.   all of these options

12. A client-centered therapist would not say, "You're right about that" because _____.
   a.   it wouldn't be genuine
   b.   the client is seldom right
   c.   it implies that the therapist is judging the client
   d.   it is not empathic

13. Reflecting back or paraphrasing what the client is saying is a part of _____.
   a.   gestalt directness
   b.   psychoanalytic transference
   c.   cognitive restructuring
   d.   active listening

14. Relaxation training is an important component in _____.
   a.   systematic desensitization
   b.   aversion conditioning
   c.   time out training
   d.   a token economy

15. People with phobias, delinquent behaviors, and eating disorders have been treated successfully with _____ therapy.
   a.   electroconvulsive shock
   b.   drug
   c.   psychoanalytic
   d.   behavior

16. The main difference between a self-help group and group therapy is that the former _____.
    a.   does not deal with psychological problems
    b.   provides more understanding and support
    c.   does not have a professional leader
    d.   all of these options

17. According to William Menninger, mental health problems do not affect three or four out of five persons, but _____.
    a.   the vast majority of people
    b.   also their families
    c.   also the therapist
    d.   one out of one

18. If a client threatens to rob a bank, the therapist can hospitalize the client for _____.
    a.   12 to 24 hours
    b.   24 to 72 hours
    c.   as long as it takes for the client to stop the threats
    d.   none of these options; this is not an indication for involuntary hospitalization

19. The policy of discharging as many people as possible from state hospitals and discouraging admissions is called _____.
    a.   biomedical downsizing
    b.   deinstitutionalization
    c.   managed care
    d.   all of these findings

20. A *Consumer Reports* survey confirmed which of these previous research findings?
    a.   most people get better with treatment
    b.   some therapies are better than others
    c.   short-term is better than long-term treatment
    d.   all of these findings

ANSWERS

The following answers to active learning exercises, crossword puzzles, fill-ins, matching exercises, and practice tests 1 and 2 provide immediate feedback on your mastery of the material. Try not to simply memorize the answers. When you are unsure of your "guess" or make an error, be sure to go back to the textbook and carefully review. This will greatly improve your scores on classroom exams and quizzes.

CROSSWORD PUZZLE FOR CHAPTER 15

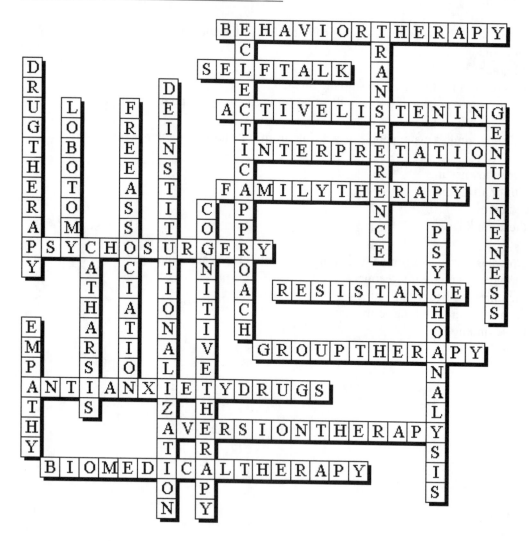

FILL-IN EXERCISES

1. depression; 2. unconscious, psychoanalysis; 3. free association, dream analysis, resistance, transference, interpretation; 4. psychodynamic; 5. Rational-emotive; 6. depression; 7. Humanistic; 8. behavior therapy; 9. Systematic desensitization; 10. deinstitutionalization.

MATCHING EXERCISES

a. 7, b. 5, c. 9, d. 8, e. 2, f. 6, g. 10, h. 4, i. 3, j. 1

PRACTICE TEST I		PRACTICE TEST II	
1. c (p. 524)	11. c (p. 538)	1. d (p. 524)	11. c (p. 541)
2. d (p. 526)	12. d (p. 538)	2. d (p. 525)	12. c (p. 541)
3. c (p. 527)	13. d (p. 541)	3. d (p. 526)	13. d (p. 542)
4. b (p. 528)	14. c (p. 541)	4. b (p. 529)	14. a (p. 544)
5. a (p. 529)	15. c (p. 544)	5. a (p. 531)	15. d (p. 548)
6. d (p. 530)	16. a (p. 546)	6. c (p. 535)	16. c (p. 550)
7. d (p. 531)	17. a (p. 548)	7. d (p. 535)	17. d (p. 550)
8. b (p. 534)	18. c (p. 548)	8. a (p. 538)	18. b (p. 552)
9. a (p. 534)	19. d (p. 550)	9. b (p. 539)	19. b (p. 553)
10.a (p. 534)	20. b (p. 551)	10.d (p. 540)	20. d (p. 554)

16 Social Psychology

OUTLINE (Survey & Question)

This outline is intended to help you *survey* the chapter. As you read through the various sections, write down any *questions* or comments that come to mind in the space provided. This is a valuable part of active learning and the SQ4R method. It not only makes your reading time more enjoyable and active, but it also increases retention and understanding of the material.

TOPIC	NOTES

I. OUR THOUGHTS ABOUT OTHERS

　　A. Attribution

　　B. Attitudes

II. OUR FEELINGS ABOUT OTHERS

　　A. Prejudice and Discrimination

　　B. Interpersonal Attraction

Gender and Cultural Diversity: Physical Attractiveness Across Cultures

III. OUR ACTIONS TOWARD OTHERS

A. Social Influence

        Critical Thinking/Active Learning: Would You Have Obeyed Milgram's Experimenters?

B. Group Processes

C. Aggression

        Research Highlight: America's Anger Epidemic

D. Altruism

Core and Expanded LEARNING OBJECTIVES   (Read, Recite & wRite)

While *reading* the chapter, stop periodically and *recite* (or repeat in your own words) the answers to the following learning objectives. It will also help your retention if you *write* your answer in the space provided. (Page numbers refer to the text Psychology in Action, 6th Ed.)

Core Learning Objectives
These objectives are found at the beginning of each chapter of Psychology in Action (6th ed.).

1. How do our thoughts affect how we explain and judge others?

2. What feelings are most important in our social interactions?

3. How do our actions toward others affect their lives and our own?

Expanded Learning Objectives
These objectives offer more detail and a more intensive way to study the chapter.

Upon completion of CHAPTER 16, the student should be able to:

1. Describe Milgram's classic obedience study (pp. 563-564).

2. Define social psychology, and describe the results of research on several commonsense statements regarding social interactions (p. 565).

3. Define attribution, explain how choosing between dispositional and situational attributions results in the fundamental attribution error and the self-serving bias, and state how culture impacts these errors (pp. 565-568).

4. Define attitude, and describe its three basic components (pp. 568-569).

5. Describe cognitive dissonance theory, the impact of dissonance on attitudes and behavior, and how culture impacts cognitive dissonance (pp. 569-570).

6. Differentiate between a stereotype, prejudice, and discrimination. Describe the four major sources of prejudice and discrimination (pp. 571-573).

7. Explain how cooperation, superordinate goals, increased contact, cognitive retraining, and cognitive dissonance can reduce prejudice and discrimination (pp. 573-575).

8. Describe the three key factors in interpersonal attraction. Discuss cross-cultural and historical similarities and differences in physical attractiveness (pp. 575-577).

9. Describe the three components that distinguish liking from loving in Rubin's research; compare romantic and companionate love; and discuss problems associated with romantic love (pp. 578-581).

10. Define conformity, and explain the three factors that contribute to this behavior (pp. 581-584).

11. Define obedience, and describe how authority, responsibility, graduations in requests, and disobedient models affect this behavior (pp. 584-585).

12. Define roles and describe their effect on the behavior of "prisoners" and "guards" in Zimbardo's classic prison study (pp. 587-589).

13. Discuss how group polarization and groupthink affect group decision making (pp. 589-591).

14. Define aggression, and explain the factors that contribute to its expression (pp. 592-594).

15. Describe three approaches to controlling or eliminating aggression. Identify five misconceptions and controversies regarding juvenile aggression (pp. 594-595).

16. Define altruism, and describe its evolutionary benefit. Compare and contrast the egoistic model and the empathy-altruism hypothesis regarding this behavior (pp. 596-597).

17. Describe Latane and Darley's decision-making model for helping behavior, and discuss how it can be used to increase the likelihood of helping (pp. 597-598).

KEY TERMS (Review)

The *review* step in the SQ4R method is very important to your performance on quizzes and exams. Upon completion of this chapter, you should be able to define the following terms.

Aggression: _____

_____

Altruism: _____

_____

Attitude: _____

_____

Attribution: _____

_____

Cognitive Dissonance Theory: _____

_____

Companionate Love: _____

_____

Conformity: _____

_____

Deindividuation: _____

_____

Diffusion of Responsibility: _____

_____

Discrimination: _____

_____

Egoistic Model: _____

_____

Empathy-Altruism Hypothesis: _____

_____

Foot-in-the-Door Technique: _____

_____

Frustration-Aggression Hypothesis: _____

_____

Fundamental Attribution Error: _____

_____

Group Polarization: _____

_____

Groupthink: _____

_____

Informational Social Influence: _____

_____

Ingroup Favoritism: _____

_____

Interpersonal Attraction: _____

_____

Need Compatibility: _____

_____

Need Complementarity: _____

_____

Norm: _____

_____

Normative Social Influence: _____

_____

Obedience: _____

_____

Outgroup Homogeneity Effect: _____

_____

Prejudice: _____

_____

Proximity: _____

_____

Reference Groups: _____

_____

Romantic Love: _____

_____

Saliency Bias: _____

_____

Self-Serving Bias: _____

_____

Social Psychology: _____

_____

Stereotype: _____

_____

ACTIVE LEARNING EXERCISES (Recite)

The *recite* step in the SQ4R method requires you to be an ACTIVE learner. By completing the following exercises, you will test and improve your mastery of the chapter material, which will also improve your performance on quizzes and exams. Answers to some exercises appear at the end of this study guide chapter.

ACTIVE LEARNING EXERCISE I

In the space next to each issue, place a number (1 to 5) in the first space that indicates your CURRENT attitude, and then enter a number (1 to 5) in the space to the right that indicates your PAST attitude (five to ten years ago).

1 = Strongly support
2 = Mildly support
3 = Neutral
4 = Mildly oppose
5 = Strongly oppose

	CURRENT	PAST
Drinking and driving	_____	_____
Gun control	_____	_____
Abortion	_____	_____
Smoking in public places	_____	_____
Divorce	_____	_____

1. Circle the top two issues you scored "highest" (either a 1 or 5). Briefly state your attitudes toward each of these issues. How did these attitudes develop? Through direct experience, indirect observation, or what? Can you remember important experiences or significant individuals that influenced these attitudes? Try to identify the three components of each of your three attitudes (cognitive, affective, and behavioral).

_____

_____

_____

2. Now compare your CURRENT attitudes to those of your PAST. Which attitudes were the most subject to change? Why? On what issues were you most resistant to change? How would you explain this?

_____

_____

_____

3. Cognitive dissonance theory asserts that "changing behavior changes attitudes." Using this theory, how would you design a program to change an undesirable attitude (in yourself and others)?

_____

_____

_____

ACTIVE LEARNING EXERCISE II

<u>Applying</u> <u>Knowledge</u> <u>to</u> <u>New</u> <u>Situations</u>   (A Behavioral Skill)

A critical thinker is able to take existing information and apply that knowledge to new or future situations. To increase your awareness of various forms of prejudice on your college campus, ask a member of the other sex to be your partner in the following exercise:

Visit one set of both male and female bathrooms in three separate buildings on your campus (e.g., the art department, business department, and psychology department). Record your observations below:

1. Did you notice any graffiti directed at certain minority groups?

_____

_____

_____

2. Was there a difference between the male and female prejudices (as expressed by the graffiti)?

_____

_____

_____

3. Did you notice a difference between the three buildings in their "graffiti prejudice?"

_____

_____

_____

4. Did you gain new insights into the causes or and treatment of prejudice?

_____

_____

_____

CHAPTER OVERVIEW (<u>R</u>eview)

The following CHAPTER OVERVIEW provides a narrative overview of the main topics covered in the chapter. Like the Visual Summary found at the end of each chapter in the text, this narrative summary provides a final opportunity to *review* chapter material.

I. Our Thoughts About Others

We explain people's behavior (make attributions) by determining whether their actions resulted from internal factors (their own traits and motives) or external factors (the situation). Attribution is subject to several forms of error and bias. The **fundamental attribution error** is the tendency to overestimate internal, personality influences when judging the behavior of others. When we explain our own behavior, however, we tend to attribute positive outcomes to internal factors and negative outcomes to external causes (the **self-serving bias**).

Attitudes are learned predispositions toward a particular object. Three components of all attitudes are the cognitive responses (thoughts and beliefs), affective responses (feelings), and behavioral tendencies (predispositions to actions). We sometimes change our attitudes because of **cognitive dissonance**, which is a state of tension or anxiety we feel when two or more attitudes contradict each other or when our attitudes do not match our behaviors. This mismatch and resulting tension motivate us to change our attitude to restore balance.

II. Our Feelings About Others

Prejudice is a generally negative attitude directed toward specific people solely because of their membership in a specific group. It contains all three components of attitudes (cognitive, affective, and behavioral). **Discrimination** is not the same as prejudice. It refers to the actual negative behavior directed at members of a group. People do not always act on their prejudices.

The four major sources of prejudice are learning (classical and operant conditioning and social learning), cognitive processes (categorization), economic and political competition, and displaced aggression (scapegoating). Cooperation, superordinate goals, and increased contact are three major methods for reducing prejudice and discrimination.

Physical attractiveness is very important to **interpersonal attraction**. Physically attractive people are often perceived as more intelligent, sociable, and interesting than less attractive people. Standards for physical attractiveness vary across cultures and historically. Physical attractiveness is generally more important to men than to women. Physical **proximity** increases one's attractiveness. If you live near someone or work alongside someone, you are more likely to like that person. Although people commonly believe that "opposites attract" (**need complementarity**), research shows similarity (**need compatibility**) is a much more important factor in attraction.

Love can be defined in terms of caring, attachment, and intimacy. **Romantic love** is highly valued in our society, but because it is based on mystery and fantasy, it is hard to sustain. **Companionate love** relies on mutual trust, respect, and friendship and seems to grow stronger with time.

III. Social Influence

The process of social influence teaches important cultural values and behaviors that are essential to successful social living. Two of the most important forms of social influence are conformity and obedience. **Conformity** refers to changes in behavior in response to real or imagined pressure from others. People conform for approval and acceptance (**normative social influence**), out of a need for more information (**informational social influence**), and to match the behavior of those they admire and feel similar to (their **reference group**). People also conform because it is often adaptive to do so.

Obedience involves giving in to a command from others. Milgram's experiment found a surprisingly large number of people obey orders, even when another human being is physically threatened. There are at least four factors that either increase or decrease obedience: the power of authority, foot-in-the-door technique, assignment of responsibility, and disobedient models.

IV. Group Processes

Groups differ from mere collections of people because group members share a mutually recognized relationship with one another. Groups affect us through the roles we play. The importance of roles in determining and controlling behavior was dramatically demonstrated in Zimbardo's Stanford Prison Study. Group membership can also lead to deindividuation, in which a person becomes so caught up in the group's identity that individual self-awareness and responsibility are temporarily suspended.

Groups are often trusted with decisions because we believe they will make more "middle of the road" decisions than individuals. Research shows, however, that if most group members initially tend toward an extreme idea, the entire group will polarize in that direction because the other "Like-minded" members reinforce the dominant tendency. This is called **group polarization**. **Groupthink** is a dangerous type of thinking that occurs when a group's desire for agreement overrules its desire to critically evaluate information.

V. Aggression and Altruism

Aggression is any deliberate attempt to harm another living being who is motivated to avoid such treatment. In looking for explanations for aggression, some researchers have focused on inborn instinctual factors, whereas others have done research on genes, the brain, hormones, and neurotransmitters. Still other researchers have studied frustration and social learning. Releasing aggressive feelings through violent acts or watching violence is not an effective way to reduce aggression. Introducing incompatible responses (such as humor) and teaching social and communication skills is more efficient.

Altruism refers to actions designed to help others with no obvious benefit to oneself. Evolutionary theorists believe altruism is innate and has survival value. Psychological explanations for altruism emphasize the **egoistic model**, which suggests that helping is motivated by anticipated gain, or the **empathy-altruism hypothesis**, which proposes that helping can also be activated when the helper feels empathy for the victim.

Whether or not someone helps depends on a series of interconnected events, starting with noticing the problem and ending with a decision to help. Altruism is also inhibited by the fact that many emergencies are ambiguous and the potential respondent is unsure of what to do. Inhibition also comes from not taking personal responsibility and assuming someone else will respond (the **diffusion of responsibility** phenomenon). To increase the chances of altruism, we should increase the rewards and decrease the costs. We can also reduce ambiguity by giving clear directions to those who may be watching.

SELF-TESTS (Review & wRite)

Completing the following SELF-TESTS will provide immediate feedback on how well you have mastered the material. In the *crossword puzzle* and *fill-in exercises*, write the appropriate word or words in the blank spaces. The *matching exercise* requires you to match the terms in one column to their correct definitions in the other. For the *multiple-choice questions* in Practice Tests I and II, circle or underline the correct answer. When you are unsure of any answer, be sure to highlight or specially mark the item and then go back to the text for further review. Correct answers are provided at the end of this study guide chapter.

CROSSWORD PUZZLE FOR CHAPTER 16

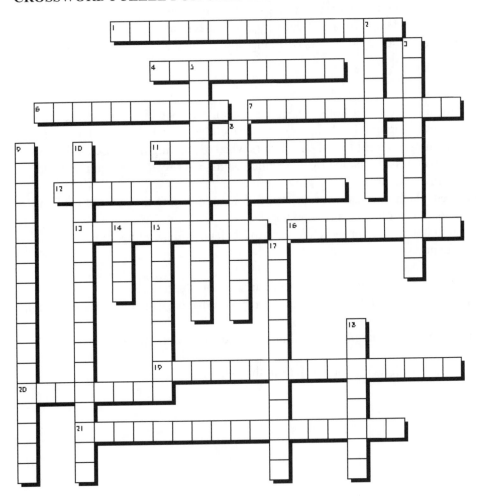

ACROSS

1 People to whom we conform (or with whom we go along) because we like and admire them and want to be like them.

4 (1) A set of beliefs about the characteristics of people in a group that is generalized to all group members or (2) the cognitive component of prejudice.

6 Any behavior that is intended to harm someone.

7 The principles people follow in making judgments about the causes of events, others' behavior, and their own behavior.

11 Negative behaviors directed at members of a group.

12 The increased arousal and reduced self-consciousness, inhibition, and personal responsibility that can occur when a person is part of a group, particularly when the members feel anonymous.

13 A type of social influence in which individuals change their behavior as a result of real or imagined group pressure.

16 A key factor in attraction involving geographic, residential, and other forms of physical closeness.

19 A strong feeling of attraction to another person characterized by trust, caring, tolerance, and friendship. It is believed to provide an enduring basis for long-term relationships.

20 A learned predisposition to respond cognitively, affectively, and behaviorally to a particular object.

21 A cognitive process in prejudice whereby members of an ingroup are viewed in more favorable terms than members of an outgroup.

DOWN

2 A generally negative attitude directed toward others because of their membership in a specific group. Like all attitudes, prejudice involves cognitions (thoughts), affect (feelings), and behavioral tendencies.

3 The tendency to focus on the most noticeable (salient) factors when explaining the causes of behavior.

5 The proposal that helping behavior is motivated by anticipated gain---later reciprocation, increased self-esteem, or avoidance of guilt and distress.

8 A condition that results when a highly cohesive group strives for agreement to the point of avoiding inconsistent information; the result is faulty decision-making.

9 A group's movement toward either riskier or more conservative behavior, depending upon the members' initial dominant tendency.

10 A sharing of similar needs.

14 Cultural rule of behavior that prescribes what is acceptable in a given situation.

15 A type of social influence in which an individual follows direct commands, usually from someone in a position of authority.

17 An intense feeling of attraction to another person, within an erotic context and with future expectations.

18 Actions designed to help others with no obvious benefit to the helper.

FILL-IN EXERCISES

1. The principles people follow in making judgments about the causes of events, others' behavior, and their own behavior is known as _____ (p. 566).

2. When judging the causes of others' behavior, we tend to overestimate personality factors and underestimate social or situational factors, a bias known as the _____; however, when judging our own behavior we take credit for successes and externalize failures, known as the _____ (p. 566).

3. There are three major components to all attitudes: the _____, _____, and _____ (p. 568).

4. According to _____ theory, a perceived discrepancy between an attitude and a behavior or between an attitude and new information leads to tension, which then encourages attitude change (p. 569).

5. A generally negative attitude directed toward others because of their membership in a specific group is known as _____ (p. 571).

6. Stereotyping represents the _____ component of prejudice, whereas discrimination is the _____ component (p. 571).

7. The three key factors in attraction are _____, _____, and _____ (p. 575).

8. A type of social influence where individuals change their behavior as a result of real or imagined group pressure is known as _____; whereas going along with a direct command from others is known as _____ (pp. 582, 584)

9. _____ refers to the tendency of groups to make decisions that are either riskier or more cautious than decisions made by individuals; whereas _____ refers to faulty decision making resulting from the group's strong need for agreement that overrules its desire for critical evaluation (pp. 590-591).

10. Evidence suggests that bystanders failed to intervene in the Kitty Genovese murder because there was _____ (p. 597).

MATCHING EXERCISES

Column A   Column B

a. Attitude   1.____ Helping is motivated by anticipated gain.
b. Self-Serving Bias   2.____ Increases attraction due to mere exposure effect.
c. Need Complementarity   3.____ Those we admire and feel similar to.
d. Normative Social Influence 4.____ Attraction to others with opposite traits.
e. Egoistic Model   5.____ Attraction to others based on similarity.
f. Romantic Love   6.____ Conforming out of a need for approval and acceptance.
g. Proximity   7.____ Based on mutual trust, respect, and friendship.
h. Companionate Love   8.____ Based on mystery and fantasy.
i. Reference Group   9.____ Learned predispositions toward an object.
j. Need Compatibility   10.____ Taking credit for successes and externalizing failures.

PRACTICE TEST I

1. Social psychologists study_____.
    a.   how others influence an individual's thoughts
    b.   how groups influence behavior
    c.   how a person's feelings are affected by others
    d.   all of the above

2. Attribution _____.
    a.   explains how people use cognitive structures for exploring the world and explaining human behavior
    b.   describes the principles we use in explaining what caused a behavior
    c.   is usually unrelated to social perceptions
    d.   describes our predisposition toward others or things

3. People engage in the fundamental attribution error because _____.
    a.   it is easier to blame people than "things"
    b.   of the saliency bias
    c.   situations are not as concrete and conspicuous
    d.   all of the above

4. A(n) _____ is the learned predisposition to respond consistently in a positive or negative way to someone, some thing, or some situation.
    a.   attitude
    b.   attribute
    c.   cognition
    d.   bias

5. Which statement does **NOT** illustrate a component of an attitude toward marijuana?
   a. the belief that marijuana is unsafe
   b. anxiety regarding the dangers of marijuana
   c. a predisposition to vote against the legalization of marijuana
   d. hallucinating while under the influence

6. Cognitive dissonance provokes a change in attitude due to _____.
   a. rational discourse between the id, ego, and superego
   b. rational discourse between people with opposite attitudes
   c. emotional thinking and reasoning
   d. psychological tension produced by personally discrepant attitudes

7. Cognitive dissonance is most prevalent in _____ cultures.
   a. Higher SES
   b. collectivist
   c. interdependent
   d. individualistic

8. Prejudice is a _____ directed toward others based on their group membership.
   a. negative behavior
   b. generally negative attitude
   c. stereotype
   d. all of these options

9. _____ is the cognitive component of prejudice.
   a. Harassment
   b. A stereotype
   c. Discrimination
   d. Ethnocentrism

10. Which of the following is an example of the outgroup homogeneity effect?
    a. "You don't belong here."
    b. "We are all alike."
    c. "You can't tell those people apart."
    d. all of these options

11. Your text defines ingroup favoritism as _____.
    a. any behavior intended to benefit your ethnic or religious group
    b. physical or verbal discrimination that favors your group
    c. viewing ingroup members more favorably than members of an outgroup
    d. purposeful and accidental favoritism of any kind

12. Research has consistently shown that physical attractiveness _____.
    a.   has little or no effect on interpersonal attraction
    b.   is one of the most important factors in liking
    c.   is associated with socioeconomic status
    d.   none of the above

13. An intense feeling of attraction to another person characterized by high passion, obsessive thinking, and emotional fluctuation defines _____.
    a.   the arousal phase
    b.   companionate love
    c.   romantic love
    d.   the sexual response cycle

14. Conforming to the typical behaviors of society out of a need for approval and acceptance is known as _____.
    a.   normative social influence
    b.   informational social influence
    c.   obedience
    d.   reference group adherence

15. Authority is most associated with which form of social influence?
    a.   informational
    b.   normative
    c.   obedience
    d.   reference group

16. In Zimbardo's prison experiment, the majority of participants with the role of prisoner became _____.
    a.   combative
    b.   defiant
    c.   passive
    d.   manic depressive

17. The tendency of a group to shift towards its initial dominant behavior or attitude is called _____.
    a.   the risky shift
    b.   the conservative movement
    c.   groupthink
    d.   group polarization

18. A group is strongly cohesive and its members have a shared desire for agreement; the members should be alert to the dangers of this in their decision making.
    a. group polarization
    b. groupthink
    c. brainstorming
    d. the "bandwagon" effect

19. Altruism refers to actions designed to help others when _____.
    a. there is no obvious benefit to oneself
    b. there is a benefit to the altruistic person
    c. they have previously helped you
    d. they are in a position to help you in the future

20. Based on Latane and Darley's theory, Kitty Genovese might have survived if she had been attacked _____.
    a. in the midwest instead of New York
    b. indoors instead of outdoors
    c. in the presence of only one neighbor who knew no one else was around
    d. during daylight hours instead of at night

PRACTICE TEST II

1. _____ percent of the people in Milgram's study followed orders to hurt a fellow participant.
    a. 15
    b. 25
    c. 65
    d. 95

2. Internal dispositions and external situations are the two basic types of _____.
    a. cognitions
    b. propositions
    c. attributions
    d. attitudes

3. One reason you look back at the ground when you trip is to signal others that there might be a(n) _____ for why you tripped.
    a. situational attribution
    b. external disposition
    c. cognitive explanation
    d. internal attitude

4. "All old people are slow drivers" is an example of _____.
    a.   the fundamental attribution error
    b.   prejudice
    c.   ethnocentrism
    d.   discrimination

5. After demeaning a member of another ethnic group, Walter experienced a brief rise in his own self-esteem. This is one way individuals learn _____.
    a.   the self-serving bias
    b.   prejudice
    c.   ethnocentrism
    d.   external attributions

6. According to _____ theorists, cross-cultural similarity in judgment of attractiveness reflects the fact that good looks generally indicate good health, sound genes, and high fertility.
    a.   sociophysiological
    b.   evolutionary
    c.   biological
    d.   none of the above

7. Similarity is the most important factor in _____ a relationship.
    a.   forming
    b.   appreciating
    c.   ending
    d.   maintaining

8. The reason _____ increases liking is that familiarity is less threatening than novelty.
    a.   mere exposure
    b.   physical attractiveness
    c.   need complementarity
    d.   need compatibility

9. According to _____, caring, attachment, and intimacy are important elements in loving.
    a.   Sternberg
    b.   Milgram
    c.   Zimbardo
    d.   Rubin

10. Rubin found that _____ was associated with admiration, respect, and favorable evaluation.
    a.   liking
    b.   loving
    c.   caring
    d.   limerance

11. Illusions are one of the foundations of _____ love.
    a.   companionate
    b.   romantic
    c.   fatuous
    d.   empty

12. What did Benjamin Franklin have to say about vision and love?
    a.   love lasts longest when your eyes are wide open
    b.   don't look before you leap
    c.   a glance is worth a thousand words
    d.   wide-eyed at first, then half closed

13. Asch is best known for his study on _____.
    a.   compliance
    b.   obedience
    c.   conformity
    d.   persuasion

14. Normative social influence, informational social influence, and reference groups are explanations for _____.
    a.   compliance
    b.   the foot-in-the-door strategy
    c.   obedience
    d.   conformity

15. Legitimate authority, distance between the teacher and learner, and _____ were several of the reasons participants in Milgram's study obeyed the researchers.
    a.   letting others assume responsibilty
    b.   the saliency bias
    c.   the self-serving bias
    d.   lack of empathy

16. Roles are based on _____.
    a.   social expectations
    b.   inborn dispositions
    c.   acquired dispositions
    d.   personal expectations

17. The classic prison study that determined the power of roles in affecting people's behavior was conducted by _____.
    a.   Milgram
    b.   Zimbardo
    c.   Bandura
    d.   Asch

18. Appointing a devil's advocate in a cohesive group would _____.
    a.   improve the group's decision-making abilities
    b.   hinder the group's decision-making efforts
    c.   have no effect on group decision-making
    d.   lead to chaos, resentment, and dissolution of the group

19. Violence in children _____.
    a.   is a natural, biological part of maturation
    b.   can be predicted by their levels of testosterone
    c.   can be increased by watching violent television
    d.   is totally unpredictable

20. If you were being mugged on a busy sidewalk, which of the following would be most likely to get you the help you need?
    a.   fighting with the mugger
    b.   yelling, "Help, help!"
    c.   crying forlornly and looking helpless
    d.   pointing to a specific person and asking them to call the police

ANSWERS

The following answers to active learning exercises, crossword puzzles, fill-ins, matching exercises, and practice tests 1 and 2 provide immediate feedback on your mastery of the material. Try not to simply memorize the answers. When you are unsure of your "guess" or make an error, be sure to go back to the textbook and carefully review. This will greatly improve your scores on classroom exams and quizzes.

CROSSWORD PUZZLE FOR CHAPTER 16

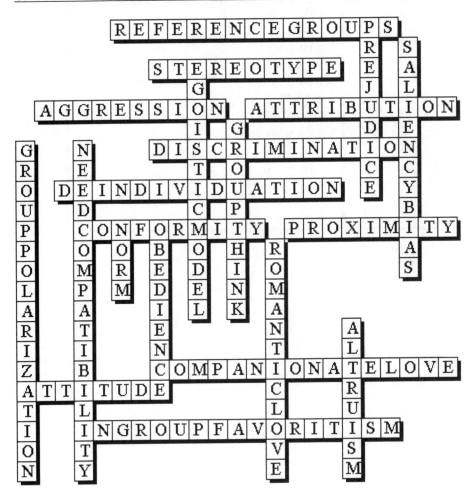

FILL-IN EXERCISES

1. attribution; 2. fundamental attribution error, self-serving bias; 3. cognitive, affective, behavioral; 4. cognitive dissonance; 5. prejudice; 6. cognitive, behavioral; 7. physical attractiveness, proximity, similarity; 8. conformity, obedience; 9. group polarization, groupthink; 10. a diffusion of responsibility.

MATCHING EXERCISES

a. 9, b. 10, c. 4, d. 6, e. 1, f. 8, g. 2, h. 7, i. 3, j. 5.

PRACTICE TEST I		PRACTICE TEST II	
1. d (p. 565)	11. c (p. 572)	1. c (p. 564)	11. b (p. 579)
2. b (p. 566)	12. b (p. 575)	2. c (p. 566)	12. d (p. 581)
3. d (p. 567)	13. c (p. 579)	3. a (p. 566)	13. c (p. 582)
4. a (p. 568)	14. a (p. 582)	4. b (p. 571)	14. d (p. 582)
5. d (p. 568)	15. c (p. 584)	5. b (p. 572)	15. a (p. 584)
6. d (p. 570)	16. c (p. 588)	6. b (p. 576)	16. a (p. 587)
7. d (p. 570)	17. d (p. 590)	7. d (p. 577)	17. b (p. 587)
8. b (p. 571)	18. b (p. 590)	8. a (p. 577)	18. a (p. 591)
9. b (p. 571)	19. a (p. 596)	9. d (p. 578)	19. c (p. 593)
10. c (p. 572)	20. c (p. 597)	10. a (p. 578)	20. d (p. 597)